From Faith to Faith

from FAITH TO FAITH

BLINDMAN'S BLUFF

Gilbert Soo Hoo
with a foreword by Thomas R. Edgar

WIPF & STOCK · Eugene, Oregon

FROM FAITH TO FAITH
Blindman's Bluff

Copyright © 2012 Gilbert Soo Hoo. All rights reserved. Except for brief quotations in critical publications or reviews, no part of this book may be reproduced in any manner without prior written permission from the publisher. Write: Permissions, Wipf and Stock Publishers, 199 W. 8th Ave., Suite 3, Eugene, OR 97401.

Wipf & Stock
An Imprint of Wipf and Stock Publishers
199 W. 8th Ave., Suite 3
Eugene, OR 97401

www.wipfandstock.com

ISBN 13: 978-1-61097-467-7

Manufactured in the U.S.A.

All Old Testament quotations are taken from the New American Standard Bible®, Copyright © 1960, 1962, 1963, 1968, 1971, 1972, 1973, 1975, 1977, 1995 by The Lockman Foundation. Used by permission.

Contents

List of Illustrations vi
Foreword by Thomas R. Edgar ThD vii
Preface ix
Acknowledgments xi
Abbreviations xii

1. Once Upon a Time 1
2. Reading Character 12
3. From the Wrong Side of the Tracks 36
4. Enter the Light 50
5. The Gift of Sight 62
6. Is It Really You? 70
7. Jekyll or Hyde? 80
8. One Step Forward, One Step Back 90
9. The Facts and Nothing But 103
10. The Lecture 119
11. Commencement 129
12. Judgment Day 140
13. End of One Story, Beginning of Another 165

Bibliography 175

Illustrations

Figure 1. Process of Maturing Faith 117
Figure 2. Healed Man's Faith Trajectory 173

Foreword

A RECENT COMMENTARY PURPORTED that it specialized in the exegesis of the Greek (original language) text of the New Testament. However, the very passages in which I was particularly interested were interpreted from a historical perspective. On these passages, the commentary was scarcely based on the biblical text. The author's interests and theological perspective were not really in accord with the literal meaning of the passage. One's theology often controls what is considered significant for discussion, as well as how it is interpreted. An author who discusses the actual meaning of a biblical text may also be accused of interpreting from a Western cultural perspective. These charges cannot be leveled against Soo Hoo's book.

In this book, Gilbert Soo Hoo discusses the narrative of Jesus' healing of the blind man in John, chapter 9. He discusses many and varied issues arising from this incident. A reader may ask, "Who would think of this question or problem?" Perhaps a reader would recognize, "I would never have thought of that." Soo Hoo's discussion provokes readers to realize that their questions and issues are not necessarily of the same importance as that of other readers. This passage would seem ideal as a launching pad for a discussion of certain social agendas, such as government healthcare. For example, some recent interpretations of 1 Corinthians, chapter 6, utterly ignore the Apostle Paul's very specific statements describing the problem he is discussing. Instead the interpretations reflect an issue between social classes—the rich versus the poor. However, there is a common trait to the various issues that Soo Hoo discusses. They all arise from the biblical passage itself. They do not function merely to promote modern social or cultural agendas, or other contemporary ideas. Soo Hoo does not ignore the more academic issues but discusses selected ones in the footnotes.

Soo Hoo brings a unique combination of background, training, and experience to his presentation. His training and experience include both the secular and theological, the academic and practical. His theological training and experience is varied. His formal theological training was in a Western institution. His practical church experience was in an Asian American church. His formal teaching experience includes some teaching in the West, but it is largely in Singapore. He is particularly competent in the exegesis of the Greek New Testament. Thus, the reader can rest assured that his perspective is not from any one cultural background or from an insulated academic outlook. Above all, Soo Hoo knows the ultimate author of John, chapter 9.

His discussion is a narrative approach that is easy to comprehend. Yet, he deals thoroughly with this passage. Perhaps the main and most enlightening point is that Jesus' healing of the blind man in John, chapter 9, is not a single, isolated event. Rather, he shows that it has a definite function in the larger narrative context. It is an integral part of John's overall presentation. I recommend this book to anyone who seeks a better understanding of this biblical passage, and how this all fits in John's Gospel.

—Thomas R. Edgar, ThD
Distinguished Professor of New Testament Literature and Exegesis
Capital Bible Seminary

Preface

IN MY YEARS OF ministry I have known many devout believers who take the Bible seriously. Some of them rival seminary graduates in their understanding of theological and ministerial issues. It is with this group of lay Christians in mind that I wrote this work. They include church leaders, Sunday school teachers, and Bible study leaders. Pastors and professional Christian workers will also benefit from this book. Yet I think that those individuals who are starting out or are struggling in their faith journey can find both encouragement and challenge through a thoughtful consideration of the healed man at the center of this study (John 9:1—10:21).

Because of the intended readership, I have relegated more technical discussions and concepts to the footnotes; and I have replaced the minimal Greek that was unavoidable with transliterations. In this manner, the interested reader may pursue more in-depth investigation by prodding through these notes, where I also introduce some of the standard technical literature. Others not so inclined can opt not to get bogged down and simply move on. And so I have brought a blend of pastoral and academic interests to the task.

A brief comment on the title, *From Faith to Faith: Blindman's Bluff*, will have to suffice here. Blindman's bluff is a children's game in which the person blindfolded attempts to catch sighted players. The game serves as a metaphor for the blind man who, although healed near the beginning of the story, must "grope" his way to a fuller understanding of Jesus.

My particular approach recognizes the narrative features of the Fourth Gospel, particularly the two-party juridical controversy embroiling Jesus and his accusers over two perceived Sabbath violations. This Sabbath conflict spans John 5:1—18:27. Unresolved, the dispute comes before Pilate (18:28), effectively converting the two-party procedure into a formal three-party trial. As the conflict intensifies, the healed man becomes first a witness for Jesus' defense and then a surrogate disputant in Jesus' absence. In the process, he gains depth of faith and understanding. The blind man's journey serves as an encouraging model for the reader.

Acknowledgments

I GRATEFULLY ACKNOWLEDGE THE contribution of friends and colleagues to the production of this work. Nadine Woods and Carol Cheng read the entire manuscript, and Evelyn Lechliter examined selected chapters to weed out conceptual incongruities and to suggest smoother English. Dr. Michael L. C. Phua reviewed sections concerning the Second Temple period. Special thanks to Dr. Thomas R. Edgar for introducing me to the art of biblical exegesis. And, most importantly, Ming lavished on me her unconditional support and love. Her enthusiasm is contagious.

Abbreviations

11QT^a	*Temple Scroll^a*
1QSa	*Rule of the Congregation* (Appendix a to 1QS)
4QD^a	Damascus Document^a
4QMessAp	*Messianic Apocalypse*
AB	Anchor Bible
Ag. Ap.	*Against Apion* (Josephus)
A.J.	*Antiquitates judaicae* (Josephus)
Bar.	Baruch (Old Testament Pseudepigrapha)
b. Ber.	Babylonian Talmud Berakhot
BDAG	Walter Bauer, Frederick W. Danker, William F. Arndt, and F. Wilbur Gingrich. See Bibliography for source information.
BDF	F. Blass, A. Debrunner, and Robert W. Funk. See Bibliography for source information.
BSac	*Bibliotheca sacra*
CBQ	*Catholic Biblical Quarterly*
CBQMS	Catholic Biblical Quarterly Monograph Series
DRev	*Downside Review*
DSS	Dead Sea Scrolls
En	Enoch (Old Testament Pseudepigrapha)
Esd	Esdras (Old Testament Apocrypha)
EvQ	*Evangelical Quarterly*

ExpTim	*Expository Times*
HTR	*Harvard Theological Review*
HUCA	*Hebrew Union College Annual*
Int	*Interpretation*
JAAR	Journal of the American Academy of Religion
JBL	*Journal of Biblical Literature*
JETS	Journal of the Evangelical Theological Society
JSNT	*Journal for the Study of the New Testament*
JSNTSup	Journal for the Study of the New Testament: Supplement Series
JSPSup	Journal for the Study of the Pseudepigrapha: Supplement Series
JTSA	*Journal of Theology for Southern Africa*
J.W.	*Jewish War* (Josephus)
LXX	Septuagint (ancient Greek translation of the Hebrew Old Testament)
m. Abot	Abot (tractate from the Mishnah)
Macc	Maccabees (1–2 Macc, Old Testament Apocrypha)
m. Pe'ah	Pe'ah (tractate from the Mishnah)
m. Sanh	Sanhedrin (tractate from the Mishnah)
m. Shab	Shabbat (tractate from the Mishnah)
m. Sukk.	Sukkah (tractate from the Mishnah)
NASB	New American Standard Bible
Neot	*Neotestamentica*
NICNT	New International Commentary on the New Testament
NovT	*Novum Testamentum*
NovTSup	Novum Testamentum Supplements
NT	New Testament
NTS	*New Testament Studies*

OT		Old Testament
PRSt		*Perspectives in Religious Studies*
Pss. Sol.		Psalms of Solomon (Old Testament Pseudepigrapha)
RB		*Revue biblique*
RevExp		*Review and Expositor*
SBL		Society of Biblical Literature
SBLDS		Society of Biblical Literature Dissertation Series
SBLEJL		Society of Biblical Literature Early Judaism and Its Literature
SBLMS		Society of Biblical Literature Monograph Series
SBLSBS		Society of Biblical Literature Sources for Biblical Study
Sir		Sirach/Ecclesiasticus
SNTSMS		Society for New Testament Studies Monograph Series
T. Benj.		Testament of Benjamin (Old Testament Pseudepigrapha)
TDNT		*Theological Dictionary of the New Testament*
Tg. Isa.		*Targum Isaiah*
T. Job		Testament of Job (Old Testament Pseudepigrapha)
T. Jud.		Testament of Judah (Old Testament Pseudepigrapha)
USQR		*Union Seminary Quarterly Review*
VC		*Vigiliae christianae*
Wis		Wisdom of Solomon (Old Testament Apocrypha)
WTJ		*Westminster Theological Journal*
WW		*Word and World*
ZNW		*Zeitschrift für die neutestamentliche Wissenschaft und die Kunde der älteren Kirche*

1

Once Upon a Time

I LOVE MY FRIENDS, so I make time in a busy schedule for them. However, these friends are not flesh and blood. Rather, they are the classics, some of which I first met in a literature course. Over the years we have become close. Of course, when I say *classics*, it is from my perspective. Charles Dickens's *A Tale of Two Cities* would be everyone's idea of a classic. But Tom Clancy's *Rainbow Six* probably is not.

I visit these friends, and read and reread them without ever getting tired of them. Familiar and comfortable, these friends invite my imagination into their world, and I become a part of their tight circle. Their presence lingers even after I return to the real world, because my imagination remains in their embrace.

I didn't realize how zealous I was for my friends until I saw *Masterpiece Theatre*'s 2006 production of "Jane Eyre." The glowing review by the *Guardian* floored me: "An excellent performance from Toby Stephens, who manages to make Rochester simultaneously macho and vulnerable, and also from Ruth Wilson as a quizzical, strong and unneurotic Jane."[1] Excellent performance? Anyone acquainted with the Charlotte Brontë original would have felt betrayed. To be sure, there was some resemblance to the plot and the characters, but that similarity raised my expectations. Had this production been a completely different story and another cast of characters, I would have had no issue. However, as I watched the film I was constantly comparing and contrasting it to the

---

1. *Masterpiece Theatre*, "Jane Eyre."

Brontë original, thinking to myself, sometimes out loud: "This isn't right; that is so off; they've omitted an entire episode!"

In the *Masterpiece Theatre* production, I felt that Toby Stephens needed to be more brooding, and he was much too young and mellow. The middle-aged Rochester's heavy brow emanated a dark perpetual scowl. Then big-boned Ruth Wilson, who stands nearly as tall as Toby's character, shattered my image of a petite Jane Eyre. I waited in vain for Jane's quick-witted retorts and saw no fiercely independent spirit. This wasn't the spirited, spunky Jane Eyre I knew so well.

So yes, I'm zealous for my friend's sake. Brontë created a world of true complexity and finely crafted dialog. She delivered rapturous descriptions of open field, babbling brook, and quiet forest; and Brontë's portrayal of the characters' moods and the dark shadows of Thornfield Hall did not make an appearance.

A DISCIPLINED APPROACH

There is another classic that has become a close friend. The author of this classic has mesmerized countless of readers by his profundity for more than the nearly two millennia since the work first appeared. The Gospel according to John, like his cousins the Synoptic Gospels, conveys the compelling story of Jesus, arguably the most intriguing person who ever lived. This combination of a great author who portrays an even greater subject makes for an "I can't put this book down until I finish" reading experience.

Although any good story should be a fascinating read, the Gospel of John's purpose is not entertainment. The author clearly states his objective (20:30–31): "Therefore Jesus performed many other signs before his disciples that are not written in this book. But these have been written in order that you may believe that Jesus is the Christ, the Son of God, and in order that by believing you may have life in his name."[2] Transformation takes place as we read Scripture, meditate on it, and obey. The Gospel of John is both great literature and Scripture, and it contains a latent power that grips the reader who, in turn, cannot remain neutral.

A few years ago my wife and I started a small group Bible study designed specifically for those individuals on the fringes of the believing

---

2. I translated this and all subsequent NT quotations from the Greek. OT quotations, however, are based on the NASB.

community. Most of these people did not regularly attend church. So we challenged them to commit three months to this new group, where we would study the Bible inductively. The three months extended beyond one year as group members developed a strong sense of belonging. I led the analytical studies and exhorted them to adopt the applications. There were ample discussions and interactions with the text. They demanded more than well-packaged answers to their questions. Their sharing often revealed some of the rawness of their lives: struggling with addiction, finding purpose in their lives, or being accepted by others. In time, they returned to church and began caring for others. Some entered into the church's discipleship ministry to be equipped for service. Disciplined Bible study can do that. I intend to provide a similarly disciplined approach to the study of one story from the Gospel of John. Let us study it together.

CONTEXT OF JOHN 9:1—10:18

John 9:1—10:18 tells about the aftermath of Jesus giving sight to a blind man. Before examining the text, an overview of John's Gospel is in order.

Comprehending Transcendent Truth

Many scholars note that the prevailing usage of symbols in the Fourth Gospel is a communication vehicle of truth.[3] One scholar, Craig R. Koester, writes: "A symbol, in the most general sense, is something that stands for something else. Here, however, we will focus on the definition: A symbol is an image, an action, or a person that is understood to have transcendent significance. In Johannine terms, symbols span the chasm between what is 'from above' and what is 'from below' without collapsing the distinction."[4]

The Gospel of John portrays a two-tiered cosmology—the realm above where the Father abides; and the world of mankind, below. The terms "above" and "below" are metaphors of that cosmology (8:23).

---

3. For example, see Schneiders ("History and Symbolism in the Fourth Gospel"), Dodd (*Interpretation of the Fourth Gospel*), and Painter ("Johannine Symbols," 26–41). In his important work, Kanagaraj connects John's background with Merkabah mysticism—based in large measure on Ezekiel 1, in which the throne-chariot of God symbolizes his glory—and perceives Jesus as the self-revelation of God in the world (*'Mysticism' in the Gospel of John*, 214–47).

4. Koester, *Symbolism*, 4.

Jesus enters into our world below through the incarnation (1:14) with the mission of revealing the Father above (1:18). In order to make the Father comprehensible to the world, Jesus and the narrator of this gospel through "asides" (narrative sections where the narrator addresses us readers directly) employ worldly symbols to communicate transcendent truths. After all, our minds are familiar only with the world below and have no actual grasp of the realm above. Thus, the things, events, institutions, and ideologies of this world are utilized in this gospel to symbolize analogous realities pertaining to the realm above.

The narrator presents his characters as not merely historical but also representative figures.[5] The narrator characterizes the disciples in terms of their faith, struggles (with understanding Jesus' teaching), and even failures; and in so doing, represents the future generations of believers. The Pharisees and the Jews represent the world's resistance to and opposition against Jesus. Jesus himself is representative. He reveals the Father in such a manner that he is able to proclaim: "The one who has seen me has seen the Father" (14:9). And then there is the man born blind in 9:1—10:18.

The blind man is representative of every person who in spite of handicap or hardship comes to faith in Jesus. The man could have been a member of my Bible study group of misfits. In his physical condition, he can depict every person who is blind spiritually. Spiritual blindness in the Gospel refers to the blindness of at least two truths—the lack of insight into Jesus' identity and the lack of the abundant life that only he provides (10:10).

---

5. Ibid., 32–73. Culpepper (*Anatomy*, 102–4, 145) notes that Johannine characters serve as foils to bring out Jesus' character and to represent the various responses to Jesus. Throughout this work I make a distinction between the real human author of the Gospel and the narrator of the story within. Narrative criticism is a reading strategy of biblical narrative, of which the Gospels are examples, that attempt to discern the different points of view expressed by the narrator who tells the story; the central character, Jesus; and the other characters who interact with Jesus. Assuming a narrator supposes that there is a story to be told, Petersen states: "The narrator reaches out of his narrative to lead his reader on an imaginative journey into the past, plucking him out of his time and place, as it were, and setting him down in another time and place" ("'Point of View' in Mark's Narrative," 101). The narrator represents an omniscient storyteller who, like the character Jesus, can read the minds and discern the motives of all the characters. The narrator guides the reader to a sympathetic assessment of Jesus and, as 20:30–31 declares, ultimately to faith in him. By comparison, the author collects and edits source material, and then writes the Gospel. In creating the story, he expresses his interpretation of the historical events and, at the same time, creates the (implied) narrator, a literary presence, to tell the story.

Blindness is symptomatic of darkness. Darkness is a symbol of the world's predicament—existence apart from God. In his prologue, John declares: "In him was life, and the life was the light of men. And the light shines in the darkness, but the darkness did not overcome it" (1:4–5). Here is the first hint of the hostility that Jesus will face, as described later in the Gospel. The coming of the light into the world, symbolic of Jesus as the revelation of God, creates a crisis of faith. An encounter with this light prompts a person to travel one path or the other. There are but two paths. Those who choose the path that leads deeper into the darkness, represented by the religious leadership, are compelled by internal forces to proceed further on that path. There is no turning back. Those who choose the path that approaches the light, however, continually face a decision—maintain the course or turn back.[6] The decision is a faith issue as encapsulated in the question: "Who is Jesus and where is he from?" The blind man represents those who come to the light. In every encounter in the first portion of the Fourth Gospel (1:19—12:50), the question is posed and answered according to one's perception of Jesus.

Two Realms

The symbolism of light and darkness characterizes the fundamental dualism of the Gospel of John. This dualism is rooted in the existence of two realms, mutually exclusive and diametrically opposed. Robert Kysar discerns a double dualism in the Fourth Gospel based on 8:23 ("You are from below; I am from above. You are from this world; I am not from this world")—a cosmic division between the divine and created realms, and a human division portrayed by the truth-falsehood axis.[7] Jesus frequently alludes to being sent by the Father, the principle manner by which he identifies himself. So characteristic is this self-reference in the narrative that Wayne A. Meeks, another biblical scholar, famously calls Jesus "the Stranger from the world above."[8]

---

6. There is a collection of secret believers in Jesus, including many of the religious authorities who, for fear of being cast out of the synagogue, do not confess Jesus publicly (9:22; 12:42). They include Nicodemus, Joseph of Arimathea, and the blind man's parents. Their secret faith takes them just so far, but no further. Ultimately they turn back and are no different than unbelievers. Theirs is a sign-based faith that proves inadequate (2:23–25). See Lincoln, *Gospel according to John*, 152, 258–59.

7. Kysar, *Maverick Gospel*, 63–67.

8. Meeks, "Man from Heaven," 71.

Jesus shares nothing in common with those of the world below. The descent-ascent motif of the Fourth Gospel that describes Jesus' cosmic journey from the realm above to the world below and back sets Jesus apart from all mankind as unique, because he alone has descended first since he alone is from above. Thus, even Nicodemus, the "teacher of Israel" cannot comprehend this alien (3:3–10). Jesus' identity and his origin remain a mystery to Nicodemus.

But Jesus' coming into the world serves as the bridge or intersection between the two realms where the transcendent has become immanent. How a person responds to Jesus determines that person's association with either the realm above or below. Faith in Jesus' self-identification or the lack of such faith is the sole determinant. As the narrative moves toward the time of his ascension back to the Father, Jesus tells his disciples who believe in him that "you are not of the world, but I have chosen you out of the world" (15:19). Their association with the realm above disassociates them from the world below. A definitive change in socio-religious location occurs.

Whereas the characters in the narrative encounter Jesus in the flesh and make a decision about him, we encounter him through the reading of the narrative. As Meeks notes, "The book functions for its readers in precisely the same way that the epiphany of its hero functions within its narratives and dialogues."[9] Our response to Jesus as measured by the vitality of our relationship with him provides a gauge to determine our affiliation with either the realm above or the world below. As the Fourth Gospel teaches, we cannot maintain intimacy with the world if we desire unity with Jesus and, through Jesus, with God.

A Different Dualism

The Johannine dualism of light and darkness is not a form of the familiar *yin* and *yang* in which the core principle is constant change.[10] Asian philosopher Bo Mou explains: "The two kinds of forces might be identified, in more or less metaphorical terms, as the negative, passive, yielding,

---

9. Ibid., 69.

10. Blofeld translates *I Ching* (or *Yi-Jing*), the ancient Chinese document predating Confucius that explains the philosophical concepts of *yin* and *yang*, as the "Book of Change" to capture the essential thought: "Change as the one unchanging aspect of the universe" (*I Ching*, 23–24).

weak, and deconstructive *yin* force and as the positive, active, aggressive, strong, and constructive *yang* force."[11]

Perhaps you, like many others, believe the world operates under some version of this *yin yang* dualism. The weather, ecology, global economics, and the alliances and conflicts between corporations and nations constantly change. You may even experience change in your life, with respect to your job, relationships, and mood.

For *yin* and *yang*, each causes its opposite in an endless cycle where one dominates for a time before the other gains dominance. When one entity dominates, its opposite does not entirely disappear. Light has some vestige of darkness and vice versa. The light-darkness motif of the Fourth Gospel, however, does not portray any endless cycle but a mutual exclusivity. Once light vanquishes darkness, only light remains. But if darkness prevails, the individual who rejects the light dwells in complete darkness. Ultimately, forthcoming judgment, however, results in final victory for the light. There is no ceaseless flow of one into the other.[12] In John, only light comes into the darkness.

Johannine dualism is not an abstraction or impersonal reality. This concept can be found in today's popular culture. For example, the Force of the *Star Wars* anthology permeates the universe with its light and dark sides. A version of dualism is also found in the ancient world. An example is the Egyptian *maat*—"the order, the just measure of things, that underlies the world; it is the perfect state of things toward which one should strive and which is in harmony with the creator god's intentions."[13] Either one conforms to *maat* or he risks disturbing the balance.

Another dualistic system, Manichaeism, features a cosmogony in which two eternal domains of light and darkness coexist.[14] Manichaeism teaches that darkness invaded the light but light will ultimately triumph. In the Fourth Gospel, however, light "invades" the darkness; and the darkness is not eternal.

---

11. Mou, "Becoming-Being Complementarity," 89. Schwartz offers a somewhat different interpretation in regarding *yin* and *yang* as but two of six *ch'i*—the others being wind, rain, darkness, and light—where *ch'i* refers to the fundamental order in the cosmos (*World of Thought in Ancient China*, 180–81.)

12. For a more positive view on *yin yang* philosophy as a hermeneutical approach to Scripture, see Kim, "Interpretative Modes of Yin–Yang Dynamics," 287–308.

13. Hornung, *Conceptions of God in Ancient Egypt*, 213.

14. Stroumsa and Stroumsa, "Aspects of Anti-Manichaean Polemics," 37–58.

From Another World

Jesus, as Meeks points out, is an alien from another world. He is not a UFO but an IFO—Incomprehensible Foreign Object. The world cannot understand him. In the Fourth Gospel, Jesus symbolizes transcendent truth for us who cannot on our own penetrate the chasm between two realities. He comes into our world to manifest the reality of another realm above, a realm so radically different from our world below that we must jettison our inadequate preconceptions of that realm above if we are to comprehend transcendent truth. Jesus has been sent to declare good news: not only can we know the Father who sent him, but we have access to the realm above if we accept the invitation to exercise faith in him. In so doing, we find grace and wisdom to live worshipful lives here on Earth.

OUR STARTING POINT

We all begin in darkness, for darkness characterizes the world below. We cannot move out of the darkness on our own. There is no way out until Jesus the light comes to show us the way. Some of us may not even be aware that we are in the dark. We regard the world as not only familiar but comfortable—perhaps too comfortable.

Thus, Jesus the light must make the first move and come into the world and into our lives. We, as the Fourth Gospel makes clear, can only react; we cannot be proactive (20:31). We, like the blind man in the story, have an opportunity to respond to Jesus through reading the man's story.

THE JOURNEY

In the following chapters, I will trace the journey of the man born blind. Even though he gains his sight immediately, it represents only the beginning of his journey. He takes a succession of steps by which he progressively gains insight into Jesus' identity. The gift of physical sight triggers a sequence of events in which the man must make decisions about Jesus. On this journey he gains wisdom to move in the right direction, and in the end he worships the author of life. The man's story can be ours if we follow in his footsteps.

Along the way Jesus is mysteriously absent, and the man has to fend for himself in his encounters with the religious establishment.[15] If

---

15. The narrative alternates mentioning the Pharisees (9:13, 15–16, 40) and the Jews

we view the Gospel narrative as an unfolding play, Jesus' absence may be attributed to the practice of ancient dramatists who allow "only two characters/groups [to] appear on 'the stage' at any given time, heightening the dramatic effect and, in these dialogues, emphasizing the force of the conflicts."[16] Others theorize that Jesus' absence "would correspond to the situation of people living one or two generations after the end of his earthly ministry."[17] However, there may also be a pedagogical explanation for his absence.[18] Like an effective teacher, Jesus assigns his "student" a project to research, and to draw conclusions on his own. In the end, the man gains the spiritual insight necessary to lead a worshipful life.

The man represents everyone. I can relate to him and so can you. The concept of us being the reader who can interact with the biblical text in a potentially transformational way is based on a rhetorical reading. The author seeks to persuade us, the readers, to respond with a change in beliefs and to adopt behavior consistent with those beliefs. We enter the world in the text to experience what the man experiences: we feel his emotions and we hear his unspoken thoughts.[19] The narrative's transformational power does not stem simply from being the conveyor of revelation, but, in reality, the narrative "is the revelation" where we encounter Jesus through reading the text.[20]

Because the Fourth Gospel engages a variety of different readers, our identities and personal issues, though different, do not really matter.[21] This Gospel offers hope to anyone.

(9:18, 22). Martyn's proposal that seven different scenes (9:1–7, 9:8–12, 9:13–17, 9:18–23, 9:24–34, 9:35–38, 9:39–41), stitched together into a continuous narrative in John 9, helps in distinguishing the two groups (*History and Theology in the Fourth Gospel*, 40–45).

16. Painter, "John 9," 36.

17. Koester, *Symbolism*, 64.

18. Soo Hoo, *Pedagogy of the Johannine Jesus*, 145–48.

19. For the classical treatment on reader-response and rhetorical criticism, see Staley, *Print's First Kiss*, 6–49. See also Kennedy, *New Testament Interpretation*, 3–113.

20. O'Day, "Narrative Mode and Theological Claim," 657–68.

21. Brown discerns seven identifiable groups associated with the Fourth Gospel both within and in front of the narrative (*Community of the Beloved Disciple*, 63–91). Koester advocates a wide readership range from different cultures and religious backgrounds ("Spectrum of Johannine Readers" 5–19).

A LITERARY CAVEAT

Allow me to make an important distinction between the story in the narrative and the narrative as the literary vehicle that communicates the story. The story follows the timeline of the sequence of events as they take place in the lives of the characters. By contrast, the narrative may compress the story's timeline with a summary, fast forward with an omission, pause to look back at the past, or slow the action with discourse. The differences between the story and the narrative signal the narrator's rhetorical strategy in maximizing the impact of his storytelling. In that sense, he guides us as we take that first step of our journey—reading his narrative with an open mind and heart.

A CRISIS OF FAITH

As we strive to know Jesus in the process of reading the Fourth Gospel, I hope we will not incur Jesus' rebuttal to Philip: "Have I been with you for such a long time and you do not know me?" (14:9).

We will examine one sign of the seven in the Fourth Gospel—the healing of the blind man. That sign represented one man's first step toward greater faith and insight; but it drove others away. That man represents us in our crisis of faith.

I faced a crisis that represented a standing-at-the-threshold moment for me at the ripe old age of twenty-eight. I had been a Christian for less than three years when I sensed a "leading" to enroll in seminary. Back then it meant major commitment—I would have to quit my job. Today Bible schools accommodate the busy minister or layperson. They offer evening and weekend classes, satellite campuses, even distance learning options. I did not have such alternatives back then. Quitting my job presented a major psychological hurdle—I would forego my sense of security, and I couldn't explain to my parents the actions I was contemplating.

A quiet evening walk alone in June is indelibly engraved in my mind. As I looked up at the stars for answers, they only twinkled mutely. I had only a vague notion about seminary. I wondered whether I would do well. I thought it foolhardy to quit my job and then flunk out. Disquieted and alone, I experienced inner turmoil.

Then in late August I burned my bridge by telling my big boss "I quit." Looking back I realize that I had to take that fateful step to move forward. But at the time I could not possibly discern it that way. That was my crisis of faith.

The healed blind man's path toward greater faith and insight lies before you, just as it did for me. You face two possible journeys, each leading to a radically different destiny. The choices will become clearer as you read on. As you trace the man's journey you will ask, "Who is Jesus to me and what difference does that make?"

In the next chapter, I lay out my hermeneutics, or principles, for approaching the narrative. After those principles are identified, I will then read the blind man's story and dovetail his story into ours starting in chapter 3. So please accept my invitation to read, and then experience your story.

2

Reading Character

In this chapter I lay out my hermeneutics, or interpretative principles, for reading the story of the blind man and his journey to fuller faith after regaining physical sight. In the next chapter we will then trace the emergence of his character as he interacts with first his acquaintances and then his interrogators.

The blind man's character determines the direction of his faith development. One's character can be dynamic and, in the blind man's case, his character continually evolves and, in the end, crystallizes. The narrative documents the development of his character through his interaction with other people in the story. The hermeneutical key of this story lies in tracking the healed blind man's progressing character definition as the gauge for evaluating the vitality of his faith in Jesus at important narrative junctures.

As I stated in the previous chapter, Bible stories confront and compel the reader to self-reflection, the first step to potential character transformation. Whether our faith matures in a similar manner, as that of the healed blind man, depends on our character and the changes we undergo as we read and respond.

BIBLICAL CHARACTERIZATION

In recent years characterization has emerged as a major topic in biblical studies as evidenced by a plethora of publication in both book form and article. The narrative genre is a natural site for events and characters that move the story forward and fulfil the narrator's agenda. Given the healed blind man's prominent role in John 9, his character and function in fulfilling Jesus' purpose ("in order that the works of God may be manifested in him," 9:3) are of paramount importance.

Lehtipuu notes the challenges of studying biblical characters. He lists three challenges in particular.[1]

First, the distance of time and culture of the characters confront the modern reader. Attempting to span the temporal and cultural divide, we realize that we do not know the socio-economic realities of blindness in the time of Jesus. How did people of this biblical time and place regard a blind person?

Second, the brevity of a character's appearance in a story (the blind man appears in 9:1 and disappears after 9:38) leaves scant data from which to develop an informed impression of his personality. Biblical narrative, unlike modern novels, does not subject characters to in-depth psychological analysis. What can be gleaned, however, deals primarily with how a character relates to Jesus. The effect seems to make the character subservient to the story plot.

And third, the reader must reconstruct characters in the story for evaluation. Here the idea of the character's symbolic depth emerges, and the reader ascertains the character's significance to himself. Of course, a reader's acquaintance with a literary character differs significantly from knowing a real person.[2] The reader cannot interact with a character in the normal give-and-take that typifies a real relationship. The reader-character relation is confined to a literary experience. Moreover, no one in real life corresponds to the omniscient narrator who can unveil a person's thoughts and motives. We must content ourselves with making inferences based on a real person's observed behavior and words. Hence, uncertainty will always cloud our assessment. That uncertainty is removed to a certain extent by narrative comments about a character. For biblical narrative we shall assume that the narrator is reliable, that he does not intentionally subvert the reading process by misleading the reader.[3]

1. Lehtipuu, "Characterization and Persuasion," 74–81.

2. Darr, *On Character Building*, 47. Although Darr writes in the context of Luke-Acts, his discussion is pertinent to biblical narrative in general.

3. Berlin, *Poetics and Interpretation*, 43. Also Alter, *Art of Biblical Narrative*, 116. For the reader's (read feminist) defiant stance toward her narrator's attempt to influence and limit her impressions on the characters, see Bach, "Signs of the Flesh: Observations on Characterization in the Bible," 61–79. Bach attempts to resuscitate the flattened female character and restore some semblance of individuality by regarding her as much more than simply a plot device. I do concur partially with Bach's objective but not at the cost of

CHARACTER CLUES

Alter identifies a "scale of means, in ascending order of explicitness and certainty" by which a narrator portrays a character.[4] Of the many ways for describing a character, his actions and appearance, located at the lower end of the scale, requires a good deal of inference on the part of the reader to ascribe traits. More objective information can be gleaned from the character's direct speech or from what other characters say about him.[5] At this location of the scale the character's interaction with other characters in the story has an important place.[6] But as Alter cautions, the speech may be more the product of the situation than a window into the person's true nature. Moving up the scale we find a character's narrated inner thoughts, which provide more objective data on his true motives. And finally, at the top end of the scale, there is the narrator's own description of the character's inner thoughts, feelings, and motives. Here the reader enjoys the greatest assurance of knowing the character with the least amount of inference.[7]

CHARACTER TYPES

Culpepper briefly surveys contemporary studies on characterization and posits two extremes that span a continuum of how the text treats

---

completely rejecting the narrative.

4. Alter, *Art of Biblical Narrative*, 116–17.

5. For an OT example, see O'Brien, "Contribution of Judah's Speech," 429–47.

6. McCracken advocates that biblical characterization is essentially interaction between characters at the threshold or boundary, where there is a crisis or scandal of faith ("Character in the Boundary," 29–42). Because the vast majority of biblical dialogue features Jesus as one of the characters, McCracken sees how someone responding to Jesus offers a glimpse of that person's character. In addition to inter-character dialogue, McCracken values the dialogic relationship between the character with the reader and the character with the narrator.

7. The reader's assurance rests on a tacit trust in the narrator's reliability and truthfulness. But the reality of the character is textual and not necessarily historical. Words paint the portrait. In a sense, he is the figment of the narrator's literary imagination. If the characterization reflects a faithful rendition of history, we the modern reader have no independent means of evaluating the faithfulness of the portrait. There may be extra-textual data, but what we know with certainty of first-century Hellenistic Palestine is quite limited. So we have no other recourse but to depend on the narrative. I assume that the Bible is a reliable faith document and that the authors were faithful agents of God tasked with communicating divine truth.

the characters.[8] At one end, the text regards characters as "autonomous beings" with a life that extends beyond the text; and at the other end, they are merely literary constructs that advance the plot. Culpepper also cites Forster's categorization of "flat" characters who serve as caricatures that portray a single quality (for example, Judas the betrayer) and "round" characters who have a more complex makeup.[9] Although Culpepper believes all Johannine characters but Jesus tend to personify a single trait, I believe that the healed blind man's narrative portrait gravitates toward a fuller personality in that he experiences growth and, so, is not static.[10]

Berlin proposes three categories of characterization.[11] First, her "full-fledged character" correlates with Forster's "round" character, that is, most life-like. Second, the "type" portrays a single quality or trait analogous to Forster's "flat" character. Third, the "agent" simply facilitates the plot. Although these categories are distinct, Berlin observes that a character may shift between any of the three categories in different portions of the narrative. That being the possibility, there is then a continuum or, in Berlin's words, degrees of characterization:[12]

> There is no real line separating these three types; the difference is a matter of the degree of characterization rather than the kind of characterization. One might think of them as points on a continuum: 1) the agent, about whom nothing is known except what is necessary for the plot; the agent is a function of the plot or part of the setting; 2) the type, who has a limited and stereotyped range of traits, and who represents the class of people with these traits; 3) the character, who has a broader range of traits (not all belonging to the same class of people), and about whom we know more than is necessary for the plot.

The text and the reader are the two primary sources for characterization. In regard to the second source, Burnett notes that in the reading process the reader must fill in the gaps of the narrative by inferring character traits from "words, deeds, relationships, and attributive propositions

---

8. Culpepper, *Anatomy*, 101–2.

9. Ibid., 102. He cites Forster, *Aspects of the Novel*.

10. Culpepper acknowledges this aspect of the man (*Anatomy*, 103).

11. Berlin, *Poetics and Interpretation*, 23–24. Berlin's area of focus is OT narrative, but much of her material is applicable to NT narrative.

12. Ibid., 32. Culpepper sees a continuum of character responses to Jesus (*Anatomy*, 104). His view is influenced by Collins ("Representative Figures," 26–46 and 118–32).

given in the text."[13] The reader's significant role of inference and even speculation is not limited to the text.[14] When a character transcends the text, he or she takes on individuality or a life of his or her own, apart from the story.[15]

In the case of our healed blind man, we witness an evolution of character. He begins his narrative existence as an agent. Jesus declares that he, in his congenital condition, is the setting by which God's works will be manifested (9:3). The blind man exists solely to serve as the device through which God will manifest himself. The blind man has no active or speaking part. He is simply there—first as a theological curiosity for the disciples (9:2) and then as a stage where Jesus will reveal his identity as the light of the world (9:3–5). We only know that he is blind from birth (9:1) and nothing more. He has no identifiable traits. In fact, those who knew him before his healing probably knew nothing more about him except that he was a beggar (9:8). Only when the narrative unfolds and the man interacts first with his acquaintances and then with the Pharisees and the Jews do his character traits emerge. As we the readers follow the intense and hostile exchange, we begin to make inferences based largely on his repartee with his interrogators.

Even so, we are never completely at liberty to draw whatever inferences we fancy. The narrative always serves as our moderator to provide parameters and constraints by which we measure our conclusions about the blind man. Because of the cosmic context of Jesus being sent from the realm above to the world below to reveal the Father, we know that what Jesus does to and through the man reveals the Father and substantiates Jesus' origin. Then there is the context of the healing and immediate aftermath, in which the man gains insight about Jesus through acknowledging the undeniable evidence of gaining his sight and processing its significance. At the same time, he exposes his interrogators as being stubbornly blind to the truth about Jesus. So both objective and subjective elements contribute to the character of the blind man.

---

13. Burnett, "Characterization and Reader Construction," 16.

14. Chatman, *Story and Discourse*, 117–18. Chatman advocates that the plot and the character are separable and "independently memorable." But for a critique of Chatman see Lee, *Luke's Stories of Jesus*, 340–41.

15. Burnett, "Characterization and Reader Construction," 16.

WHAT IS IN A NAME?

Burnett states that a character's proper name is the "crucial factor in the construction of a character" and helps create the sense of individuality for the reader.[16] I disagree with Burnett on one important point. Since the healed blind man remains anonymous throughout the narrative, we would be handicapped, according to Burnett, in our attempt to characterize him. But we are not handicapped in the least—we can characterize the blind man quite effectively. Even so, the narrator's tactic of leaving him nameless, especially since he is the principle protagonist for much of the narrative, mystifies us.

According to Beck, the very anonymity of the healed blind man serves an important rhetorical role.[17] When a character is named, a distance is created between the character and the reader. But if the character remains nameless, there is an implicit invitation to the reader to identify with him. The reader can enter into the story and experience what the character experiences. The healed man is everyman and everywoman, especially if the reader shares something of the man's alienation from society, family, and religious community.[18]

This rhetorical premise, the man's anonymity serving to invite us to identify with him, lies at the core of what I am attempting to do in this book. As Beck observes, the anonymous Johannine characters with significant narrative presence are the very ones, for the most part, who respond favorably to Jesus.[19] Whereas I think Beck makes some valid points, I believe that named characters can also have the potential of invitation

---

16. Ibid., 17–18. Burnett quotes Barthes, *S/Z: An Essay*, 67–68.

17. Beck, "Narrative Function," 147–53. But, as Beck notes, anonymity does not inherently signal significance (p. 147). Background characters, for example, who form part of a story's setting or who make a fleeting appearance remain nameless because individually they are unimportant. They hardly warrant the reader's attention. Some are nameless in order not to distract the reader from the named character. But Beck goes too far in suggesting that the Samaritan woman and the healed blind man are nameless in order to maintain the spotlight on Jesus. In the Fourth Gospel, as well as in the Synoptic Gospels, Jesus always remains the focus. In spite of his absence for the majority of the story (John 9), Jesus weighs heavily on the minds of all the characters present and he is the subject of their exchanges.

18. Ibid., 153.

19. Ibid., 150–55. Beck, however, paints too positive a picture of the lame man who, unlike the other nameless characters, does not ever respond to Jesus in faith. We would not want to identify with that man, as Beck suggests.

to the reader to enter into the story or, at least, to relate elements of the story to his or her life situation. The complexity of Peter's character, for example, invites us to examine the messiness of our lives.[20] We have experienced times of clarity, as when Peter confesses Jesus to be the Holy One of God (6:68–69). And we have stumbled badly as when Peter denies the Lord (18:17, 25–27). Yet in our identifying with the nameless man born blind, we can trace his steps toward growth in our insight and faith. We see our faith having a mental and a psychological aspect. Like the blind man, we must think through the evidence at our disposal in order to draw logical conclusions about Jesus. And like the blind man, we must face with courage and perseverance whatever challenges and obstacles that may be strewn across our path.

A READING STRATEGY

Four distinct reading strategies emerge from a survey of representative literature on the Fourth Gospel.[21] These strategies represent the ways in which scholars have wrestled with the seemingly glaring anti-Semitism of the Fourth Gospel, wherein "the Jews" are condemned for rejecting Jesus.[22]

The first approach provides a blatantly anti-Jewish "compliant reading" regarding the Jews as the children of the devil who slay Jesus.[23] The second sides with the Jews, but rejects Jesus in a "resistant reading." The third reading assumes that the Fourth Gospel reflects the historical, cultural, religious, and political context of the time of composition. The first readers of this Gospel comprised the so-called Johannine community of disciples expelled from the synagogue by an edict labelled Birkat

---

20. Tannehill observes that when readers make a positive evaluation of a disciple, they may identify with the disciple ("Gospel of Mark as Narrative Christology," 69–70). Whereas that may be true, I believe it also true that we can readily identify with a "rounded" character who realistically portrays both positive and negative traits. For a fuller treatment on positive and negative evaluations of the disciples specifically for Mark, see Danove, *Rhetoric of the Characterization*, 90–126.

21. Reinhartz proposes these reading strategies in her recent survey ("Judaism in the Gospel of John," 386–93).

22. Cook, for example, readily acknowledges that the Gospel is undeniably anti-Jewish but also advocates that other themes subordinate the anti-Judaic aspect ("Gospel of John and the Jews," 259–71).

23. Ashton appears to favor this rendering ("Identity and Function of the ’ΙΟΥΔΑΙΟΙ in the Fourth Gospel," 40–75). But at the same time, he acknowledges the symbolic reference to unbelief in Jesus and *the Jews* becomes the *world* in the Farewell Discourse.

Haminim ("blessing of the heretics") sometime after the destruction of the temple and Jerusalem in 70 CE.[24] And a fourth way of reading this Gospel places the historical and sociological context as the backdrop and thrusts to the foreground theological issues with regard to Jesus' identity and what he offers mankind.

Reinhartz asks a fundamental question by way of these four strategies: "Is there really only one path to God, only one way to be in covenantal relationship with God?"[25] For Reinhartz, a Jewish reader of the twenty-first century, the answer is no. She goes on to raise a few more questions, which I find poignant. How do modern readers live out their faith with a conviction that there is but one path or, by contrast, are there many paths? If the Gospel is part of the sacred canon, how should people relate to it? Must they uphold all of it or, if they cannot, must they reject all of it? Can they uphold parts of the canon while rejecting other parts? Reinhartz laments the anti-Semitism that has been extracted from the Fourth Gospel to justify the divide between people groups over the centuries. In her struggle with these questions, she forges her own path in which she can admire the literary artistry of this Gospel but, at the same time, reject its theology, or, as I see it, its Christology.

I respect Reinhartz's choice of response to the Fourth Gospel. I do not agree with her, for I too have made a choice, howbeit, a different choice. She has chosen to treasure the vehicle and to reject the message. I choose to value both. Every reader must make a choice that only he or she can make. No one can choose for him or her. This is the rhetorical agenda of the author. But at the same time we should heed Culpepper's call for "a hermeneutics of ethical accountability" that sensitizes us to possible readings that may counter a polemic against Jews and the marginalized.[26]

Of the four readings that Reinhartz delineates, I find no real distinction between the first and fourth readings, the compliant and the engaged readings (Reinhartz's terms), respectively. In regarding the Jews as

---

24. Martyn influenced a generation of Johannine scholars to read the Gospel at two levels, the story level and the historical level, in his seminal *History and Theology in the Fourth Gospel*. See, for example, Horbury, "Benediction of the *Minim* and Early Jewish-Christian Controversy," 19–61; and Painter, "John 9 and the Interpretation of the Fourth Gospel," 37–40. For a proposed reconstruction of the Johannine community, see Brown, *The Community of the Beloved Disciple*. But for a cogent rebuttal of this historical hypothesis, see Reinhartz, "Judaism in the Gospel of John," 389.

25. Ibid., 392.

26. Culpepper, "Gospel of John as a Document," 107–27.

representative of those who reject Jesus in hardened unbelief, I see them not exclusively as Jewish but as human. They represent anyone, ethnically Jew or Gentile, who reject Jesus' truth claims. In the Farewell Discourse (14:17, 19, 22, 27, 30–31; 15:18–19; 16:8, 11, 20, 33), this representative resistance to Jesus is "the world."[27] The broadened term points to a wider referent. If my reading of the Fourth Gospel is resistant, then I am of the world that hates Jesus and, because of him, his disciples. But if my reading is compliant and engaged, I—like the blind man who sees—will perceive Jesus as the way, the truth, and the life; and I will see the world as condemned for rejecting the truth and thus will grope hopelessly for the way.

A HISTORICAL READING

An engaged reading of the Fourth Gospel recognizes the importance of the historical and sociological backdrop of Jesus' cosmological journey to the world below from the realm above, and back again. But unlike a number of scholars, I strive to curb my speculative nature and not postulate the existence of a Johannine community whose struggles with late first-century Judaism resulted in expulsion from the synagogue. Hence, I do not read the Fourth Gospel at two different levels, historical and literary. Rather, I read the Christological message in order to respond in faith.

There are a number of historical questions stemming from our text that begs for answers, provided we want a better understanding of the ramifications for our faith journey today. Our main protagonist was congenitally blind and reduced to begging. What were the socio-economical realities facing a blind beggar in Jewish society of ancient Palestine? Which group today would readily identify with this man? Who were "the Jews," a group that apparently welded sufficient authority to invoke fear among the constituents? Are they to be identified with the Pharisees as one monolithic group, or were there significant differences between the two even though they may have gathered for common causes? Who today would we label the Jews? Do we regard any oppressor as the Jews? What did it mean to be excommunicated from the synagogue? Does the setting for this story antedate or postdate the catastrophic events of 70 CE? What are the implications for interpretation in dating the narrative? How is Jesus, always the main character of any gospel story, although uniquely

---

27. Strictly speaking, John 17 is not a discourse to the disciples but an intercessory prayer for the disciples.

absent for much of the present story, to be located in the socio-political spectrum in the ancient world? Is he to be classified as a charismatic authority figure, as Darr proposes?[28] How do we interact with Jesus today?

In matters of history and culture that form the context for the Johannine stories, we must rely on resources available during the period, known as Second Temple Judaism. The sources are primarily literary, although archaeology can provide important information. This treasure trove forms the basis for the extra-text: the corpus of Second Temple literature, excluding the Fourth Gospel. Scott provides a good overview and summary of this repository.[29] Among the more important sources are the Hebrew OT and the Greek translation of the OT, the LXX, particularly when the NT writers showed a closer affinity to the LXX in their citations of the OT, and when there are discernable differences between the Hebrew and Greek versions in matters of the text and content.[30] A major distinction is the inclusion of the Apocrypha in the LXX that was a product of the Second Temple period due in large measure to Hellenization that rendered devout Jews illiterate with regard to the Hebrew Scriptures. Another important resource of the period is the OT Pseudepigrapha, representing a wide range of literary genres composed between 200 BCE and 200 CE.[31] Some other ancient sources from the period include the Dead

---

28. Darr, *Herod the Fox*, 101–36. A charismatic, according to Darr, is one who is substantiated by "the unusual gifts of spirit, mind, and body possessed by the charismatic leader and recognized as such by other people" (p. 101).

29. Scott, *Jewish Backgrounds*, 29–39. For a good introduction to the period, see Tomasino, *Judaism Before Jesus*.

30. Hunt asserts that the Hebrew OT reached canonical status with the Torah in 621 or 450 BCE, Prophets between 450 and 165 BCE, and Writings between 200 BCE and 100 CE ("Examination of the Current Emphasis," 58–60). But Josephus (*Ag. Ap.*) made the earliest mention of 22 canonical books in 90 CE (p. 60). Based on available data, Vanderkam states more accurately that a closed canon agreed on by all Jewish sects was not achieved by 100 CE (*From Revelation to Canon*, 10–29). The Qumran community, for example, viewed *1 Enoch* and *Jubilees* as sacred. But it cannot be verified that all Jewish sects concurred. Nor can one confirm that Josephus, with Pharisaical tendencies, was representative of the Pharisees' idea of the canon. Consensus on the Hebrew canon would not come until later. Grisanti contends that books like the Psalter underwent a lengthy process of composition and editing in which the product was canonical at each step ("Inspiration, Inerrancy, and the OT Canon," 577–98). However, only the final form of the text in the canon is viewed as inspired (Klein et al., *Introduction to Biblical Interpretation*, 187).

31. Charlesworth gives a precise definition of pseudepigrapha: "those writings(1) that, with the exception of Ahiqar, are Jewish or Christian; (2) that are often attributed to

Sea Scrolls; the NT, which even Jewish scholars regard as an historical document; the writings of Philo Judaeus and Flavius Josephus, two first century Jewish writers; the rabbinic literature, which came from a later period but may offer a glimpse into some of the Jewish practices from Second Temple times; and contemporary Greco-Roman literature with references to Jewish customs.[32]

EXTRA-TEXT: BLINDNESS

I will now survey the available literature of the Second Temple period.

OT and Apocrypha

In the OT, including the Apocrypha, God shows compassion toward the blind and heals them (Lev 19:14; Ps 146:8; Isa 29:18; 35:5), but he afflicts with blindness either literally or figuratively those who sin against him (Deut 28:28–29; Jer 39:7; 52:11; Zeph 1:17; Zech 11:17; Wis 19:17).[33] An unacceptable defect, blindness disqualified people from serving as priests (Lev 21:17–21) and animals from being offered to the Lord (Lev 22:19–22; Deut 15:21; Mal 1:8). Metaphorically, blindness expresses compromising one's integrity in matters requiring justice (Exod 23:8; Deut 16:19; 1 Sam 12:3; Sir 20:29). Of the forty-two references to blindness, twenty-four cases point to a physical ailment and the remaining occurrences are metaphorical. The condition does not necessarily imply begging. Several times a prohibition warns against taking advantage of those so afflicted. However, the rather lengthy treatment on the subject of helping the poor, assuming the inclusion of the blind, in Sir 4:1–10 suggests society's responsibility to the less fortunate (also Sir 7:10, 32).

---

ideal figures in Israel's past; (3) that customarily claim to contain God's word or message; (4) that frequently build upon ideas and narratives present in the Old Testament; (5) and that almost always were composed either during the period 200 B.C. to A.D. 200 or, though late, apparently preserve, albeit in an edited form, Jewish traditions that date from that period" ("Introduction for the General Reader," xxv).

32. For a fuller list and discussion, see Scott, *Jewish Backgrounds*, 30–34.

33. For the LXX's characterization of the blind and the poor, see Roth, *Blind, the Lame, and the Poor*, 103–6 and 112–39, respectively. The latter survey also covers the OT Pseudepigrapha. He draws three conclusions: the blind are divinely designated to receive human kindness, they may be healed by God or his agent, and they will be healed eschatologically (p. 106).

OT Pseudepigrapha

In the OT Pseudepigrapha, references to the blind or blindness are metaphorical in eleven incidences; physical in seventeen occurrences, of which only one reveals an explicit connection with begging; and two possible cases of judgment. In *T. Job* 17:3, a distribution list of those who receive alms features three distinct classes of people: beggars, the blind, and the lame. Interestingly, the list separates beggars from the blind and the lame, the physically handicapped. In any case, all receive alms.

Qumran Literature

A survey of the DSS yields similar findings with fourteen and sixteen incidences of metaphorical and physical uses of blindness, respectively. The metaphorical use of blindness always conveys a negative connotation of spiritual ineptitude and moral compromise. Through the use of simile, a number of physical references to blindness describe those guilty of willful sin and injustice.[34] The blind are portrayed as easy targets for victimization.[35] Blindness is considered a serious blemish[36] and is grouped with the lame and paralytic,[37] the humpback,[38] and the twisted, presumably a reference to twisted backs.[39]

Tobit

The deuterocanonical work of Tobit, a second century BCE composition, merits separate treatment because one of its major protagonists becomes

---

34. For example, the guilty are like the blind who grope for the path (4QDa col. 2:1–2). Or they are likened to those who go astray (4QpsDanc ar [4Q245] frag. 2:3). 4QpsDanc ar is the third of three pseudo-Daniel manuscripts written in Aramaic found in Cave 4 at Qumran.

35. 4QDd (*olim* Df) [4Q269] frag. 9:2, 4QDe [4Q270] frag. 5:15, and 4QDf (*olim* Dc) [4Q271] frag. 3:9, all of which refer to Deut 27:18, specifying judgment for leading the blind astray. These documents are three different copies of the Damascus Document found in Cave 4.

36. 11QTa col. 52:10.

37. 1QSa col. 2:5–6; M [1Q33] col. 7:4.

38. Hodayot-like Text A [4Q433] frag. 1:3. Hodayot means "thanksgiving" and refers to the *Thanksgiving Scroll*, a collection of poetic compositions, many of which thank God; found in Cave 1. A number of fragmentary manuscripts bearing varying degrees of similarity to the Hodayot are called Hodayot-like in the literature.

39. 4QMessAp frag. 2 col. 2:8.

blind for a period of time.[40] The story depicts Tobit's isolation in Assyrian exile far from Palestine, his homeland (1:2), when he incurs the king's wrath for burying fellow Jews slain by the king (1:18–19).[41] The king confiscates all of Tobit's property and takes away his wife and son (1:20). But with the succession of a new king and the intervention of a relative, Ahiqar, the chief cupbearer, Tobit returns home and reunites with his family (1:21—2:1). But he is mocked by other Jews for burying yet another slain Jew (2:7-8). Although isolated from homeland, kinsmen, and, for a time, his family, Tobit claims to maintain his faithfulness to God (1:3–12) and concern for his people (1:16–18). Then to make matters worse, he suffers blindness by the absurdity of having his eyes smeared by bird dung and the ineptitude of the physicians (2:10). Immediately, however, Tobit, as the narrator, foretells that his blindness will last four years.[42]

At the message level, the book of Tobit is really about the world being out of order in which several prominent inversions form the framework for the unfolding narrative and God ultimately intervenes to right what is wrong.[43] The fundamental inversion is the subjugation of Israel under Gentile rule. Scattered into the Diaspora with no obvious means of returning home, God's people languishes until God enters into the human experience dramatically in the person of Raphael ("God heals"), one of the seven angels before the glory of the Lord (12:15), who comes in response to both Tobit's and Sarah's prayers (3:16–17). Over the course of

---

40. For an excellent discussion of the Aramaic of Tobit that helps date the work, see Fitzmyer's "Aramaic and Hebrew Fragments," 655–75. Others like Coogan, however, date it earlier to the fourth or third century BCE (*Old Testament: Historical and Literary*, 533).

41. See Portier-Young for her treatment of Tobit's isolation ("Alleviation of Suffering," 37–45).

42. Zimmerman notes the transition from first-person account to the third person in 3:7 that becomes more evident in 3:16–17 (*Book of Tobit*, 6). But 3:7 offers no reference to Tobit. The switch takes place at 3:16 when Sarah, Tobit's future daughter-in-law, and Tobit are alluded to in the third person. McCracken explains this shift in Tobit's role as narrator and character—Tobit-as-narrator looks back after the events concerning Tobit-as-character have played out ("Narration and Comedy," 404–7). Tobit becomes the narrator when commanded by the angel to record the events (12:20). What Tobit writes down becomes the first-person account in the early part of the book (ibid., 405).

43. Cousland, "Tobit: Comedy in Error?" 535–53, especially 548–52. Cousland lists as inversions Tobit's wife, Anna, assuming the man's role in being the breadwinner; Sarah, Tobit's distant relative, failing to be fruitful and multiply, contrary to Gen 1:28a; birds and fish having the upper hand over humans, contrary to Gen 1:28b; and injustices in this life not being rectified.

the rest of the story, Raphael in the guise of a human rescues them from their respective predicaments. At the end of the narrative the Jews are still exiled under foreign rule. But in a psalm of praise (13:1–18), Tobit expresses hope of an eventual return (13:10–11, 13, 17–18). He anticipates the rebuilding of the tabernacle (13:11) and Jerusalem (13:17).

A number of observations that I have made about Tobit's blindness may provide a glimpse into how the affliction was viewed, and how certain elements of the narrative suggest a possible parallel between Tobit and the blind man in the Fourth Gospel.[44]

Not surprisingly, the family reacts with grief to Tobit's blindness (2:10). They see his condition as tragic. But one relative, Ahiqar, refuses to become despondent and responds with charity by way of supporting Tobit for the first two years. Then Tobit's wife, Anna, finds employment.[45] Thus, Tobit is portrayed as unemployable and totally dependent on his family. One can imagine the helplessness and shame associated with the affliction. Another important observation finds that Tobit's family proves reliable, and so he does not need to beg. Even though the narrative limits the condition to four years (Tobit as narrator manifests an omniscience characteristic of narrators), as a character in the story he does not know he will be blind for a limited time. No situational hint prompts him to anticipate facing anything other than a permanent condition.

Almost immediately, Tobit displays a perceptual blindness: he wrongfully accuses his wife of theft when she brings home a young goat, a bonus from her employers in addition to her wages (2:12–14). He refuses to believe her explanation, and so solicits her sarcastic reply (2:14e): "And where are your acts of mercy? Where are your righteous deeds? Behold, these are known about you." Tobit proves incongruous

---

44. In a somewhat reverse manner, Novick focuses on Tobit's use of the canonical OT in a manner that generalizes a biblical, historical situation and applies it to a nonbiblical situation ("Biblicized Narrative," 755–64). Novick is one of many who study Tobit's intertextuality. See, for example, Di Lella's, "Deuteronomic Background," 380–89, and "Tobit 14:10," 497–506, and Weitzman's, "Allusion, Artifice, and Exile," 49–61. However, I do not suggest that the author of the Fourth Gospel intentionally modelled his characterization of the blind man after Tobit. I seek instead circumstantial generalizations that might have a bearing in our understanding of the Gospel's blind man.

45. Portier-Young notes the Greek term "nourish" with regard to Ahiqar's support for Tobit (2:10) and the expression "womanly work" (2:11) in describing Anna's employment in order to highlight Tobit's helplessness ("Alleviation of Suffering," 41). Cousland, however, regards Anna negatively as someone who should have trusted God more and not enter into "the man's role" ("Tobit," 544, 549).

with his reputation for being merciful and just.[46] His perceptual blindness has turned him against the one person who sacrifices herself to provide for his sustenance.

Feeling justified, he demands that Anna return what he thinks is a stolen goat. His refusal to believe his wife's claim of innocence aggravates his faulty perception. He has judged her guilty and no amount of pleading will change his verdict.

His predicament—a combination of the murder of a fellow Jew (2:3–5), the lack of his neighbor's sympathy in his burying the victim (2:8), his blindness, and finally what he wrongly perceives to be his wife's thievery—moves him to pray to God (3:1–6). First, he acknowledges God's righteous judgments in exiling his people for their sins. Then he recognizes God's just punishment for his sins. Here he appears to allude to his physical blindness and to his grief over his wife's supposed thievery. Finally he comes to the main thrust of his prayer—he prays for death. His sense of humiliation is too much to bear.

Through Tobit, we see a correlation between blindness, both physically and perceptually, and grief, humiliation, and an overwhelming sense of isolation, although other attendant matters complicate his situation. There is a cause and effect relationship. For Tobit, divine punishment for sin results in blindness. But rather than stoically enduring the consequences, he desires death. It is the only conceivable means of escape from present suffering. He prays that God mercifully takes away his life. Yet, he requests more than simply an end to his physical life. He pleads (3:6e): "Lord, command that I should be released from this distress. Release me to the eternal place." Whatever this "eternal place" may be in Tobit's understanding, it may represent some kind of afterlife.[47] It is eternal destiny he desires; however, he wants entry sooner than later.

But he does not remain in physical and perceptual blindness. He eventually gains both sight and insight. The narrative turning point (3:16) is the divine response to two prayers—Tobit's and Sarah's. Unbeknownst to him, Sarah, his future daughter-in-law, simultaneously prays to express her grief and desire to die (3:11–15). She too has suffered greatly because

---

46. Overall, however, Tobit is portrayed as a righteous man who regularly gives alms. See Di Lella, "Study of Tobit 14:10," 504–5. In fact, Di Lella advocates that almsgiving "is a major theme of the book" (p. 504).

47. Cousland states that the book of Tobit entertains no belief in the afterlife ("Tobit," 548, 550).

a demon has slain seven successive husbands on each of her wedding nights and, as a result, has been harshly reproached by one of her maids. There is a switch of narrators. Up to this point Tobit has been the narrator-character; but the shift from a first-person to a third-person account cues the reader that Tobit is now strictly the character in the story and that another has assumed the role of narrator. The new narrator comments that God hears both prayers (3:16). Alerted, the reader anticipates a change in the fortunes of both petitioners.

God sends an angel to heal both Tobit and Sarah (3:17). Tobit will supernaturally gain his sight and see the "light of God" and Sarah will finally have a husband who survives the wedding night when the demon is driven from her. Here we find a loose parallel with the Fourth Gospel, where God sends an emissary to earth. The emissary supernaturally heals the blindness. And, as Tobit will see the "light of God," Jesus will demonstrate that he is the "light of the world"—and the man he heals will see him as that light. Both Tobit and the man Jesus heals endure a process that consummates in final healing.

There is another parallel. Tobias, Tobit's son, applies fish gall on his father's blind eyes and peels off the white film from the eyes so that he may regain his sight (11:11–13). Neither the fish gall nor Tobias has any inherent power to heal. Rather, Tobias obeys the angel's instruction in facilitating the healing. In like manner, the blind man follows Jesus' instruction to go wash at the pool and gains his sight. In both situations, obedience to the emissary's instruction is crucial to the healing.

A significant difference between the two accounts of healing, however, centers on the angel Raphael disguising his true identity by taking human form; whereas unbelief hides Jesus' true identity from his opponents. In the former case, the angel simply appears human; but in the latter case, Jesus becomes human through the incarnation. Yet, another difference is that Jesus heals a congenitally blind man. Tobit, on the other hand, has normal sight until a bizarre incident blinds him. Also, the families of the two men demonstrate different attitudes and relationships with them. Tobit's family, although grieved, provides support to meet all his material needs. But the congenitally blind man must beg for a living, and his parents abandon him in his moment of testing.

With this overview and comparison of Tobit and the Fourth Gospel accounts of blindness, I draw a number of conclusions. First, blindness, a grievous affliction, renders these two people helpless. Tobit is unemployable and must rely totally on his family for support, and the blind man in the Fourth Gospel goes begging in the public arena. Second, Tobit offers a unique opportunity to enter into the psyche of the blind. If Tobit is in any sense "typical," I infer that the blind man suffers both emotionally and spiritually, and may regard his condition as divine judgment for his sins. Viewing his dilemma as irrevocable, he may harbor a death wish. If he is at all religious, he may pray for death. But he is not suicidal. He does not take matters into his own hands. There may be an overwhelming sense of isolation. He has no friends and even his family feels the burden of caring for him. He may feel distant from God, for God seemingly has abandoned him. Third, there is no cure for blindness short of supernatural intervention. It is a hopeless condition. A person must resign himself to his fate and make the best of a desperate situation.

New Testament

In the Gospels, the blind beseech Jesus for mercy and receive their sight (Matt 9:27–30; 12:22; 15:30–31; 20:30–34; 21:14; Mark 8:22–25; 10:46–52; Luke 7:21; 18:35–43). Of these incidences, only two cases identify the blind explicitly as beggars (Mark 10:46; Luke 18:35). A third case involves the blind man in our narrative (John 9:8). Again, the NT refers metaphorically to blindness as a spiritual or moral condition that cannot detect the light of the gospel (2 Cor 4:4), as lacking things related to godliness (2 Pet 1:9), as hating one's brother (1 John 2:11),[48] or as lukewarmness (Rev 3:17–18).

Josephus and Philo

Josephus mentions the blind or being blind seventeen times. Five times the blind are mentioned simply as a part of society without any reference to begging.[49] Three times judgment results in blindness.[50] And the remaining nine occurrences are metaphorical.[51] Of the ninety-two occurrences of the blind, or being blind, in Philo's writings, metaphorical references account for sixty-eight cases. Physical allusions make up the bulk of the remaining twenty-four incidences in which the blind are stereotyped

---

48. Marshall, *Epistles of John*, 110, 133.
49. *A.J.* 1.267; 7.61; 15.283; *Ag. Ap.* 2:15, 23.
50. *A.J.* 1.202; 10.141; *J.W.* 5.343.
51. *A.J.* 7.169; 8.30; *J.W.* 1.515; 5.572; 6.138; *Ag. Ap.* 1.214, 226; 2.132, 142.

as those who cannot see and so stumble about, not being able to make their way around. Not once does either writer link the blind with begging.

Roman Literature

A number of Roman authors from the third century BCE through early third century CE offer some insight into the attitude toward the unfortunate. The early playwright Titus Maccius Plautus, living in the third to second century BCE, has one of his characters denounce an accomplice as being "lame, blind, dumb, defective, and weak" for failing to complete a mission (*Mercator* 3.4).[52] Dismissively, Plautus classifies lameness and blindness figuratively as ineptitude. Pliny the Elder, a first-century CE historian, describes blind Fortune (or Fate) in *The Natural History* 2.5. Metaphorically speaking, Fortune, being totally random, gropes about without any sense of direction, like the blind. He also labels a person's lack of perception as blindness (*Natural History* 9.20; 11.54). Similarly, Titus Livius, another historian, calls a lack of perception blindness (*The History of Rome* 21.54; 22.6; 25.21; 26.13; 31.10; 37.43; 38.17; 40.13; 42.47, 55). On one occasion, Livius attributes men's blindness to Fortune in making them insensible to the consequences of their actions (*History* 5.22). In another incidence, blindness is the result of punishment meted out by the gods (*History* 9.29). The author Cornelius Tacitus, of the late first and early second centuries, offers a metaphorical use of blindness in his *The Annuals* 1.32 and in *The History* 1.49. Exceeding the bounds of credibility, a contemporary of Tacitus, Roman administrator Gaius Suetonius Tranquillus, ascribes divine-like powers to the emperor Vespasian in healing a blind man with spittle (*The Lives of the Twelve Caesars* 7). Born in the middle of the second century, Cassius Dio (or Dio Cassius, Lucius Cassius Dio Cocceianus), authored the eighty-volume *Historiae Romanae*, completing it in the first third of the following century. Dio made no explicit mention about the blind and their status within the empire; but several tangential comments about the afflicted or destitute may be pertinent. In the First Punic War (264 to 241 BCE), Regulus, one of the Roman generals, was reputedly so impoverished that the public treasury supported his family to enable him to concentrate on the war (11.43.20). On another occasion, due to the exigency of war, Julius Caesar intervened

---

52. http://www.perseus.tufts.edu/hopper/ contains all the literature cited in this section.

in the often-contentious disputes between lender and borrower at home, and in the process offered some protection for the borrower (41.37.3). Finally, Agrippa advised Octavian to pity those who meet with misfortune (52.4.8), and to mete out justice to the masses when any are wronged (52.37.7).

Early Christian Literature

A survey of some early Christian writings likewise yields a rather uncertain picture of the blind in ancient Palestine. In the late first century, *1 Clement* (*First Epistle of Clement to the Corinthians*) admonishes the strong not to neglect the weak, and the weak to respect the strong, and the rich to help the poor (38:2).[53] Then toward the end of the letter a prayer beseeches God to show mercy upon the lowly, to lift up the fallen, to manifest himself to the needy, feed the hungry, raise up the weak, and comfort the fainthearted (59:4).[54] Ignatius, martyred in 107 CE, wrote seven letters that survive to this day.[55] In his *Epistle to the Smyrnæans*, he exhorts the poor among his readers to maintain their dignity (6.2). Polycarp instructs presbyters to provide for widows, orphans, and the poor (*Epistle of Polycarp to the Philippians* 6.1). Another early second-century document, *Epistle of Barnabas*, categorizes the withholding of justice from the widow and orphan, and pity for the poor with murder, idolatry, and hypocrisy (20.2). The *Didache* (*Teaching of the Lord through the Twelve Apostles to the Nations*) is perhaps to be dated in the early second century.[56] Chapter four admonishes the reader not to turn away a brother in want; and chapter five seems to echo *Barnabas* (or is it the other way around?) in likening the withholding of pity from a poor man to such evil as murders, idolatries, and hypocrisy. Then the instructions about supporting true prophets in chapter 13 direct Christians to give to the poor if there are no prophets to sustain. The early Christian writings examined so far do not explicitly mention the blind. We have to assume

---

53. Schnelle dates the letter 96 CE (*History and Theology*, 352). http://www.earlychristianwritings.com/ features the documents reviewed in this section.

54. Lightfoot's translation differs from the Coxe version, *Apostolic Fathers*, 5–21. Coxe's version omits 57.7–63.4, which Lightfoot's includes. According to Coxe, his exemplar lacks a whole leaf (p. 20 n. 15).

55. Ibid., 48.

56. Schnelle, *History and Theology*, 355; and Brown, *Introduction to the New Testament*, 837. Debate over the dating of this work continues.

that they are subsumed under the category "poor." A second-century work, the *Gospel of Thomas* consists of Jesus' sayings, many similar to that found in the Synoptic Gospels.[57] A puzzling saying states that it is harmful to give alms (saying 14). But the clearest reference to blindness anticipates two blind men falling into a pit if one should lead the other (saying 34), recalling Matt 15:14 and Luke 6:39. Another second century work, *Shepherd of Hermas* contains one of the most extensive discussions about the poor from among early noncanonical Christian writings. The last six verses of Parable 2 condemn the rich for being poor toward God unless they help the poor who is rich toward God in terms of intercession. Since this work makes no mention of the blind, again we infer that they are included among the poor.

Mishnah

The Mishnah, completed toward the end of the second-century CE, represents the rabbinic interpretation of the law, both written and oral, preserving for posterity the traditions of the elders.[58] Tractate *m. Pe'ah* ("Gleanings") 8:7–8 provides for the poor. Then *m. Pe'ah* 8:9 articulates a curious curse on someone who pretends to be lame, dumb, blind, or stammering and refers to metaphorical blindness due to bribery.

Conclusions

As I review our survey of ancient literature, I find that the DSS, Tobit, and the canonical writings present the clearest and most helpful commentary about the blind in ancient society. The other works rarely mention the blind. As a result, I broadened our investigation to the all-encompassing strata of the poor with the underlying assumption that the blind were categorized with the widow, orphan, destitute, oppressed, and materially poor. Analogously, the lame would probably be included as well. These, if mentioned, were consistently objects of compassion in Christian literature, both canonical and noncanonical, whereby the author admonished his reader to provide for their sustenance. These brief glimpses suggest that society, particularly Roman society in the person of the ruler, had some sense of responsibility toward the poor. The general populace, however, did not appear to have any

---

57. Brown counts seventy-nine sayings that have Synoptic parallels (ibid., 839–40).

58. Danby, *Mishnah*, xiii–xiv. In particular, the Mishnah preserved the religious system of the Pharisees and not that of the Sadducees.

imposed obligation. None of the other noncanonical literature evidenced any intentional concern for the poor.

This literary survey does not imply, however, that ancient society showed no mercy toward the poor, including the blind. These unfortunates were clearly a part of society. But were they cared for? Most, if not all, of the ancient noncanonical writers examined here dwelt on the big issues of the day, either of a political, military, or historical nature. Simply, the masses formed the backdrop of the then-current events. Only the OT, NT, and noncanonical Christian literature, not surprisingly, have any real regard for those who struggled. The writing of Tobit is exceptional; but Tobit's physical blindness bears strong symbolic significance in portraying perceptual blindness and may well be a divinely appointed affliction to showcase God's covenantal mercy and power. Clearly, since God cares for the poor and destitute, his people must reflect that concern in practice. Any conclusions that we draw about the poor in general and the blind in particular remain tentative. The available data is simply too scant. In our examination of the blind man in John 9, I will have to make some inferences in order to fill in the gaps in our knowledge. In some ways our protagonist was probably "typical." But in certain other ways he was unique in that he emerges as a hero who triumphs against his adversaries. Samson (Judg 16:21–31) and Tobit form the closest parallels in the ancient literature.[59]

The bulk of the frequent metaphorical allusions to blindness deals with being blinded by greed or ambition and the like, or with those who act as the blind because they are groping in the dark. In the canonical writings, figurative blindness indicates either a deficient moral or spiritual condition, or signals divine judgment. Often the two alternatives overlap, in that God judges those found deficient.

CHARACTERIZATION OF THE BLIND MAN

The preceding review of the ancient literature attempts to identify the extra-text, pertinent readings from Second Temple literature excluding

---

59. The ancient literature reviewed in this chapter defines the scope of my comment. Other ancient literature, of course, dealt with blindness. For example, Sophocles' tragedy *Oedipus the King* (or *Oedipus Rex*) featured the motif of physical and metaphorical blindness, as ironically personified by Oedipus who was "blind" to his parentage and incest until he blinded himself, and by the blind seer Tiresias who "saw" the true state of things quite clearly.

the Fourth Gospel, that forms one of three sources by which we may understand the man born blind. The other two sources are the text that contains the story of the man (John 9) and the reader. The extra-text provides a glimpse of the social conventions that typified the historical setting of the story. However, our knowledge of that remote period will always be imperfect. The conventions of the time were intimately familiar, for both the author and his original readers; so much so that the familiarity was assumed and left tacit.[60] We modern readers have too few clues with regard to those ancient conventions. We can only speculate about how the other characters of the story regarded and interacted with the blind man, the kind of life the man led, and his perception of the world around him. We do not know whether people respected or despised him, and whether he felt stripped of his dignity with no sense of place in society. His relationship with his family remains a mystery. Obviously illiterate, he may still have received some religious education as a Jew. Perhaps a low quality of life prodded him to survive as a scavenger of sorts. People conceivably viewed him as an untouchable. We do not have definitive clues.

We can know nothing of his personality unless the text informs us. But we can extract something of his character from the narrative. As readers of the text, we bring into the reading experience the social conventions of our time and our prior experience with the blind. In doing so, we fill in the story's gaps, and so fill out the missing pieces in the man's portrait. We have no other recourse. Mindful of the limited information at our disposal, we guard against becoming dogmatic. We can speculate to some extent but we also acknowledge that our conclusions are tentative, that other possibilities of interpretation may exist.

My experience with blindness is embodied in two people who were legally blind—Aunt Sylvia and a member of my former congregation. In both cases, the family was instrumental in helping each person cope. My devoted uncle facilitated my aunt's daily routine. I recall the visit my family paid to them. As we left their home for lunch at a local restaurant, I extended my hand to help Aunt Sylvia out the door. Almost immediately my uncle pushed my hand away and took her arm. Slowly they made their way to the car. Years later I witnessed the same care the young woman in my congregation received from her mother. My experience is quite limited, confined to those whose family spared

---

60. Alter, *Art of Biblical Narrative*, 47–49.

no effort or resources toward their well-being. Neither one begged or depended on welfare. In fact, the young woman's employer provided a special computer monitor to this visually challenged sister in Christ because she still had some residual vision.

But I have also encountered blindness in public venues. The sight-impaired would position themselves on crowded sidewalks, usually sitting on a small stool with a donation reciprocal in front. If musically gifted, they would sing, play an instrument, or both. I often wondered whether they received enough for each day's sustenance. I don't recall ever seeing a full bucket before any of them. I also wondered how they managed to get themselves to and from their spot each time.

Based on my personal background and what I can glean from the ancient literature, I come to the Fourth Gospel and make a few inferences about the life of the blind at that time.[61] First, the blind could not become self-supporting. The ancient occupations of farmer, merchant, skilled craftsman, and soldier were not viable options. Second, they must have then depended on the charity of others, whether from the family or society (God may be the benefactor tacitly). Third, they were not viewed as assets to society because they could not contribute in a meaningful way to society's well-being. Fourth, if the family could not provide for all their needs, they turned to the only recourse open to them—begging. Hence, not surprisingly, the blind man of our text was a beggar (9:8).

But these inferences are stereotypical, and they threaten to diminish the individuality of this blind man. Whereas, if he had had a sense of humor or a gregarious nature, or had been philosophical about his condition or unique in some way, we have no way of knowing unless the text tells us. We cannot simply make up something in order to make our character special. The text's reticence both precludes and suggests.[62] The author may invite the reader to speculate through omissions. This engages

---

61. There are a significant number of the blind throughout history who did not fit the stereotype, but who were major forces in the sciences, politics, culture and the arts. For a partial list, including Homer (although uncertainty surrounded his life), see Braille Works' "Famous People with Visual Impairments," lines 34–44. Significantly, the ancient Iranian poet and ballad singer Abu Abdullah Jafar ibne Mohammad Rudaki was born blind. See "Iranian Poetry," lines 1–34. The blind man of the Fourth Gospel will also be non-stereotypical primarily because of God's plans for him and how he will respond to God's election.

62. Alter focuses more on the possibilities of interpretation in view of the author's omissions (*Art of Biblical Narrative*, 114–30).

the imagination to fill in the narrative gaps, and so rhetorically draws the reader in to become an active player who can contribute to the reading process. There is, then, a three-member collaboration of extra-text, text, and reader that results in a reading that prompts the reader to respond intellectually, emotionally, and, ultimately, spiritually.

Conditioned in part by the OT and entertaining a misunderstanding of retributive justice, Jesus' disciples see the blind man and make unfounded assumptions. In response, Jesus gives a surprising reason for the man's congenital condition. We will study their brief exchange and the man himself in more detail in the coming chapters. And in the end we will have a proposed characterization of the man by which we can measure ourselves. I suspect that we will be quite challenged.

3

From the Wrong Side of the Tracks

> And when he passed by, he saw a man blind from birth. And his disciples asked him, "Rabbi, who sinned, this man or his parents, that he was born blind?" Jesus answered, "Neither did this man sin nor his parents, but that the works of God may be manifested in him."
>
> —John 9:1–3

As the man born blind proceeds on his journey, he gains greater insight into Jesus' identity and, as a consequence, experiences a change in association. He no longer associates with the world that dwells in spiritual darkness; but he joins the community of those who live in a privileged union with Jesus and the Father. But let us not get ahead of the man's story.

Our imagination enables an effective reading of the Fourth Gospel narrative. We strive to picture ourselves as participants in the story rather than as dispassionate readers of it. Slipping into his shoes, we imagine ourselves as the blind man. In this story only he experiences movement. Both Jesus and the disciples are static. Jesus does not need to change. The disciples should change but do not, at least not until later.

The man represents our condition. He starts out blind in lacking the insight into Jesus' true identity. As the blind man comes to a fuller grasp of the person Jesus, he makes certain choices despite pressure from the religious establishment to choose otherwise. His choices reveal a new set of convictions about Jesus that, in turn, gives him the courage to stand firm. Our life choices and convictions reveal whether we really know Jesus or not.

And now on with the story.

The story begins as a continuation of an ongoing narrative with "and" being the first word of 9:1. Jesus had left the temple, the target of stoning for alleged blasphemy (8:59). His crime was declaring, "Before Abraham came on the scene, I have been around" (8:58).[1] This self-declaration of preexistence, an essential attribute of divinity, forms the immediate backdrop for the sign of the blind man gaining sight. It sets the stage for the subsequent drama.

We cannot determine with any certainty the timeline of the story. A gap of some duration separates 8:59 and 9:1. Two time markers confine the successive events to within the Feast of Tabernacles (7:2) and before the Feast of Rededication (10:22). But from the perspective of the narrative, Jesus coming upon the blind man follows immediately upon his departure from the temple. Given the apparent isolation of the incident that afforded uninterrupted interaction between Jesus and his disciples, and his interaction with the blind man, the episode occurs some distance from the temple. The Jews do not spot Jesus, and the man's acquaintances who interact with him later (9:8–12) are not present.

DIVINE APPOINTMENT

The narrative states that when Jesus passes by he sees the man, blind from birth. A number of questions arise in our minds. Is this a chance encounter or is it a divine appointment? We learn from 4:4 that Jesus had to pass through Samaria on his way to Galilee, although alternative routes existed. Only after the narrative depicts his offer of living water (4:10, 13–14), his self-identification as the expected Messiah-Christ (4:26), and the subsequent belief of the Samaritan woman's hometown neighbors (4:39–42), do we understand the "necessity" of Jesus' mission to Samaria. He intentionally went through Samaria. In like manner, there may be an implicit divine imperative to pass by the blind man. Also, how does Jesus

---

1. Jesus literally said, "Before Abraham became, I am." The contrast of verbs conveys the intended meaning—the first verb infers a change, that is, Abraham was born; in contrast, the second verb is stative in declaring Jesus' existence. Abraham experienced change; Jesus does not. He ever exists as the unchanging one. The Jews correctly interpret his statement, but refuse to accept it. Hence, they sought to stone him for blasphemy according to the Law.

know he was born blind? Perhaps we can ascribe to Jesus divine insight. But how do the disciples know the man's personal history? The narrative does not answer these questions.

INADEQUATE WORLDVIEW

As it turns out, we are not the only ones with questions. Upon seeing the blind man, the disciples ask Jesus, "Rabbi, who sinned, this man or his parents, that he was born blind?" (9:2). The disciples' worldview prompts the question. They believe the world operates on the principle of retributive justice. You do good deeds—you will be blessed. You do wicked things—expect punishment.

I myself learned that principle early. The house rules were clear; and the consequences for breaking them were painfully clear as well. I grew up thinking that my father's love was conditioned on obedience. Infractions incurred a penalty swiftly meted out. Not washing the dishes properly resulted in a strong verbal rebuke. Accidentally breaking a dish meant a well-aimed shoe thrown in my direction. Talking back was not tolerated. In most households this last rule is normal. But my father expanded the rule to include voicing a different position on subjects he had a firm opinion, especially if I dissented in the presence of guests. It showed disrespect. It did not take too many run-ins with father to learn to keep my mouth shut.

Retributive justice reduces God. He becomes predictable. If we act a certain way, we expect him to respond in a certain way. But God is not predictable because he does not fit neatly into our categories. Hamlet affirms that reality when he says: "There are more things in heaven and earth, Horatio, than are dreamt of in your philosophy."[2]

Much of the pertinent literature concerning retributive justice relate to the book of Job, the classic discourse on the subject.[3] Sylvia H. Scholnick makes an important distinction between jurisprudence and sovereignty in rendering the two uses of "justice" in Job.[4] Job seeks vindication in court; but God acts according to his sovereign authority. Instead

---

2. Shakespeare, *Hamlet*, act 1 scene 5.

3. For example, Clines, "Shape and Argument of the Book of Job" 125–39, especially 130–39; and Tsevat, "Meaning of the Book of Job," 73–106.

4. Scholnick, "Meaning of *mišpāt* [Justice]," 521–29.

of answering Job's request for the charges against him point for point (Job 13:23), God reviews his dominion over the created order (Job 38–41).

Suffering and affliction may or may not have a ready explanation. Paul relates the Corinthian Christians' suffering, and in some cases even their demise, to their desecrating the sanctity of the Lord's Supper (1 Cor 11:27–30). The consequences were swift. In 1 Tim 5:24, we find the biblical perspective: "The sins of some people which go before into judgment are evident, but for others they follow afterwards." Some people experience the consequences of their sins in this life; but others will face the consequences after death. No one escapes judgment. From a big picture perspective, no one is justified in calling God unfair or unjust.

Jesus' disciples do not ask whether the blind man is an example of retributive justice. They assume it. He suffers for sin in this life. Divine justice has been measured out now. Their question has to do with who is culpable—the man or his parents. There is no sympathy. In their estimation, he clearly deserves his condition. However, given his congenital condition, there is the possibility that he suffers through no personal fault of his own. Then surely his parents must be guilty. Perhaps the disciples recall the Mosaic legislation that requires succeeding generations to pay for the iniquity of the fathers until the third and fourth generation (Exod 20:5; 34:7; Num 14:18; Deut 5:9). It must have been a serious offense, they think.

MORE THAN A RABBI

Even before Jesus responds to their inquiry, we discern that the disciples do not have an adequate grasp of the situation. In addressing Jesus as "Rabbi," the disciples, while respectful, fail to realize that Jesus is more than a rabbi. They do regard him, at least, as the Messiah (1:41), and even as the Son of God and the king of Israel (1:49). But they are shackled with the Judaic comprehension of these titles.[5] In his covenanting with David,

---

5. For ancient Jewish messianic expectations, see Wolters' review of Qumran specialists, Collins (*Scepter and the Star*) and Wise (*First Messiah*), who mine the DSS for messianic references ("Messiah in the Qumran Documents," 75–89). Wise posits one messianic figure and Collins four, portrayed as the object of eschatological hope—king, priest, prophet, and heavenly Messiah. The last category can be human or quasi-divine. Stuckenbruck looks at documents that antedate or are contemporaneous with early Christianity ("Messianic Ideas," 90–113). He finds a diversity of messianic ideas: the eschatological agent is human or ascribed divine sonship. Oegema examines the Maccabaean and Hasmonaean period and also finds multiple messianic figures

God declares, with regard to Solomon: "I shall be a father to him and he shall be a son to Me. When he commits iniquity I will reprove him with the rod of men and with the strokes of the sons of men" (2 Sam 7:14). The disciples recognize Jesus as the Son of God in the long line of Jewish kings beginning with Solomon. But to see Jesus as one greater than Solomon (Matt 12:42; Luke 11:31) awaits a later time (20:28).

Bound by their Jewish traditions, the disciples view Jesus as merely human. Similarly, retributive justice is a long-accepted principle within their tradition (Deuteronomy 28–31), informing their worldview.

But Jesus shatters their preconceptions with his reply: "Neither did this man sin nor his parents, but that the works of God may be manifested in him."

OBJECT OF CURIOSITY OR PERSON?

Before proceeding further, we can profit by entering into the blind man's mind for a short time. We strive to imagine what he must be thinking and feeling. Being a Jew, he is a product of his times and may have the same worldview as the disciples. Therefore, disturbing questions may haunt him: Must I resign myself hopelessly to this bitter fate? What heinous sins did my parents do? How should I feel toward them? Will no one take pity on me? Will God never show mercy?

There is a story about a man who watches a wheelchair-bound war veteran outside a baseball stadium. Before the game, the veteran makes

---

(*Anointed and his People*, 73–102). Pomykala studies Judaic literature of the Hellenistic and Roman periods, especially the *Pss. Sol.* a first-century BCE work which features, according to Pomykala, the most extensive treatment of a Davidic king from that era, and finds three characteristics: divinely appointed, idealized but human, and rules over restored Israel (*Davidic Dynasty Tradition*, 159–65). Shepherd studies *Tg. Isa.*, particularly the fourth servant song (Isa 52:13—53:12), that predates the NT ("Targums, the New Testament, and Biblical Theology," 55–56). He finds that in Judaism the Messiah will not suffer and die an atoning death. In this aspect, the NT and Targum diverge. Expectations focus on a king who restores the land and rules over the nations (Novenson, "Jewish Messiahs," 357–73). Rivkin delineates Pharisaic criteria for a messianic figure: descends from David, performs signs, follows Elijah the forerunner, preserves the written and oral law, and teaches accepted doctrine ("Meaning of Messiah," 397). Limited resources from this period make conclusions tentative. The sectarian nature of the Qumran material, for example, expresses ideology from only one segment of society. Generalizations representing the majority of Jews must be tentative. Within these limitations, we extract expectations and requirements that give some idea of why the Jews reject Jesus' claims that transcend their concept of a Messiah. Although the disciples do not reject him, they do not understand him because of their religious traditions.

his way to one of the entrances in the midst of the rush of spectators. He struggles to mount a curb. No one stops to help. In fact, some fans are annoyed with him being in their way.

The man watching finally comes over to help. There is a brief exchange, and the veteran parks himself against the wall. He places a box on his lap to collect alms. There he waits for contributions. Most ignore him. But there is the occasional cutting remark or putdown hurled his way. Each time he closes his eyes as if to absorb the blow before opening them again.

After some time, the man watching approaches to place money in the box, and initiates a conversation. He asks, "How can you take the abuse and say nothing?" "I don't let it bother me," replies the veteran, "I just close my eyes until the hurt goes away."

We take away two things from this story. First, people can be quite callous when they are self-absorbed. As a result, they can dehumanize another person. The veteran was not seen as a human with feelings, but as an annoyance. Second, we see rejection. The spectators were in too much of a hurry to catch a game to be bothered with someone who needed their generosity for his next meal.

The disciples are not in a hurry nor do they hurl abuse at the blind man. But we do not detect any compassion for him either. He is simply a curiosity, someone who prompts the question of whose sin resulted in his present condition. Apparently, it was customary for the blind to beg from passersby (cf. 9:8).

The Synoptic Gospels record two other accounts of the blind sitting at the roadside (Matt 20:30–34; Mark 10:46–52). Matt 20:30 does not explicitly state that the two blind men beg. It only indicates that they sit by the road. But we infer from the posture and location of the blind men that they situate themselves at a well-traveled locale to receive alms. We find it insightful that the two cry to Jesus for mercy upon hearing of his coming. They address him as the Son of David, indicating some understanding of his identity. The blind man in Mark is explicitly labeled a beggar. The blind man in the Fourth Gospel has additional handicaps—no one tells him that Jesus is passing by and he has no clue to Jesus' identity. And only he, compared to the other blind men in Matthew and Mark, seems to be blind from birth.

In the Fourth Gospel, as the disciples walk by the blind man they make no sympathetic overtures to him. The disciples express no regard for his feelings and suffering. They have a money box from which they can give something to the poor (13:29), but they do nothing. They are calloused. The blind man is not even worthy of the compassion reserved for the poor. He is lower, perhaps at the same level of lepers, for he is condemned. But the blind man will not stay down; he will ultimately surmount all obstacles triumphantly.

Belief in retributive justice hardens a person toward the plight of others. People suffer because they deserve what they got. The disciples are judgmental—the blind man is guilty—no ifs, buts, or maybes. It is a black and white world, a humanly contrived dualism—the righteous expect rewards and the wicked face judgment. Interest in the man is purely academic—who is culpable?—they have no intentions of doing anything for him. They are ready to move on and forget him once their curiosity is satisfied. They reject him.

Before we become too hard on the disciples we need to ask ourselves, "Have I adopted something of the mindset of retributive justice?" We see prodigal children and we conclude "terrible parents." We hear of strained relationships in a marriage and we think "someone's having an affair." Many times we are not that blatant. But too often we judge. We can be as guilty as Jesus' disciples in their disregard for the blind man's dignity and humanity. Retributive justice focuses more on the offense and offender than on the suffering and individual needs. If we misplace our focus we do what the disciples did, even if we do not overtly subscribe to retributive justice.

We can be unfeeling. I remember someone suffering from depression with accompanying mood swings and emotional instability. She felt no one liked the way she dressed or talked. Her self-esteem plummeted. Some from the congregation were critical of her behavior and separated from her, worsening her sense of isolation. A few even criticized her to her face.

Of course, depression is a complex issue that may require professional help. But isn't the church a place where someone hurting should find grace? A recent book release in the United States entitled *ReChurch: Healing Your Way Back to the People of God* written by Stephen Mansfield, a former pastor, documents the all-too-prevalent phenomena of Christians suffering a "church hurt" and then leaving the church. Mansfield describes his own exodus and reentry back into the local church. The book offers hope and guidance to hurting Christians. But it also serves as a warning to churches. A church ought to examine the quiet exodus out the backdoor as it strives to bring people in through the front door.

The practice of any aspect of retributive justice, although unwitting, hurts and alienates. People are seen as objects, not to be loved and affirmed, but to be measured according to the "justice" of the one passing judgment. If, for example, someone hurts me, he deserves payback. I look to get even. That is so intuitive I don't need to think about it. But to treat my offender with grace and love I must be intentional because it is not natural (Lev 19:18). I must leave the redress of wrong to God (Deut 32:35).

A RAMIFICATION OF TIT-FOR-TAT THEOLOGY

Some people consider "small" sins as being inconsequential.[6] Emboldened, they move on to a "bigger" sin.[7] If they still suffer no adverse consequence, they might conclude the following: one, sin is not a big deal; or two, God is not a factor. Retributive justice is tit-for-tat theology.

This fallacious thinking mirrors that of a young child. The mother sets a boundary, for example: do not play in the living room because it has been cleaned in preparation for company that evening. So what does the child do? He brings some toys to the living room. Mom frowns and says, "Don't play in there, Johnny." Okay, I can go this far, rationalizes the youngster—no consequence of substance. Next he brings his paint set. Mom's voice is louder, "No!" accompanied by a menacing step toward the boy. Johnny quickly retreats, paint set in tow. The child is testing his parent for the *real* boundary.

Some young people tell me that they admire and even envy their non-Christian friends who seem to be more successful and happier without God than they with God. So why bother living as if God matters? God did not zap their non-Christian acquaintances with lightning—their

---

6. Such thinking is unscriptural. Jas 2:10–11 teaches that the one who breaks one aspect of the law while keeping the rest, even the majority, of the law is guilty of the whole law. The law of God is an integrated whole. A person cannot divide and compartmentalize the moral law of God, evaluating one aspect as more or less important. Then he has set himself up as being above the law in judging the law. However, there may be degrees of severity in judgment based on the severity of the sin (Matt 10:15; 11:20–24; Luke 10:10–16).

7. The process may also be driven by a progressively desensitized conscience.

conclusion being that it is too hard living conscientiously by faith without the perks; so it is not worth it.

This theology smacked me in the face one day. I was meeting with a young adult from my congregation for lunch. She had been a leader in our campus ministry. As we ate, she had the temerity to look me, her pastor, in the eye and say, "I don't want to work too hard at being a Christian. I'm going to heaven anyway; why try so hard?" It was not the food in my mouth that made me speechless. I was stunned. I could not believe what I heard from across the table. Here was a former spiritual leader who thought and talked this way, without any hint of embarrassment.

That is the challenge facing those who practice tit-for-tat theology. They have myopic vision. They cannot see beyond this life. Eternal consequences mean nothing. If God does not strike them down right then, and he does not reward them either, they don't worry about him.

Thus, the presupposition of rewards and punishment in this life shape convictions. Motivation is conditioned by immediate consequences, good or bad. If I get rewarded for doing right, then I will be motivated to do right.

This thought pattern is precisely Satan's argument with God (Job 1:9–11)—Job is righteous because God has handsomely rewarded him to be righteous; take away the perks and Job will lose any motivation to be "blameless and upright." We have to wonder whether Satan is not really the author of tit-for-tat theology. If that is so, we who subscribe to retributive justice have been duped by the father of lies (John 8:44). Then we have degenerated into a state of mind no higher than that of Pavlov's dog's conditional reflex. We simply react.

GOD'S AGENDA

Fortunately for the blind man, Jesus does not judge a person according to the principles of retributive justice. The man is not condemned nor is his predicament hopeless. Rather, unbeknownst to him and to the disciples, he is a platform in preparation by which God's works will be showcased. Jesus says, "Neither did this man sin nor his parents, but that the works of God may be manifested in him" (9:3).[8] At this point of the story the blind

---

8. I have artificially divided Jesus' response to the disciples at the end of 9:3 to form two parts—9:3 and 9:4–5. In actuality, his words span 9:3–5 in what Staley calls a pronouncement ("Stumbling in the Dark," 64–65). My reason for doing so is heuristic in facilitating your, the reader's, reading experience and journey. In the next chapter, I will

man is an "agent" in the parlance of characterization theory. He serves as a plot device by which Jesus may correct the disciples' faulty theology and announce that he, Jesus, is the light of the world. The blind man is the venue for God's works, with no individuality ascribed to him. He is simply an object, human but barely so.

Jesus anticipates what he will do to and for the blind man. The giving of sight represents but one work, and yet Jesus says "works," implying a multiplicity. Embedded in the plural form of the word, anticipation refers to not just the healing at this time, but to future activity. The motif of "works" in the Fourth Gospel provides a contrast in significance and function with the similar motif in the Synoptic Gospels. In Matthew, Mark, and Luke, Jesus' works primarily manifest supernatural power that substantiates the entry of God's kingdom into the world with the presence of Jesus.[9] But in John, works have a symbolic or revelatory role.[10] This work of healing the blind man reveals God to the world.

The stage set, the man was born blind for a higher purpose. With Jesus' coming upon him, the curtains lift.

But before proceeding with the drama, we should reflect. Something may befall us, provoking the cry, "Misfortune!" But we can interpret it as an opportunity. For the blind man, however, anticipating Jesus requires a premonition. At times, God manifests himself through divinely appointed opportunities that the world calls misfortunes. He would have no platform for a never-before-accomplished miracle without the man being born blind (9:32).

The man represents us in our affliction. Two possible readings emerge from John: a physical reading permits us to relate to the blind man in our physical infirmities; and a spiritual reading facilitates our relating to him in our spiritual shortcomings. We will consider the latter reading in the following chapters. But for now, we explore the former reading, that of the physical.

---

look at Jesus' pronouncement in its entirety when I include 9:4–5.

9. For a fuller treatment on this topic, see Brown, *Gospel According to John*, 525–31.

10. In addition to Brown, see Moloney, *Signs and Shadows*, 120–21. The rhetorical purpose associated with Jesus' works, labeled "signs," is to foster the reader's faith in Jesus (Howard, "Significance of Minor Characters," 64). Grassi presents a chiastic structure based on seven signs, replacing Jesus' walking on water with his crucifixion ("Role of Jesus' Mother," 67–80). According to Grassi, the first six signs point to the seventh, the crucifixion, the fullest revelation of Jesus.

GOD IS GOOD BUT...

In his bestseller *When Bad Things Happen to Good People*, Harold S. Kushner grapples with the paradox of the innocent suffering in a world supposedly governed by retributive justice. When his son was diagnosed with progeria (premature aging), a deadly genetic disorder, Kushner's worldview crashes. The righteous should not be hurt, and the wicked should not get away with evil. Yet, there are countless real life examples that seem to counter that simplistic belief. Through much soul-searching and a rereading of Job, Kushner concludes that God is good but not all-powerful:

> Let me suggest that the author of the Book of Job takes the position which neither Job nor his friends take. He believes in God's goodness and in Job's goodness, and is prepared to give up his belief in proposition (A): that God is all-powerful. Bad things do happen to good people in this world, but it is not God who wills it. God would like people to get what they deserve in life, but He cannot always arrange it. Forced to choose between a good God who is not totally powerful, or a powerful God who is not totally good, the author of the Book of Job chose to believe in God's goodness.[11]

And in the end of his book he pleads:

> Are you capable of forgiving and loving God even when you have found out that He is not perfect, even when He has let you down and disappointed you by permitting bad luck and sickness and cruelty in His world, and permitting some of those things to happen to you? Can you learn to love and forgive Him despite His limitations, as Job does?[12]

Kushner concludes that the world does not conform to tit-for-tat theology because God cannot enforce it. His power is limited, although he is good and loves us. It is not God's fault; suffering is due to fate. But if we blame God, let us also forgive him because he is trying his best.

---

11. Kushner, *When Bad Things Happen*, 42–43. Kushner's proposition (A) is part of three truth statements that are universally accepted (p. 37):
—A. God is all-powerful and causes everything that happens in the world. Nothing happens without his willing it.
—B. God is just and fair, so people get what they deserve. The good prosper and the wicked are punished.
—C. Job is a good person.
12. Ibid., 148.

Whereas we lament Kushner's personal tragedy and loss, and must acknowledge that many of us have not experienced the depth of pain and grief he endured, we cannot agree with his conclusions about God and life. The God of Harold Kushner is not the God of the Bible, and is certainly not the God of Job.

Kushner's suggestion that the leviathan in Job 41 may be symbolic of chaos and evil has merit, but this suggestion requires consideration of the immediate context and overall monotheistic view of the book. Even though the author of Job uses figurative language, the reference to the leviathan may be literal.[13] The description of the animal's physical attributes is very detailed and lengthy. The level of detail suggests an actual beast. We compare, for example, the briefer Isa 27:1 ("In that day the Lord will punish Leviathan the fleeing serpent, with His fierce and great and mighty sword, even Leviathan the twisted serpent; and He will kill the dragon who is in the sea"). The passage speaks "of great evil powers whether cosmic or political in terms of monstrous creatures."[14]

Regardless of how we may interpret the leviathan in Job 41, be it literally or symbolically, the emerging theology takes precedence. Kushner sees a God who struggles against the bad that happens in the world, and, according to him, God barely has the upper hand. Kushner then concludes that misfortune does not represent God's punishment, and, in fact, does not come from God at all.

A GOD WHO ANSWERS TO NO ONE

We can agree that misfortune is not necessarily divine justice on display. But Kushner missed the point of Job 41—it has nothing to do with God contending with chaos or misfortune; rather Job 40–41 is a repudiation of any human claim to control in the natural realm. The obvious implication is that God alone is the Almighty (40:2), all-powerful, and all-wise.

There is a solution to the apparent paradox of the righteous suffering and the existence of an all-powerful God who is also good. But it does

---

13. Harris, "Book of Job," 21–22. The article is a reprint of Harris' earlier article by the same title in *Grace Journal* 13 (1972) 3–33.

14. Smick, "Mythology and the Book of Job," 106. Smick acknowledges the evidence in Job that the author may have borrowed from the language of contemporaneous polytheistic mythology to formulate his metaphors without also bringing in the mythology. The strong monotheistic affirmation of the book indicates that the author simply used the terminology to enrich his poetic expressions. See also Smick's "Another Look," 213–28.

not eliminate his power, as Kushner has proclaimed. Rather, this solution realizes that tit-for-tat theology wrongfully boxes God in a very neat and tidy manner that is humanly comprehensible. This solution recognizes that tit-for-tat theology humanizes God at the expense of his deity. The book of Job presents a transcendent God who defies human reason and the human sense of fairness. Like Job, we must learn not to contend with God by demanding a day in court. And, like Job, we may never learn the reasons behind specific incidences of misfortune and suffering.

The answer is not found on the lips of Job's friends who champion retributive justice. Nor is the answer to be found in Kushner's bestseller. Job 38–41 proclaims that God answers to no man. We may not be able to reconcile with and explain his sovereign power and immeasurable goodness in regard to life, the good and the bad. An irresolvable tension in our lives yearns for answers, but we will get no satisfaction. It takes faith to live with that tension.

We can agree with Kushner to not judge those who suffer, but come alongside and offer what support and comfort we can as fellow pilgrims. But comfort cannot be in the form of bad theology.

FIRST STEP

Let us return to John 9:1–3. Nothing has happened yet, or so it seems; just a brief exchange between Jesus and his disciples. The man is still blind and he has not experienced anything. Or has he?

Conceivably he overhears the exchange. It seems reasonable that the disciples stop in front of the man to pose their inquiry to Jesus. Or, what may be more likely, Jesus stops upon seeing him. The disciples follow Jesus' gaze that, in turn, prompts their question.

The man hears that he is not cursed because of sin. In fact, he will experience a visitation from God, whereupon God will perform works in him. At this juncture, we wonder about the man's thoughts. He may experience a mixture of wonder and befuddlement. He learns that he is not condemned. This should be wonderful news. But his condition remains unchanged and he cannot anticipate what works of God will occur in him. And so he may be mystified. Perhaps he eagerly waits for what will happen next.

Earlier we made the case that, for many, the blind man is no more than a curiosity and, at worst, an object of scorn and condemnation. He himself may be thinking likewise. Now for the first time in his life he hears good news.

He hears that God has plans for him. The Jew of Jesus' day would have been conditioned by the Deuteronomic stipulations of blessings for obedience and curses for disobedience. Because the blind man and his parents are not condemned as sinners according to Jesus, then he can expect blessings through the works of God in light of Jesus' pronouncement.

Being noticed by the Lord marks the first step in the man's journey. The Lord sees him not as a sinner but as a potential for God's works. He will experience God's glory. Already the man rises from the depths. He is being humanized. God has taken note of him and will do something in his life.

Let us recognize this as our first step as well. God has taken note of us and knows our condition. He has plans that will ennoble us. May we, like the blind man, anticipate the next step.

4

Enter the Light

> Jesus answered, "Neither did this man sin nor his parents, but that the works of God may be manifested in him. It is necessary for us to do the works of the one who sent me while it is day. Night is coming when no one can work. When I am in the world, I am the light of the world."
>
> —John 9:3–5

WE FIND THE BLIND man at the first step of his journey. Although Jesus speaks to the disciples, the man is within earshot. He cannot be a neutral listener since he is the subject of Jesus' words. The man represents us, so we too listen with interest for what Jesus says applies to us also.

JESUS' SAYINGS

In response to his disciples' inquiry about the man born blind, Jesus issues a pronouncement. Actually, two pronouncements and a discourse characterize this story of receiving sight. Robert C. Tannehill identifies the "pronouncement story" as a distinct and important literary genre in Synoptic Gospel studies.[1] Even though he limits his study to the Synoptic Gospels, I believe the genre to be pertinent to the Fourth Gospel.

Tannehill defines this genre as "a brief narrative in which the climatic (and often final) element is a pronouncement [poignant declaration] which is presented as a particular person's response to something

---

1. Tannehill, "Introduction: Pronouncement Story," 1–13.

said or observed on a particular occasion of the past."[2] He finds six kinds of pronouncement stories: correction stories, commendation stories, objection stories, quest stories, inquiry stories, and description stories. Hybrid pronouncement stories combine at least two of the six fundamental types.[3] As we will see, John 9 is a hybrid pronouncement story incorporating an inquiry pronouncement (9:3–5), by which Jesus answers the disciples' question about the man born blind (9:2), and a commendation pronouncement (9:39), where Jesus makes a positive comment about the man as one who now sees in a spiritually perceptive way. Moreover, a negative judgment against the Pharisees, who discern the judgment as being directed toward them (9:40), follows Jesus' commendation.[4]

Although many commentators break the narrative at 9:41, with 10:1 beginning a new section, no break interrupts Jesus' speaking in 9:41—10:18. Actually, because of its length, 9:41—10:18 is a discourse rather than another pronouncement. Nothing like this appears in the Synoptic Gospels. Jesus' statements, brief in 9:3–5 and 9:39 but protracted in 9:41—10:18, drive the story in 9:1—10:18. Jesus' sayings reveal the significance of the events that take place in the story. Without his comments we cannot put the unfolding narrative into proper perspective. The prominent feature of the narrative is not the giving of sight, miraculous though the healing may be, but Jesus' statements. In fact, the description of the healing is quite cursory (9:6–7). Jesus' sayings situate the healing in the overall symbolism of the Fourth Gospel. This sign of a man born blind receiving sight has a revelatory function in confirming Jesus' self-disclosure when he says, "I am the light of the world."

Then Jesus' words constitute an important component of the man's journey and, by association, a key feature of our journey as well. His words explain the meaning of our condition and Jesus' identity, particularly in relation to us. He is the light that has entered into the blind man's world and into our lives. His entry initiates a chain reaction. But, as we shall see,

---

2. Ibid., 1.

3. Ibid., 11–12; and Tannehill, "Varieties of Synoptic Pronouncement Stories," 101–19.

4. Tannehill observes that most commendation stories in the Synoptic Gospels are hybrids, creating a tension that is "designed to move the reader away from one attitude toward the attitude which Jesus represents" (ibid., 105). I will make additional comments on the reader's response to 9:39 in a later chapter of this book.

how the sequence of events plays out depends on our response to Jesus. The man models the correct response. Let us study him well.

Jesus states explicitly that sin did not cause the man's blindness. Hence, we may erroneously conclude that the man has no sin. We recall the healing of the paralytic that provides dramatic proof of Jesus' authority to forgive sins (Matt 9:2–8; Mark 2:3–12; Luke 5:18–26). We cannot infer, however, the blind man's innocence since his condition symbolizes the world's condition (1:5, 9). The prologue declares that faith in Jesus is the prerequisite to receiving authority to become children of God (1:12). The blind man does not as yet have such faith. But he will. In fact, the paralytic receives forgiveness because of faith both his and that of his friends. We can infer, based on the prologue, that as the light of the world, Jesus offers eternal life to the world (1:4). The blind man too will be forgiven of his sins. We infer this result based on Jesus' condemnation of the Pharisees (9:41b): "But now you say, 'We see.' Your sin remains."

"WORKS OF GOD"

The expression "works of God" encompasses all that will happen to and in the man. The plural *works* goes beyond the one act of giving sight. Receiving sight is but the first of a series of works. These works of God point to the active agent—God portrayed as active in the affairs of men. One cannot see God. But, like the wind (cf. 3:8), one can see the effects of it. The effects indicate God's presence in the world.

The conflict between Jesus and his disciples highlights a sharp difference in theological viewpoints. Although they exercise faith in him (6:68–69), they do not have full understanding of important truths conveyed by Jesus' pronouncement (9:3–5). His pronouncement is not a rebuke but more a correction of their fallacious thinking.[5]

The disciples, however, fade into the background when Jesus speaks and will have no further part to play in the remainder of the narrative. They have served their purpose—a foil for Jesus' first pronouncement. They provide him with the opportunity to explain the significance of the blind man's condition. We can even say the disciples represent a

---

5. Patte holds a similar view about the conflict between Jesus and his disciples in the Synoptic Gospels ("Jesus' Pronouncement," 3–42). The conflict is not of the same nature as that between Jesus and the religious establishment; see Asiedu-Peprah, *Johannine Sabbath Conflicts*, 29–38. On the contrary, favorably disposed toward Jesus, the disciples' inquiry is not an attack or challenge against Jesus.

plot device of setting the stage for the subsequent drama. Seen in this manner their characterization seems contrived. That may well be the case; but we should note that with their disappearance our attention is more riveted on Jesus and the blind man. Then after performing the healing even Jesus himself will disappear for a time and the healed man takes center stage. And in this way, the blind man becomes our hero, someone worthy of emulation.

The disciples, however, do not quite disappear just yet, for Jesus states: "It is necessary for us to do the works of the one who sent me while it is day." The plural *us* includes them with Jesus in doing the works of God.[6] However, only Jesus performs the healing this time.[7] He implies that they will have responsibility for carrying out God's work in the future.[8] Here is an early indication of the union comprising of Jesus and his disciples that he will state explicitly later through the extended metaphor of the vine and its branches (15:1–8). Other explicit statements refer to this organic and functional union (14:20, 23; 17:21–24, 26) by which they will continue his works and perform even greater works (14:12).

CONFRONTATION WITH THE WORLD

Jesus' statement, "it is necessary," clearly intimates a divine plan and purpose in which both Jesus and his disciples have an active role. The

---

6. There is a divided reading on the pronoun *us* among the ancient Greek manuscripts and early versions. A number of manuscripts feature the plural form and a greater number have the singular *me*. Whereas the earliest witnesses, including two key papyri, support the plural form, the bulk of later manuscripts have the singular. How one decides which reading to be more likely original depends on his criteria. Many scholars regard the earliest witnesses to be superior in quality, and hence, favor the plural pronoun. But one of the early witnesses has both forms—the plural in its original version and the singular in its corrected version—thus threatening to muddy the issue.

7. The plural *us* alludes to the disciples present. See Brown, *Gospel According to John*, 372; and Ridderbos, *Gospel according to John*, 334. I agree with Asiedu-Peprah who sees a two-part reference in which the immediate situation is "referring primarily, if not exclusively, to Jesus alone" and to the disciples in the future (*Johannine Sabbath Conflicts*, 123). They witness the anointing of the blind man's eyes. However, I believe the blind man goes to the Pool of Siloam alone. When Jesus fades from the scene, so do the disciples. In the foot washing episode (13:4–17), the disciples are passive observers and only Jesus is active. He sets before them an example for them to do likewise. Jesus does something similar with the blind man before the disciples. He models "the works of God." In a way then they are involved in this sign.

8. Moloney, *Signs and Shadows*, 121.

disciples, like the blind man, have a representative function in the narrative. Although we cannot with certainty establish their presence during Jesus' confrontation with his detractors,[9] they too will face confrontations with the world after Jesus' departure to the Father (15:18-21). For the present time while Jesus is in the world, the blind man will have his day in "court." Both sets of characters, the blind man and the disciples, are representative. These characters invite the reader, you and me, to face our hour of challenge and to prove our mettle. The blind man faces conflict with his detractors immediately upon his healing. On the other hand, the relatively inconspicuous disciples will not experience conflict with the world until later, after Jesus' return to the Father (15:18—16:4). The time differential between the immediacy of the blind man's conflict and the deferred conflict of the disciples speaks of an ongoing conflict with the world. For as long as a disciple resides in the world and stays true to Jesus, no truce can ever be called.

Conflict with the world derives from one's association with Jesus. The world hates the one whom Jesus has chosen, for there is an accompanying disassociation from the world upon being selected (15:19). A disciple faces conflict because of Jesus' name (15:21).

Jesus proclaims, "When I am in the world, I am the light of the world." He continually affirms that he has been sent by the Father. As the Father's agent he faithfully accomplishes his assignment (5:17, 19-23, 26-30; 7:16-18, 28-29; 8:26, 28-29). In a similar manner, the disciples will be sent by Jesus as agents into the world (13:14-17, 34-35; 14:21, 23-26; 15:8-17, 27; 17:18, 20-23). His mandate is to reveal the Father so that those who believe in Jesus may have life (3:14-17).

As his witnesses in the world, the disciples lead others to believe and become Jesus' disciples. Compelled not only by Jesus' commandments, they cling also to his promise: "Truly, truly, I say to you, the one who believes in me will also do the works that I am doing, and greater works than these will he do, because I am going to the Father" (14:12).

---

9. Culpepper, *Anatomy*, 117. The narrative does not mention their return with Jesus (9:35). Given their portrayal in the Fourth Gospel, we may conclude that a disciple follows and accompanies Jesus (de Jonge, *Jesus: Stranger from Heaven*, 14). It is not the only characteristic, of course; for a fuller treatment see Collins, *These Things Have Been Written*, 1-45. Thus, we assume their presence when Jesus encounters the healed man a second time.

Jesus admonishes the disciples to become the light upon his departure back to the Father. They represent the continuity in doing the Father's will—first Jesus, then his disciples.

The narrative relates the blind man and the disciples in their respective journeys and representative roles in a complementary way. Both are models for you and me. But because we confine ourselves to 9:1—10:18, the blind man alone is our example in the present study. The journeys of the blind man and the disciples toward full faith have the same destination, but the trajectories differ. For the disciples, their trajectory encompasses most of the narrative (1:35—21:23) and beyond. But for the blind man, the narrative greatly compresses his trajectory (9:6–38). The focuses of their respective journeys differ as well. The narrative documents the disciples' failures, as attested by Peter's denial and the disciples abandoning Jesus at his arrest. Yet, they have a mandate to be the light. Ultimately, they will overcome their failures and fulfill their mission because of Jesus' promise of another Paraclete, the Spirit of truth (14:26; 16:7, 13–15). But for the blind man, no mandate and no documented failure emerges, only a steady progression to full faith in Jesus.

From both the blind man and the disciples we can draw encouragement. They all will succeed in spite of fierce opposition. We can relate to them—to the blind man's initial ignorance of Jesus' identity and whereabouts (9:11–12) and to the disciples' failures (13:38; 14:5, 8–10; 16:6–7, 12, 17–22, 29–32; 18:17, 25–27; 20:19, 25). They will overcome through Jesus' victory over the world (16:33). We too can overcome our obstacles.

ENCOUNTERING THE FATHER IN THE SON

The expressions "the works of God" (9:3) and "the works of the one who sent me" (9:4) form a significant parallelism. Taken as a form of synonymous repetition, we can identify "God" with "the one who sent Jesus." God himself sends Jesus. The sending motif is prominent in the Fourth Gospel (3:34; 4:34; 5:23–24, 30, 36–38; 6:29, 38–39, 44, 57; 7:16, 18, 28–29, 33; 8:16, 18, 26, 29, 42; 9:4; 10:36; 11:42; 12:44–45, 49; 13:20; 14:24;

15:21; 16:5; 17:3, 8, 18, 21, 23, 25; 20:21).[10] The motif testifies to a union of the Father and the Son. They enjoy the most intimate of relationships.[11]

That union continues even when Jesus descends into the world below. He substantiates this remarkable truth when he declares: "Do you not believe that I am in the Father and the Father is in me? The words that I am saying to you I do not speak on my own, but the Father abiding in me does His works" (14:10). There is synchronization between the Father above and the Son below working in tandem. The Father performs his work in the world by working in and through his Son.[12]

When the Son sees the blind man (9:1), it is as if the Father sees the man. But unlike surrogates or avatars, the Son has a separate identity and life. Strikingly, the Father and Son see the man not as a condemned untouchable, but as one who will manifest God. The disciples do not see what God sees; they behold a theological curiosity—a nonhuman, an object that prompts idle inquiry. The blind man's acquaintances see only a pitiful beggar (9:8). How many have treated him with the dignity every human being deserves? The encounter with Jesus will ennoble the man and place him center stage to testify for Jesus. Jesus forges a new partnership with the blind man because of what God sees in him. God does not

---

10. For a fuller treatment of the sending motif, see Ferreira, *Johannine Ecclesiology*, 166–200. He makes a distinction between two verbs, *pémpō* and *apostéllō*. Translated "send," both, on occasion, are interchangeable. However, Ferreira argues that the first has a Christological significance in referring to Jesus' origin and unity with the Father. The second is soteriological, focusing on Jesus' mission in the world with the Father's authority. However, as Gignac points out, the two verbs are supplemental forms in the Fourth Gospel, and so no distinction in meaning can be pressed ("Use of Verbal Variety," 192–93).

11. The second clause of 1:1 reads "and the Word was toward God." The preposition "toward" is the Greek word *pros*, depicting a facing toward someone or something, often with the idea of accompanying movement (Porter, *Idioms of the Greek*, 172–73). Moloney characterizes the relationship as dynamic between two parties in which there is a mutual turning toward one another (*Belief in the Word*, 28). The next clause, "and the Word was God," further characterizes the relationship as being "so close that what one is, the other also is" (ibid.).

12. Jesus answers the accusation of Sabbath violation: "My Father is working until now, and I am working" (5:17). The Father continually works even on the Sabbath in divine activities—giving life and judgment (Dodd, *Interpretation of the Fourth Gospel*, 320–23). The Jews' murderous intent toward Jesus (5:18) indicates that they understand the implication of his linking his Sabbath work with the ceaseless work of the Father—that he "as Son of God, has both authority and power to exercise the two divine functions of 'giving life' and 'judgment'" (ibid., 324; I have translated Dodd's two Greek terms for "giving life" and "judgment").

see the blind man in his present state but his potential. But there is a caveat—the blind man must do his part by faith.

ENCOUNTERING ONE ANOTHER

What do people see when they look at you? In the previous chapter, I gave an example of the sports fans outside of the baseball stadium who beheld a wheelchair-bound war veteran begging for a livelihood. The fans perceived the veteran to be a nonentity at best, and at worst a nuisance and a target for verbal abuse.

I recall a young man who attended our worship service for young adults some years ago. A lot of people have come and gone over the years, but I remember him well—he wore a gorilla mask one Sunday morning and stood with everyone else for praise.

I never did learn why he did it. But I learned that he was socially awkward. When I visited him, I found him quite intelligent. He required psychiatric counseling to deal with the emotional scars from being raped. Maybe the mask was a cry of "look at me; I am somebody" or "I don't want you to see the real me." Maybe he had a strange sense of humor. He was not a believer at the time. Many in our congregation treated him as a nonentity. Thankfully, some reached out to him with kindness and included him. But he did not reciprocate. People had to approach him. He was simply there; and in a sense, he was not there. To include him meant giving him rides and paying the bill when young adults do what young adults typically do—go hang out somewhere. He was a student without income; and he carried a lot of baggage.

We can look at others the way people typically do, or we can see others the way God does. As a former pastor, my mandate was to develop people through discipleship and mentoring. In order to be effective, I needed to see past the raw material to behold the polished product, past the seed to discern the ripened fruit. We can excuse ourselves by saying, "Listen, I am not a pastor. So I am not equipped to shepherd ugly sheep."

We can practice tit-for-tat theology and say, "I only associate with beautiful people because they are worthy of my attention." But we remove grace from the equation.

Taking Jesus' last commandment—that we love one another as Jesus loves us—to heart demands that we follow Jesus. His love for the blind man initiated a chain reaction; our love for others can start a chain reaction too. Because of what Jesus sees in the blind man, the blind man experiences healing. Our love empowers others to experience healing and make progress in their journey of faith. Amazingly, love reciprocates. Our love facilitates our progress in our journey also.

Our journey, yours and mine, is a contemplative one. It involves a meditative approach, a delving into the heart and a baring of the soul. Who am I and what makes me tick? What is my baggage that can slow me down? Who can I become through a relationship with Jesus?

Someone reading this may think, "I don't think I can do this." But before giving up, consider the blind man. He was the lowest of the low in the culture of his day—a beggar with a congenital condition that blares out, "Guilty!" If anyone should be called hopeless, he is our prime example. The Scriptures of Jesus' time records no miraculous healing of a person born blind (cf. 9:32). The lame man of John 5 can at least hope to dip in water. Elisha healed Naaman of his leprosy (2 Kgs 5:14). The blind man, however, is in a league all his own. Not only is he guilty, he is incurable!

As a result, the blind man becomes the perfect prospect for Jesus to recruit for a journey that showcases the works of God. His potential as a symbol of hope for the downtrodden, the disenfranchised, for the misunderstood and oppressed, is enormous.

The young man with the gorilla mask was a victim—weak, isolated, and targeted for hurtful profiling. Even though he did not yet know Jesus, he willingly came to our worship services. For a time he faithfully attended, in spite of being invisible. But people seemed to look right through him as if he was not there. For a time I wondered why he continued to attend our services and largely be ignored.

Then it occurred to me. He was giving us a chance. Would we see the opportunity and seize it, and in so doing acknowledge not so much his presence but his person? He had heard it all before, that the church was a gathering of Christians who love with the love of Jesus. He came to see if it was true. He came to experience Jesus.

URGENCY OF THE "DAY"

At the end of John 9:4, Jesus injects a sense of urgency: "It is necessary for us to do the works of the one who sent me while it is day. Night is coming when no one can work."[13] Here he introduces two metaphors with

---

13. Morris, *Gospel according to John*, 426. Morris interprets "day" as an opportunity

symbolic value—"day" and "night." At the literal level, the thought is clear. In a predominantly agrarian setting, "day" represents the daylight hours during which someone may labor in the field and "night" represents a time when it is too dark to perform meaningful field work. This picture would be meaningless to a reader living, for example, in New York City or Singapore; the former is "the city that never sleeps" and in the latter, office hours often extend past sunset. On a visit to New York City, I awoke at 4:30 a.m. to loud voices outside, below my room. On the sidewalk, people were talking and laughing. Evidently, a party had just broken up. This was a Wednesday morning, hardly an early start on the weekend. And, likewise, at the school where I teach in Singapore some of my colleagues work past midnight.[14]

So at another level of the reading, Jesus' words connect with everyone, whether working and living in an urban, suburban, or rural environment. If Jesus speaks of his physical presence in the world, then the "day" connotes the duration of his descension and the "coming night" refers to his ascension.[15] However, the inclusive "it is necessary for us to do the works of the one who sent me while it is day" involves the disciples in the "day-night" schema. His presence will be extended through the ministry of the disciples.[16] But the words "night is coming when no one can work" go beyond even the company of disciples. The referent of "no one" has no bounds and includes "everyone."[17] We must accept this invitation to partner with Jesus in manifesting the works of God "while it is day," in our lifetime.

The night of death is inevitable. The sense that the opportunity can easily slip away invokes an urgency that compels us to act now, before it is too late. No one knows his allotted time—be it twenty more years or one more day. But while we live we must act.

---

to work and "night" as when it is too late to do so (n. 14).

14. "Are Singapore teachers overworked?" lines 3–24. This news blurb chronicles a "typical" Singaporean primary school teacher's daily routine.

15. For this connotation, see Ridderbos, *Gospel according to John*, 334; and Witherington, *John's Wisdom*, 183.

16. Moloney, *Signs and Shadows*, 121.

17. Brodie includes all humanity as the referent (*Gospel According to John*, 346); however, I believe the context limits the scope to believers who alone can participate in the works of God. But I agree with Brodie's interpretation that "night" alludes to death when all work ceases.

Recently, both the first principal and the chaplain of our school passed away. One had over seventy years of faithful service to the Lord, the other over fifty years. Remarkable! Their unstinting labor continued for the duration of their "day." Now "night" has fallen and they have ceased working, having gone home to be with the Father.

We have a journey that takes us ultimately to our Father—the final destiny of both Jesus and each of us. Our "day" has already begun. Will we be faithful while it is yet day? Night is coming when no one can work. As we track the blind man's journey may we be encouraged to do likewise.

A CHRISTOPHANY

If we seek the disciples' reaction to Jesus' corrective pronouncement (9:3–5) in response to their inquiry (9:2), we will look in vain. The narrative omits it. We do not know how they respond because they simply disappear. Conceivably, Jesus' answer does not persuade either them or readers sympathetic to their worldview.

Jesus seems so intent on the blind man that he appears to give them a cursory reply before devoting his full attention to the blind man himself. Is this some kind of brush off?

Their theological position, captured in a brief inquiry, spawned a whole book—Job. One might expect more discussion from Jesus and his disciples here, not unlike the thirty-six chapters where Job and his friends pontificate their respective dogmas. But we do not have that in John.

However, a literary parallel exists between Job and John 9:1–5. Following the discourses of Job and his friends over the implications of their worldview on Job's suffering, a theophany (Job 38–41) ends all discussion and Job repents (Job 42:1–6). We have something similar here in 9:5 when Jesus concludes his pronouncement with "when I am in the world, I am the light of the world."

The "I am" declarations by Jesus characterize the Fourth Gospel.[18] The Feast of Tabernacles defines the context in which the symbols of water and light are most prominent in the minds of the Jewish celebrants.[19]

---

18. Brown surveys different uses of the "I am" formula (*Gospel According to John*, 533–38). He notes that 9:5 is a predication where Jesus claims uniqueness—no one else is like him with regard to the predicate in question. Other examples include "I am the bread of life," "I am the good shepherd," and "I am the resurrection and the life."

19. For the symbolic significance of the Feast, see Rubenstein, "Sukkot," 161–95; Mullins, *Gospel of John*, 208; and Moloney, *Signs and Shadows*, 67–70. The celebrants

The great last day of the Feast of Tabernacles extends from 7:37 to 10:21. Thus, Jesus' "I am the light of the world" first uttered in the presence of the celebrants (8:12) is repeated here in 9:5. He declares himself to be the fulfillment of Israel's eschatological hope. He is the new temple (2:19–21). Through believing in him, one may have access to living water (7:37–39) and receive the light. A bold Christological claim, followed immediately by the miraculous giving of sight (9:6–7), forms a Christophany. Thus, all discussion ends.

---

have an eschatological expectation of God's renewed presence among his people through the temple in postexilic Judaism (House, *Old Testament Theology*, 342–45).

5

The Gift of Sight

> After he spoke these words, he spat on the ground and made mud from the spittle and anointed his eyes with the mud. And he said to him, "Go. Wash in the pool of Siloam" (which is interpreted "Sent"). Then he departed and washed himself and came seeing.
>
> —John 9:6–7

UPON DECLARING "WHEN I am in the world, I am the light of the world" (9:5), Jesus immediately anoints the blind man's eyes with mud.[1] But the blind man does not receive his sight until he goes to the pool of Siloam to wash himself. The healing is a two-phased process— Jesus is present in the first phase but is absent in the second. This remote healing recalls Elisha's healing of Naaman in absentia (2 Kgs 5:10–14). But unlike Elisha instructing Naaman through a messenger, Jesus speaks directly to the blind man. On another occasion, Jesus heals the royal official's child remotely (John 4:46–53). In that incidence, Jesus merely says to the official, "Go. Your son lives." (4:50) Jesus does not interact with the child but with the father. The narrative comments: "The man believed the word which Jesus spoke and went" (4:50). The father believes and exercises faith in Jesus, not the child.

---

1. One significant early Greek manuscript features the alternative reading "to put on," whereas two important early third-century papyri followed by a number of early Greek manuscripts and the mass of manuscripts from the thirteenth–fifteenth centuries altogether representing different geographical localities offer "to anoint." The strong manuscript tradition favors the reading I adopt here.

The narrative of the Fourth Gospel conveys an important contrast between the official and the many who believe in Jesus because of his signs (2:23). The official believes, based solely on Jesus' words before the healing.[2] Many others believe only after Jesus performs the signs.[3]

On the other hand, the similarity of accounts between the royal official and the blind man is striking. Jesus commands both men to go.[4] Both men obey immediately, and later experience miraculous healing. The narrative attributes faith to the official explicitly but demurs in 9:6–7 about the blind man's faith. Neither has tangible confirmation of healing at the time Jesus speaks. Confirmation comes only later.

We do not know whether the blind man possesses faith like the royal official or if he is merely submissive. The official knows Jesus' identity; the blind man may not. Jesus' persistent self-testimony of having been sent from above to the world below emerges as a prominent motif of the Fourth Gospel. Faith in him must be conditioned on belief that he descended from the Father. Any other basis for faith renders that faith inadequate, as evidenced by those who believe him only because of his signs. The blind man does not have the faith of the official because the blind man's response does not clearly acknowledge Jesus' identity.

So why does the blind man go when Jesus commands him to do so? If indeed the blind man hears the disciples' inquiry and Jesus' pronouncement, he at least knows Jesus is regarded a rabbi. He knows of Jesus' claim to be the light of the world. Yet, when asked by his neighbors for the identity of the one who healed him, he simply answers: "the man called

---

2. For an informed discussion on the nuances of the verb "to believe" followed by different prepositions or the dative case, see Moloney, *Belief in the Word*, 186, n. 42. In "the man believed the word" (4:50), "the word" in the dative case follows the verb. Regarding the father's faith as authentic is based not so much on the syntax as on the context, in particular the parallel with 2:1–12 within the "Cana-to-Cana" section (2:1—4:54). In 2:5, Mary instructs the servants: "Do whatever he says to you." She demonstrates full trust in Jesus' word that something will transpire as a result of what Jesus will say.

3. To explain the tension created by the second mention of the official's belief after his son miraculously recovers (4:53), Morris differentiates the first incidence of believing as "giving credence to Jesus' words" and the second as becoming a Christian (*Gospel according to John*, 259). But Ridderbos correctly regards the second incidence as confirmation of the first—the servants' report that his son recovered at exactly the moment Jesus declares, "He lives" confirms the official's faith (4:50) (*Gospel according to John*, 177–78).

4. The author portrays Jesus using two different words for "go" in his commands to the father and the blind man. But there is no semantic difference.

Jesus" (9:11).[5] For him, as for the disciples, Jesus is only human. Although the pronouncement may mean nothing to him, he still goes.

The blind man goes, not because of any overt faith in Jesus; that comes later. He goes because of, pardon the pun, blind hope. He has nothing to lose. Why not? Jesus speaks authoritatively and the man complies— a simple psychological response. At this juncture the blind man has only a seed of faith, the potential for germination into something much more.

THE PROPS

As I read the narrative, questions arise. Why does Jesus bother making mud from the dirt and his spittle? Why doesn't he simply say, "Let there be sight!"?

The extra action Jesus takes in healing the man will prompt the Pharisees to accuse Jesus of violating the Sabbath (9:14–16). In response to their inquiry into how he gained his sight, the man states: "He placed mud on my eyes and I washed and I see" (9:15). The man only admits that Jesus placed mud on his eyes. He does not say explicitly that Jesus granted him sight. But in that simple application of mud they condemn Jesus.[6] Making mud and granting sight are apparently subsumed in the act of applying it to the eyes.

A major motive for the mud, then, is to invoke a Sabbath conflict (9:14). It is in this crucible of a fiery "trial" that the blind man faces his adversaries alone and forges his faith. The process affords him an opportunity not to fend for himself but to develop clearer insight. He must decide for himself which beliefs to adopt. Faith is both self-determined and a gift. There is the gift of sight; and there is the hammering out of one's convictions.

---

5. Jumping ahead in the narrative, as I do here, violates one of the tenets of reader-response criticism, namely the *"description of successive reading activities"* (Resseguie, "Reader-Response Criticism," 317). The reader reads through the narrative sequentially (Fish, *Is There a Text in This Class?*, 27). He does not go back to reread or jump forward in the reading. He may anticipate what lies ahead based on what he reads so far, and his anticipation will be confirmed valid or not upon further reading. But he does not skip intervening text. However, in the interest of understanding Jesus' actions in the now of the narrative, we look ahead to see the ramifications of his deeds.

6. Ridderbos suggests that Jesus violates one of the laws forbidding the kneading of dough on the Sabbath (*Gospel according to John*, 335, n. 257). But that strains the semantic bounds of the term "mud" to mean "dough." The standard lexicons and Rengstorf ("*pēlós*," 6:118–19) consistently render it "clay" or "mud."

I wonder whether our Lord does not on occasion inject things into our lives that place us in a crucible in order to test and clarify our faith. James rejoiced at the prospect of trials, knowing that such trials represented the potential for character development (Jas 1:2–4). We must recognize our time of testing, and then persevere. As I mentioned in the first chapter, we all will face crises of faith. Moreover, just because I have experienced crises in the past, I cannot assume there will be no more in the future.

Yet, I believe there is another motive for the mud. The mud is for the reader of the story, rather than the character in the story. The author's lexical choice of "to anoint" rather than "to apply" the mud on the blind man's eyes suggests a desire to impress upon the reader the fact that Jesus applies the mud as an anointment. The mud in Jesus' hands may seem to have special properties that ordinary mud does not. However, the mud does not have inherent power to heal. But the deliberate manner by which Jesus smears it on the man's eyes connotes symbolism. If Jesus is the light of the world as he claims, surely he gives sight. The specific procedure is immaterial; rather, the focus is on his person.

The added step of having to go to the pool of Siloam and to wash away the mud suggests another symbol. Because the water has no inherent healing properties, attention gravitates to the name "Siloam." The narrative aside explains the meaning of Siloam as, "which is interpreted 'sent.'" This aside draws the reader's attention to the significance of the name, and it is privileged information given only to the reader and not to the characters in the story. However, it is possible that the blind man and disciples do know the meaning of Siloam.[7] But what the characters may know represents background knowledge that resides in their subconscious. With the explicit interpretation, this knowledge moves to the foreground and alerts the reader to the significance of "sent."

Siloam communicates meaning on two levels. On one level the name refers to the blind man being sent to the pool to regain his sight.[8] And on

---

7. They may have been cognizant of the cultic and prophetic significance of the waters related to Siloam. See Grigsby, "Washing in the Pool of Siloam," 227–35. The Rabbinic material Grigsby cites in his discussion, however, postdates the period portrayed in the Fourth Gospel. But if the material reflects earlier tradition, then we might make some inferences.

8. Witherington, *John's Wisdom*, 183.

another level it points to Jesus as the sent one.[9] But in the context of the Feast of Tabernacles, the latter connotation assumes prominence—Jesus is sent into the world as the light (1:9).

The symbols *mud* and *Siloam* identify Jesus. The narrative is spare yet loaded with meaning. The discerning reader moves along on a thoughtful journey. By means of words, metaphors, and symbols, the narrator urges the reader to move with the blind man, to travel along as both character and reader to gain greater insight. The impending crucible of testing prompts two thoughts: the exorbitant cost of acknowledging Jesus and the willingness to pay.

BLIND STEPS

Significantly, the man blindly makes his way to the pool. The only movement is that of the man. Jesus and the disciples do not move or offer further assistance.[10] Except for Jesus' brief instruction to him, the man is on his own—so typical of his life; his parents offer no support.[11] The narrative does not explain how he manages to find the pool. But he does. The trek cannot have been easy. Perhaps he walks tentatively, probing with a stick to detect potential obstacles along the way, or stops frequently to ask for directions. However he does it, he makes it to the pool. We infer his determination.

That he bothers to go at all amazes us. He does not know Jesus' identity, and yet he obeys Jesus. Jesus does not explain the reason he wants the blind man to go, nor does he give any promises of receiving sight. The anointing of the eyes provides the only clue. Early literature mentions

---

9. Moloney, *Signs and Shadows*, 122. Also, Lincoln, *Gospel according to Saint John*, 281–82. The sending motif will feature yet another slant when the Father (14:26) and Jesus (16:7) sends the Spirit, and Jesus sends his disciples into the world (17:18).

10. Thompson states that the disciples witnessed Jesus' signs based on 20:30 (*Incarnate Word*, 62). The verse refers to "many other signs . . . which are not written in this book." But that does not imply their presence at all the signs. The narrative indicates no further interaction between Jesus and the man after he departs for the pool. If Jesus was present at the pool, the man would have expressed gratitude to Jesus then and there. If Jesus was not present, as I contend, then it goes against the Johannine pattern if the disciples went along with the man without Jesus.

11. They only acknowledge him as their son but distance themselves from him before his inquisitors out of fear of the Jews (9:18–22). If their behavior typifies the general relationship with their son, then he has been on his own for a long time. The fact that Jesus first finds him by himself supports, though not conclusively, that thought.

miraculous healings with the use of eye-salve.[12] If the man is familiar with such traditions, he may have an inkling of the import of Jesus' action. But that is only an assumption. The man says nothing. He asks no questions. He simply obeys.

AN ALMOST CURSORY ACCOUNT

Devoid of embellishments, the narrative expends two verses to cover the miracle. It is a matter-of-fact account, no frills, just bare bones, omitting the usual awed wonder associated with such events. No one witnesses the actual healing except for the man himself. And we have no record of his reaction—no joy or dancing in celebration. Not informed, we can easily gloss over this sign and move on in our reading with hardly a raised eyebrow. Obviously the narrator downplays the healing itself. He focuses more on the consequences of the man's gaining his sight. The narrator ushers us quickly forward to the man's subsequent interaction, first with his neighbors and then with the religious establishment.

As we will discover, the narrative analyzes the man psychologically and spiritually, as he progresses toward greater insight into Jesus. The narrator guides us in our examination of the man, and, in the process, we enter into self-examination. The man's faith development and, in contrast, the religious leaders' plunge into greater spiritual darkness, take center stage.

The miracle is almost incidental, being primarily revelatory. This sign and Jesus' pronouncement that he is the light of the world constitute a Christophany. The effects of this Christophany are played out as the narrative continues. When a person experiences Jesus, he or she will respond in one of two ways; one cannot remain neutral. The blind man and the religious leadership represent the two possible responses to Jesus.

INCIPIENT FAITH

Earlier I indicated that the blind man possesses only incipient faith in Jesus. Still he obeys Jesus' word to go wash at the pool of Siloam. In this act he parallels the actions of the royal official who believed. I also suggested that the props of the mud anointment and the interpretation of "sent"

12. The rabbinic literature and ancient inscription cited by Köstenberger post-dates the apostolic era but still provides a helpful glimpse of the period (*John*, 92–93, n. 277–78).

provide clues about something impending and momentous. However, only the first prop, the mud, may be readily apparent to the blind man because the second prop resides in an aside directed only to the reader.

The props arouse anticipation. Even if, as I had mentioned, the blind man obeys in blind hope, he does so in anticipation. Hope is an ally of faith.

I believe the blind man harbors the seed of faith although he is ignorant of Jesus' identity.[13] That seed predisposes him favorably to Jesus. And because the Fourth Gospel characteristically portrays all the characters as having one of only two possible responses to Jesus, the man is already moving in the direction of those who believe in the one who is sent from above.[14]

In large measure, our response to the written word determines our response to Jesus. This unfolding narrative, as I pointed out earlier, is revelatory. We too can experience a Christophany through reading and interacting with this Fourth Gospel. Our response reveals our identification with one of only two kinds of people depicted.

I CAN SEE!

"Then he departed and washed himself and came seeing." The staccato effect in reading this sentence creates a dramatic reading experience. It highlights the man's "radical obedience."[15] He demonstrates a strong sense of purpose, even fearlessness in blindly navigating to the pool, and returns triumphantly seeing.

The two verbs "departed" and "came" share a common lexical root to form the outer ring of a chiastic arrangement, the inner ring being "washed himself." Going, the man was blind; coming, he sees. The difference in the manner of his movement is found at the center ring—"he washed himself." Brodie suggests that the process evokes the ideas of creation and rebirth.[16] If this interpretation is correct, then Jesus reenacts his role as both Creator and Redeemer.[17]

---

13. Kysar makes a similar point in terms of faith and experience (*Maverick Gospel*, 79).

14. Later I will discuss the faith of those in between the two polar positions of total unbelief or full faith as portrayed, for example, by Nicodemus. They can go in either direction. Eventually all will gravitate to one of the two poles.

15. Moloney, *Signs and Shadows*, 122.

16. Brodie, *Gospel According to John*, 347.

17. Brown, *Gospel According to John*, 380–82. But Brown goes too far in seeing sacra-

The now seeing man undoubtedly is euphoric, a "mountain top" experience. But as the narrative quickly moves forward, the moment proves to be brief. He does not enjoy the gift of sight for long before he enters his crucible. As he will discover, he still has a long way to go before he sees Jesus clearly.

I have discovered an occasional pattern in my own life that troubles me. There have been times when I too enjoyed the all-too-brief "mountain top." Another event would quickly follow, and I soon found myself in the depths. The slide exposed my vulnerability. Stunned, I immediately forgot the good that I experienced. Feelings of resentment, depression, even anger, surfaced. I would lose my spiritual composure and feel distant from God.

But that was not the healed blind man's story. Continually, I learn from him. The high points in life are just that, points. We, like the man, travel on a journey that consists of many points or steps that are all interconnected. We can be grateful for our high points, just as the blind man must have been. But we need to be mindful that another point connects with each high point. From that perspective we must maintain our spiritual composure and be ready for the next point, knowing that, in the end, when we have played out all the points, we will truly be on higher ground.

Like the blind man in the story, let us respond and cling to Jesus' word by faith as we move on to that next point. True faith is founded on belief in his word and not on wonderful experiences. That is what the Johannine signs really represent—wonderful experiences. And we know how Jesus regards faith grounded only on signs (2:23–25).

---

mental undertones with a baptismal interpretation of the blind man's washing.

6

Is It Really You?

> So his neighbors and those who saw him formerly as a beggar were saying, "Is he not the one who sat begging?" Some were saying, "He is." Others were saying, "No. Rather, he is like him." He said, "I am he." So they said to him, "How then were your eyes opened?" He answered, "The man called Jesus made mud and anointed my eyes and said to me, 'Go to Siloam and wash.' Then when I went and washed myself, I gained sight." And they said to him, "Where is he?" He said, "I don't know."
>
> —John 9:8–12

ONLY AFTER HE RETURNS from the pool of Siloam, now seeing, does the formerly blind man encounter those who know him in his former condition. No one was present; no eyewitnesses were there when he gained his sight. His neighbors and others must rely on his testimony as to what happened. They ask for a statement. In answering, the man speaks for the first time in the narrative.

The narrator emphasizes the spoken word rather than the action. His concern centers on the faith of the characters in the story and of the readers. Faith predicated on the spoken word is the Johannine portrait of true faith.[1] A signs-based faith cannot be trusted (2:23–25). Such an

---

1. Thompson, *Incarnate Word*, 56–63; and Moloney, *Belief in the Word*, 103–4. However, those who group Jesus' words and deeds together as the basis for true faith include Lincoln (*Truth on Trial*, 193); Hawthorne who adds people's testimonies but notes that faith initiated by signs is weak ("Concept of Faith," 117–26); and Gaffney ("Believing and Knowing," 215–41). Black classifies Jesus' speeches as grand, according to classical rhetoric, and evoke "powerful feelings, intellectual stimulation, and religious wonder-

inadequate faith has potential to become genuine, but the journey toward realization is not guaranteed. As the narrative moves forward, we will see whether the formerly blind man attains true faith. He has not even attained a signs-based faith. But he will wrestle with a miraculous phenomenon when he faces the incredulous reaction of his neighbors and the religious leadership.

As expected, when those who know the man encounter him seeing for the first time, they react with astonishment and skepticism. Some are sure he was formerly blind and had somehow gained his sight. Others deny the identification, inferring that such a miracle did not and could not have taken place. They are divided in their acceptance of the healing. This is the first of three separate times when the interlocutors of the man or Jesus experience a schism among themselves. The second time occurs when the Pharisees divide over Jesus as miracle-worker (9:16), and the third time when the Jews divide (10:19–21) over Jesus' discourse in 9:41—10:18.

ACCEPTANCE

The divisions among the people and the Pharisees point to an important initial step of faith—acceptance of a transformation. Something happened to the man, which some people cannot deny. Others refuse to believe it until the man speaks up and affirms "I am he." His simple testimony speaks volumes. Yes, he was blind, in fact congenitally blind. Yet, now he sees as well as any of them. He claims a change that no one in recorded biblical history has ever experienced. Gaining sight is spontaneous—no lengthy medical procedure. No normal process explains it. It must have been a miracle. The man infers it as such when he affirms his identity.

As soon as he speaks, all disputes among his acquaintances ceases. No one doubts or challenges his identity further. We infer that everyone accepts the fact that he was blind but now sees. They accept the miracle. But they wonder how he gained his sight. They ask, "How then were your eyes opened?"

Once they settle the issue of the man's identity, the identity of the miracle-worker becomes important. The miracle-worker must be unique to have accomplished what no man has ever done before. On one level their question of identity is natural and to be expected. But on another

---

ment" ("'Words That You Gave to Me,'" 221–23).

level they fail to direct any acknowledgement to God. The miracle-worker must be an agent of God to be able to perform this sign (9:16). If they accept the occurrence of a sign, they should accept God working in their midst. The agent is of secondary importance in comparison to the one who empowers him.

The man concisely responds: "The man called Jesus made mud and anointed my eyes and said to me, 'Go to Siloam and wash.' Then when I went and washed myself, I gained sight." Interestingly, the man's diction and manner of expression echoes that of the narrative and Jesus' sayings.[2] The author gives voice to the narrator and to each of the characters as he shapes the material, including Jesus' words, in order to enhance the rhetorical effectiveness of his gospel to the reader.

We, the readers, can readily affirm the fidelity of the man's recollection. He is as concise and Spartan as the narrator in recounting what happened.[3] In doing so, the man keeps Jesus in focus, and the healing itself to a low profile. The man's acquaintances immediately follow up on his self-identification (9:9) with a question about the means of his healing. That provides the opportunity for him to introduce "the man called Jesus."

In Jesus' absence, the man takes center stage of the unfolding drama. He becomes Jesus' spokesman in unveiling the connection between Jesus and the sign of his healing.[4] More precisely he is the proof that a sign did occur, dispelling initial doubt on the part of some. Confronted by

---

2. By "narrative" I mean the narrator's commentary, for example 9:6. Carson, Moo, and Morris, among others, have noted the stylistic and lexical unity where the differences in the language of the narrative and the words of Jesus are nearly negligible (*Introduction to the New Testament*, 152, 155–57). The authenticity of the Fourth Gospel is not adversely impacted if the author does not quote Jesus verbatim. Unlike modern-day reporting where a person is quoted and even videotaped, the Gospel writers were interpreters of Jesus, even theologians.

3. Staley considers the man loquacious in comparison to descriptions of characters in Hebrew narrative ("Stumbling in the Dark," 57).

4. The healed man bears witness in behalf of the accused, Jesus in the present case, in a two-party juridical controversy between Jesus and his accusers: the Jews and the Pharisees (Asiedu-Peprah, *Johannine Sabbath Conflicts*, 21, 31–32). I will deal with this genre, the two-party juridical controversy, a little later. I believe that Jesus is not only the sent one (Siloam), but he also sends the man to his accusers as his witness. Hence, Jesus being sent by the Father as the Father's witness to the world parallels the healed man being sent by Jesus as Jesus' witness to his accusers. The intent is to "win" his accusers over to his point of view.

the man, and, through him, confronted by the sign and the one who performed the sign, the man's acquaintances shift their attention to the absent Jesus. Shortly, the Pharisees will set their sights on Jesus as well (9:15). The issue of accepting Jesus' identity because of the revelatory function of the sign takes center stage. Although absent physically, Jesus is very much on everyone's mind.

THE PRISM

As the scene quickly unfolds, the formerly blind man finds himself in a reactionary mode. He does not voluntarily proclaim Jesus. Rather, people pepper him with questions and he responds with short answers. He acknowledges his limited knowledge honestly when they ask him, "Where is he?" He can only say, "I don't know."

Ignorant of Jesus' whereabouts and with everyone, it seems, wanting to know more, he may feel suddenly inadequate and abandoned. Where is Jesus when you need him? The man does not have all the answers. People are pressing him and all he can do is shrug his shoulders.

The man is what R. Alan Culpepper calls a *ficelle* who "exist[s] to serve specific plot functions, often revealing the protagonist, and may carry a great deal of representative or symbolic value. In John, Jesus is the protagonist and most of the other characters are ficelles. . . . They are in effect the prism which breaks up the pure light of Jesus' remote epiphany into colors the reader can see."[5]

The man serves as a prism by which we may see and better appreciate Jesus. And just as important in a representative or even symbolic way, the man serves as the means by which we may see ourselves better.

When the people in the story ask the man, "Where is he?" we may echo his response with "I don't know." Jesus disappears after he sends the blind man to the pool. The narrative remains silent about his whereabouts, leaving us the readers mystified. We do not know where he goes. More importantly, we do not know why. This portion of the narrative is the longest section of the Fourth Gospel in which Jesus is not present.

We will never learn where Jesus hides himself; but we will understand why he goes away when he reappears (9:35). Until we reach that point in our narrative reading, we lack the answer. We feel that Jesus abandons the man to face his interrogators alone. We think it unfair. He, unlike the royal

---

5. Culpepper, *Anatomy*, 104.

official, does not request healing. Jesus commendably takes the initiative; but he heals on the Sabbath. He also healed a lame man on a Sabbath (5:9), resulting in both the man and Jesus getting in trouble with the Jews (5:10–18). Jesus appears to be intentional in placing the now seeing man in his precarious position so that alone he will face the displeasure of the religious establishment for being party to a perceived Sabbath violation (9:14, 16). To put the situation in modern parlance: the man is set up. He is an unwitting victim of Jesus' agenda. We empathize with the man and wonder at Jesus' cold-heartedness. Rhetorically, the man functions as a prism that breaks the narrative reading into several components. We follow the story line as the tension between the man and his interrogators intensifies. At the same time, we are puzzled at Jesus' absence and wonder why. What purpose does his uncharacteristic absence serve? How can the healed man possibly fend off his opponents alone and remain unscathed? This thought process of ours challenges us to look below the surface of the story and to perceive the underlying dynamics of God's work in action. Giving the man physical sight represents only the first step of Jesus doing "the works of the one who sent me" (9:4). Even when absent, Jesus still works within the man through the man's interrogation. At the end of our mental exercise we will change our opinion about Jesus and better appreciate him by traversing the path the man takes.

A PATTERN

We find a parallel episode of a lame man Jesus healed also on the Sabbath in 5:5–18.[6]

The similarities and differences sensitize us in our reading. We discern a pattern in the Fourth Gospel. If Asiedu-Peprah is correct, a Sabbath conflict encompasses a significant portion of the Johannine narrative (5:1–47; 9:1—10:21) in the form of a two-party juridical controversy.[7] A two-party juridical controversy involves a dispute between two parties, the accuser and the accused, that does not involve outside mediation, typically a judge or arbitrator. In the course of the dispute, if

---

6. For comparative studies on the two pericopae, see Culpepper (ibid., 137–40); Staley, "Stumbling in the Dark," 55–80; Howard who depends heavily on Culpepper ("Significance of Minor Characters," 63–78); and Collins ("From John to the Beloved Disciple," 359–69). But they do not present the functional unity of the two.

7. Asiedu-Peprah, *Johannine Sabbath Conflicts*, 24–34. I find his arguments for the genre convincing.

either party accepts the arguments of the other, then a peaceful resolution and reconciliation can be accomplished. If no agreement can be reached, the dispute may escalate to a trial.[8] After healing the lame man, the Jews accuse Jesus of violating the Sabbath law. Jesus is the accused and the Jews are the accusers. The dispute between the two remains unresolved at the end of John 5 and will resume when Jesus heals another man, this time born blind, on the Sabbath.

I find Asiedu-Peprah's mapping of the dispute helpful:[9]

    a. Event leading to controversy (5:1–9b)

    b. The accusation (5:9c–16)

    c. Additional accusations and intended sanction (5:18)

    d. Response of the accused (5:17, 19–47)
        Reasons justifying action (5:17, 19–30)
        Invocation of witnesses (5:31–40)
        Transformation of defense into accusation (5:41–47)

    e. Sabbath controversy not yet concluded

    f. Resumption of the juridical controversy (9:1—10:21)
        Event leading to controversy (9:1–15)
        Restatement of accusation (9:16)
        Call of witnesses (9:17–27)
        Defense controversy and its aftermath (9:28–38)
        The use of juridical parable and its application (9:39—10:18)

    g. Conclusion of the Sabbath juridical controversy (10:19–21)[10]

The ongoing conflict between Jesus and the Jews and Pharisees—over Jesus' alleged violation of the Sabbath and claims to be equal with God—spans John 5 and John 9–10. There are two rounds in this conflict: round one centers on Jesus healing a lame man and round two involves Jesus healing a blind man, both on a Sabbath. After Jesus' extended

---

8. The controversy in 9:1—10:21 is not a trial scene as no mediator appears. Contra Ridderbos calling 9:8–23 "preliminary hearings," often used as a technical term associated with trials (*Gospel according to John*, 337). Ashton sees the dispute extending through much of the Fourth Gospel (John 5–10; 18–19) as a trial (*Understanding the Fourth Gospel*, 226–29). Lincoln adds to Ashton's list of passages the Farewell Discourse(s) in John 13–17 (*Truth on Trial*, 22). See also Dodd, *Interpretation of the Fourth Gospel*, 354.

9. Asiedu-Peprah, *Johannine Sabbath Conflicts*, 24–25.

10. I differ slightly with Asiedu-Peprah in viewing the juridical controversy as inconclusive at 10:19–21.

response to their accusations (5:17, 19–47), the accusers do not respond. There is no resolution of the controversy as round one ends. Neither side has acquiesced to the other. The narrative continues with "after these things Jesus departed to the other side of the Sea of Galilee of Tiberias" (6:1). Jesus simply leaves the scene.

The conflict resumes when Jesus encounters the blind man on another Sabbath. The Jews' and Pharisees' animosity toward Jesus continues unabated and simmers just below the boiling point. Aware of their hostility, Jesus intentionally aggravates the tension between himself and them. We will understand his motive for doing so when he returns at the end of round two and declares, "I have come into this world for judgment, in order that those who do not see may see and those who see may become blind" (9:39). I defer a fuller discussion of this statement to a later chapter.

At the end of round two there is still no resolution, although the Jews are divided among themselves about Jesus (10:19–21). There will follow a third round in this conflict when the two-party juridical controversy changes to a trial with the appearance of Pilate (18:28—19:16). Jesus' coming before the high priest (18:13–24) does not constitute a trial because the high priest is included among the accusers.[11] There would be a breach of protocol if he serves as both judge and accuser. In fact, the high priest does not have the authority to pass sentence.[12] And so, the interchange between Jesus and the high priest is a precursor to the trial, that is, a pretrial where the accusers clarify their charges against Jesus.

A WITNESS

Given the overview of the juridical controversy, we have a better understanding of the once blind man's role. Jesus has called him forth to be a witness in his behalf as the accused. The man is uniquely qualified. He has experienced a Christophany and so is an eyewitness. Only he does not know it yet. In fact, as we note his ignorance of Jesus' whereabouts we have a suspicion that he is not yet quite ready to be Jesus' witness.

It seems to be a gamble on Jesus' part. We do not understand why he does not inform the man of his role. What if the formerly blind man

---

11. Both Annas and Caiaphas are called high priest in the narrative. Only Caiaphas is in office at the time; but Annas retains great influence in high priestly matters and so bears an honorific title. See Lincoln, *Gospel according to John*, 451–52.

12. In 18:31 Pilate urges the Jewish leadership to judge Jesus in a religious trial; but they want a criminal trial by which Jesus might be condemned to die.

fails to fulfill his part? It all seems haphazard. Jesus depends on his plan dovetailing into circumstances, although the narrative offers no hint of such a preconceived plan. But earlier the narrator informed us that Jesus understands all men (2:24–25). The connotation appears negative, but that depends on the individual. Toward those not predisposed toward him, Jesus casts a wary eye. But to others who will believe in him, Jesus entrusts himself. Jesus entrusts the healed man with the weighty responsibility of being his witness.

Jesus does not tell the man ahead of time about his role because he knows the man must progress spiritually toward becoming an effective witness. Informing him prematurely would hinder his development. The man must naturally grow into his role. Jesus counts on this process because he knows "what is in man" (2:25).

The "crucible" I mentioned earlier is a positive experience, howbeit a painful one. Even when absent, Jesus maintains control. Initiating a chain reaction that will result in an anticipated end, he foresees the healed man responding to circumstances in such a way as to gain spiritual insight. He also foresees his accusers, the man's interrogators, moving in the opposition direction. He foresees all this because he knows "what is in man" (2:25).

Informed by the prologue, we should not be surprised by narrative developments. Jesus is the light that "shines in the darkness, and the darkness did not overcome it" (1:5). The pejorative "overcome" points to the hostility of the darkness toward Jesus the light. "He was in the world, and the world came into existence through him, and the world did not recognize him. He came to his own, and his own did not accept him" (1:10–11). The prologue unfolds through the narrative. On the other hand, the characters in the story have not read the prologue and do not have our anticipation. Our admiration for the formerly blind man increases when we compare him with the healed lame man.

Both men experienced a Christophany and, as a result, have the potential to become Jesus' witness in his juridical controversy with the Jews and Pharisees. The healed men stand in between two realms, one above and the other below. They are to bear witness of the realm above to the world below. The privilege is theirs if they accept it. The formerly lame man does not; but the formerly blind man does.

In order to better appreciate the role of witness, we note the witnesses who are already testifying for Jesus: John the Baptist (5:33, 35),

Jesus' works (5:36), the Father (5:37–38), and the Scriptures (5:39). Jesus adduces them because his accusers should accept them as reliable witnesses.[13] Now Jesus recruits the two men to be his witnesses by healing them. What makes them potentially acceptable to Jesus' accusers is that they represent the works Jesus performs. Their healing is undeniable, and hence, should be acceptable. To be included with the Father and the Scriptures as a witness is a lofty honor.

Tragically, the Jews and Pharisees reject Jesus' witnesses. He indicts them when he says: "You search the Scriptures because you think that in them you have eternal life. These are witnesses for me. But you do not desire to come to me in order that you may have life." (5:39-40) He will render final judgment at the conclusion of round two with a condemnatory discourse (9:41—10:18). Throughout this juridical controversy the accusers fail to be persuaded by Jesus' defensive arguments. The dispute between accused and accuser remains unresolved. That does not imply Jesus' failure to convince but rather their failure to accept the testimonies of reliable witnesses. That failure condemns them.

If their hardness is already evident in round one of the juridical controversy, why does Jesus bother pursuing round two? He can hardly expect them to change. I will explore these issues further at a later time.

OUR WITNESS

Representative, both healed men extend an invitation to us the readers. We too are to be Jesus' witnesses to the world. As the Jews and Pharisees represent those who should accept reliable witnesses but do not, so we too face those who will ultimately reject our witness.

Yet, the healed men represent two kinds of witnesses. The healed lame man failed to be a reliable witness by collapsing in the face of opposition and deflected criticism against himself to Jesus.[14] The healed

---

13. Asiedu-Peprah, *Johannine Sabbath Conflicts*, 99–100. Asiedu-Peprah regards the Father's testimony to be in the form of Jesus' works, and so does not separate them into two witnesses (p. 97). One can also argue that the Baptist having been sent by God (1:6) is really the Father's witness.

14. Many writers evaluate the healed lame man a failure in not standing up to Jesus' accusers. See, for example, Morris, *Gospel according to John*, 271–72; Moloney, *Signs and Shadows*, 6–7; and Witherington, *John's Wisdom*, 138. However, Brodie suggests the possibility of a positive interpretation (*Gospel According to John*, 239). The chief difference between the two witnesses lies in their response to increased pressure imposed by the accusers. The healed lame man quickly blames Jesus for the Sabbath violation because

blind man became a reliable witness and paid the price when many rejected his testimony.

As we read the narrative and vicariously participate in the juridical controversy centered on Jesus, we realize that we will become a witness of one kind or the other, depending on our willingness to pay the price.

Admittedly, we do not share an exact parallel with the two healed men. Neither of them evidences faith in Jesus before their encounter with him. We the readers, by contrast, have professed Jesus as Savior. But our response to an encounter with Jesus establishes common ground. We can shirk our responsibilities as a witness or we can accept them with boldness. One response moves us further from Jesus (cf. 5:15). The other strengthens our bond with him and deepens our insight in things pertaining to him.

---

he merely followed Jesus' instructions (5:11). And once he learns Jesus' identity, he immediately reports him to the accusers and disappears (5:14–15). The healed blind man, on the other hand, stands his ground resolutely and addresses the accusers' accusations point for point.

7

Jekyll or Hyde?

They led him, the one who was formerly blind, to the Pharisees. Now it was the Sabbath on the day Jesus made mud and opened his eyes. So again the Pharisees also asked him how he gained his sight. And he said to them, "He placed mud on my eyes, and I washed myself, and I see." Thus some of the Pharisees were saying, "This man is not from God because he does not keep the Sabbath." But others were saying, "How is a man who is a sinner able to perform such signs?" And there was a division among them.

—John 9:13–16

STRICTLY SPEAKING, ROUND TWO of the juridical controversy between Jesus and his accusers begins with the healed blind man meeting the Pharisees. The controversy involves two parties—the accused and the accuser. But only one party is now present, the accuser as represented by the Pharisees. As a witness for the accused, the man defends the absent Jesus before the accusers. The subsequent interchange between the man and the Pharisees, and later the Jews, constitutes what Asiedu-Peprah calls a defense controversy, part of the ongoing juridical controversy that began in John 5 and resumes here in John 9.[1] The healed man supplies evidence that supports the validity of Jesus' claims and that undermines the validity of the accusers' case.

---

1. Asiedu-Peprah, *Johannine Sabbath Conflicts*, 21. Asiedu-Peprah carefully states that the defense controversy is not a separate dispute nor does it signify a discontinuation of the two-party juridical controversy between Jesus and his accusers.

As soon as the man's acquaintances reach an impasse with his "I don't know" in regard to Jesus' whereabouts (9:12), they lead him to the Pharisees (9:13). They instigate the resumption of the unresolved juridical controversy. When Jesus changes his self-defense into a counter-accusation against his accusers (5:37b–47),[2] the accusers do not respond. As a consequence, the tension between the two parties remains high.

When the healed blind man identifies his healer as "the man called Jesus" (9:11), his acquaintances immediately recall that this Jesus healed the lame man earlier, and that event resulted in the dispute between Jesus and the Jews (5:10, 15–16, 18). In the present situation, the accusers are named the Pharisees (9:13, 15–16, 40) or the Jews (9:18, 22; 10:19). Evidently, then, the labels "the Pharisees" and "the Jews" are interchangeable.[3]

THE SABBATH FACTOR

The trigger that prompts the formerly blind man's acquaintances to bring him to Jesus' accusers is the Sabbath factor (9:14).[4] Once again, the accusers note Jesus working on the Sabbath. In particular, he made mud and opened the blind man's eyes. The very act of bringing him to Jesus' accusers reveals which side of the juridical controversy the man's acquaintances take. The man becomes the lone witness surrounded by those adversarial to his role. Totally isolated, he is very much on his own with the whole weight of the controversy and the validity of Jesus' claims resting solely on him. Or so it seems.

---

2. Although there is general consensus on Jesus' counter-accusation, writers identify different starting points. In regarding 5:37b as the starting point, I follow Lincoln (*Truth on Trial*, 79) and Hendricksen (*Commentary*, 208). Contra Asiedu-Peprah who sees 5:41 as the starting point (*Johannine Sabbath Conflicts*, 110).

3. Culpepper distinguishes the Pharisees as leaders of the Jews until they become blended with the Jews after 9:17 (*Anatomy*, 130–31).

4. The conjunction that introduces 9:14 normally functions as an adversative "but." Here, however, it ushers in an explanation and so is translated "now." There is the possibility, then, that 9:14 explains why the man's acquaintances bring him to the Pharisees. Carson does not detect any malice in the man's acquaintances other than the desire to see what their religious leaders make of the healing (*Gospel according to John*, 366–67). Even if the man's acquaintances were not present in round one of the juridical controversy, most likely they were aware of the Sabbath conflict and the Jews' resultant edict because his parents were aware (9:22). So the man's acquaintances seek a condemnatory verdict from the authorities with regard the latest Sabbath healing.

I think it insightful to recall the witnesses Jesus summons in the earlier Sabbath conflict involving the lame man—John the Baptist, Jesus' works, the Father, and the Scriptures (5:33–40). Jesus brings forth none of them for round two. Instead, he recruits the now seeing man for the witness stand.

Puzzled, we question Jesus' strategy. If the four earlier witnesses did not persuade his accusers, we do not understand how the healed blind man can be more effective. True, the man represents a most unusual case in that no one born blind has ever gained sight. But then the man is merely one of many examples of Jesus' works that his accusers have already rejected.

Jesus' strategy, however, does not simply involve presenting the man as healed. That proved woefully inadequate with the healed lame man because no corresponding inner healing accompanied the external healing. After the healing, Jesus warned him, "See, you are healed. Sin no longer lest something worse happens to you" (5:14). Jesus addresses a present situation, an ongoing pattern of behavior.[5] The condition typifies the world's dilemma. In the Fourth Gospel, "the world's sin consists of its rejection of Jesus as Messiah."[6] In response to the warning, "the man departs and reports to the Jews that Jesus was the one who made him whole" (5:15). The healed lame man fails to acknowledge Jesus. Significantly he moves away from Jesus to the Jews. He sins in his unbelief.

In contrast, the healed blind man moves to Jesus in faith, thereby becoming a reliable witness. Jesus utters no warning about sin. The now seeing man is not entrapped in unbelief. His potential for gaining greater faith and insight will be actualized through the interrogation with the Pharisees and the Jews. Jesus sees the man (9:1) not simply as a physical object sitting blind by the wayside nor as a sinful object that prompts the disciples' curiosity, but as someone who can and will become a viable witness because of a faith that emerges triumphantly. Jesus displays penetrating insight (2:24–25).

---

5. Jesus uses a contrast of verb tenses. The perfect tense conveys a stative condition. The man is healed, that is his state or condition. The present tense expresses action in progress in Jesus' admonition, "sin no longer." The adverb "no longer" suggests that the man is sinning and he must stop lest something worse happens to him. The particular sin is unbelief (Asiedu-Peprah, *Johannine Sabbath Conflicts*, 72–73).

6. Köstenberger, *Theology of John's Gospel*, 464.

The Sabbath constitutes a critical element of Jesus' juridical strategy that will confirm his claims and invalidate the claims of his accusers. The man's faith, not so much his healing, proves juridically effective.

OUR SABBATH FACTOR

We harbor a Sabbath factor in our lives. Defining our convictions and governing our practices, it is something we regard as sacrosanct. Specifically, our interpretation of Scripture and, more to the point, our application bind or free us.

Jesus' accusers condemn him for violating the Sabbath according to their interpretation of the law.[7] In the disputation, Jesus disagrees for two reasons. First, his Sabbath work is legitimate because the Father also works on the Sabbath (5:17, 19). This point, of course, implies equality with God, which provokes the Jews' murderous intent for perceived blasphemy (5:18). Second, healing or doing good deeds on the Sabbath fulfills the law (7:21–24). Jesus cites the regulation concerning circumcision that must be performed on the eighth day even if it coincides with the Sabbath. He argues from the law.[8] Circumcision is the means by which a person obtains life by entering into a covenant relationship with God and being incorporated into his people. Jesus, as the greater gift that supersedes the gift of the law (1:16–17), offers life through his healing work. Essentially, the Jews missed the truth in their particular interpretation of the Sabbath (7:24).[9] They misunderstand the law, in particular circumcision, and Jesus' identity. Their misunderstanding unfortunately defines their Sabbath factor and makes them obtuse to Jesus' Sabbath activities.

Alan Noble offers pertinent thoughts in his blog.[10] The focus of his article is not the effects of pop culture on the integrity of our faith or the potential adversarial effects on a "weaker" brother created by our indulgence in pop culture (which are legitimate concerns), but the potentially dire effects of our practice of Christian culture on new believers and those outside of the faith looking in. By Christian culture he means our

---

7. I will discuss the Jews' interpretation of the law more fully in a later chapter when I examine excerpts of the Mishnah, the rabbinic compilation of Pharisaical regulations with regard to the written and oral traditions.

8. For a fuller discussion on Jesus' argument, see Moloney, *Signs and Shadows*, 78–80. Blomberg offers a similar but condensed discussion (*Historical Reliability*, 135).

9. Lincoln, *Truth on Trial*, 222–25.

10. Noble, "Rethinking the Stumbling Block," lines 1–102.

"Christian" preferences, tastes, and choices. For example, our preference for Christian music can become a stumbling block for others. Noble identifies two major dangers. First, we may inadvertently conflate our faith with Christian culture so as to equate faith in Christ with the necessity to watch a movie with overt Christian themes. An observer may conclude that to be a Christian means he or she should and even must watch only Christian films. Second, we may conflate the Christian community with Christian culture. An example is our use of Christian jargon. It represents an insider's code for communication. A believer not conversant in this jargon can feel excluded.

I do not criticize Christian culture. Rather, I advocate sensitivity to other people's perceptions and differences in preference, taste, and choice. Our Sabbath factor is our interpretation of the boundaries of acceptable Christianity. I do not believe we can avoid defining those boundaries. In one sense we have the responsibility as conscientious Christians to do so. But we should align our perception of "acceptable" with Scripture truth. We need to exercise constant vigilance in assessing and insuring that our boundaries are biblical.

One day I was driving with a co-worker in ministry. We stopped at an intersection to wait for the light to change. Another driver pulled up alongside with his windows down and his stereo revved up. Rock and roll thundered across the short divide between our two vehicles. My companion turned to me and made a face of displeasure and said, "This is the devil's music." I did not audibly respond; but my mind did. I thought the music was kind of cool. Then I thought maybe our personal backgrounds explained the difference between us. He grew up in Vietnam as an ethnic Chinese and had barely escaped the Communist regime by swimming across a bay. He survived a year in a squalid refugee camp before making his way to America. I, on the other hand, grew up on a steady diet of the Allman Brothers and Journey bands.

But on further reflection I noted our similarities. We were equally devoted to the Lord and diligent in our ministry. We worked well together and were good friends. But we differed in our sense of liberty in Christ. Then as now, I oppose questionable lyrics and the lifestyles of some performing artists as much as anyone. But I cannot justify condemning a musical genre because some samples of it are morally deficient. To confine the matter to one of musical taste oversimplifies the issues. I also listened to Eddy Arnold and, since becoming a Christian, I appreciate Bill Gaither and Michael W. Smith.

My friend lives by a clearly defined Christian culture. That is his Sabbath factor, and it influences the way he perceives things and colors his assessment. He sees people through the lens of his Christian culture, which affects the relationship he has with them and they with him. He and I still get along quite well whenever we cross paths, so long as we don't discuss music. I do not share his point of view on a number of things; but there are areas where he and I overlap. I know that I have a Sabbath factor also. Sensitized, I keep close watch on possible interference with someone else's faith and freedom. In the very act of self-policing, I detect an openness to deal with this issue and attempt to change, if necessary. I would hope to change so that I do not erect artificial barriers with others and, most importantly, so that I do not hinder another person's relationship with Jesus and his people.

THE POWER OF FAITH

We return to a point raised earlier—the now seeing man's faith identified as the critical element in Jesus' strategy in his disputation. In round one of his juridical controversy, Jesus cites four witnesses in his defense: John the Baptist, Jesus' works, the Father, and Scripture. These failed to convince the Jews of the validity of Jesus' truth claims. Obviously in round two it would be pointless to raise them again. Jesus requires a different witness for the defense. Although the miraculously healed lame man failed to be effective, an internal difference sets the healed blind man apart and promises that he can substantiate Jesus' cause. Unshackled by unbelief, the healed blind man can progress to full faith without hindrance even though he does not yet believe in Jesus as the one worthy of being worshipped.

A comparison of the verbal witness of the two healed men yields insight. What they say to their interrogators is quite brief. In reply to the Jews' accusation ("it is the Sabbath and it is not lawful for you to carry your pallet"), the healed lame man defers blame: "The one who made me whole said to me, 'Take your pallet and walk'" (5:11).[11] Later he identifies Jesus as the one who healed him (5:15).

---

11. Carson, *Gospel according to John*, 245.

When the Pharisees ask the healed blind man the seemingly innocuous question of how he gained his sight, he replies, "He placed mud on my eyes, and I washed myself, and I see" (9:15). His answer omits Jesus' pronouncement to the disciples that he is the light of the world, his making mud, and his command to go wash at Siloam. He only mentions Jesus applying mud to his eyes before admitting to washing his own eyes. In contrast, he allows Jesus a larger role before his acquaintances: identifying Jesus as the one who made mud and anointed his eyes before directing him to go to Siloam to wash (9:11).

We observe two things from the healed blind man's two answers. First, he changes the verbs from "anoint" before his acquaintances to "apply" before the Pharisees. And second, he abbreviates Jesus' role even further between his two answers, thereby giving himself an equal share in his healing. The net effect reduces Jesus' role.[12]

The man seems aware of the dynamics of the situation.[13] Perhaps he knows the Pharisees have accused Jesus of Sabbath violation before. Others know, including his parents (9:22). He appears to be shielding Jesus from being accused of another violation.

Unlike the healed lame man, this man is not so quick to pass blame. He shows some backbone.[14] Not easily intimidated, he will stand up for the truth and, being a principled man, he speaks according to his convictions, a quality that serves the defense well. Jesus later declares, "I am the way and the truth and the life" (14:6). The man desires one thing—the truth about Jesus, particularly the truth about his identity and origin. Any effective witness Jesus calls forth must affirm this truth. Jesus discerns the man's character (9:1) and selects him as his witness.

As he stands his ground against his interrogators' challenge, the man's faith and insight into Jesus develops. Amazingly, Jesus does not choose someone already possessing full faith in him. He chooses instead someone with only the potential for full faith. Jesus accomplishes two purposes here. First, he develops the man spiritually through the juridical process. Second, he progressively exposes his accusers' blindness through the man's developing faith. Hence, two corresponding but opposite movements stand in stark relief—the man comes to Jesus' light and the accusers

---

12. Staley suggests the possibility of the man protecting Jesus from being accused of another Sabbath violation ("Stumbling in the Dark," 67).

13. At the very least, he is cautious. See Hendricksen, *Commentary*, 81.

14. Barrett, *Gospel according to John*, 212–13.

willfully move away from that light into the darkness. The man serves as a point of reference, even as a rebuke to Jesus' opponents. The blind man's trajectory should have been theirs.

THE POWER OF OUR FAITH

The blind man's example encourages. We do not have to be fully mature in the faith to be Jesus' witness. Our growth trajectory can be powerfully influential. We might object to that assessment, in that the healed man "failed" to win his interrogators over. But I contend that he succeeded in exposing their true condition and rendered their position in the juridical process indefensible. Positively, he showcases what Jesus can do in a life fully open to him.

In ministering to young people, I often hear the excuse "I'm not qualified to serve" or "I lack the experience." Jesus reserves the prerogative to evaluate our qualifications. He is the light of the world that shines in our lives. He chooses us as he chose the blind man. One criterion of consequence should concern us—our character as a person of principle. Our quest converges on the truth as it pertains to Jesus.

Although outnumbered by his interrogators and acquaintances, the healed man stands his ground. No matter how fierce the assault against his testimony, the man proves unshakable. He pays a heavy price, but he will accrue dividends; for Jesus says: "If you remain in my word, you are truly my witnesses; and you will know the truth and the truth will liberate you" (8:31b–32).

THE RIPPLE EFFECT

One constant emerges clearly and even dramatically as we read the Fourth Gospel. Whoever encounters Jesus responds in one of two possible ways. Either he believes in Jesus or he does not, leaving no third option. However, a momentary struggle to decide what one thinks of Jesus may ensue. Such is the case with the Pharisees.

Divided in their reaction to the man's testimony (9:16), they dispute among themselves: Is he from God, as he claims, or is he a sinner? Using more modern terms, is Jesus a Jekyll or a Hyde? The Pharisees struggle in coming to terms with what the healed man says. The miraculous healing proffers a clear implication—there is a miracle worker. This issue confronts the Pharisees, the very matter Jesus intends to raise when he says, "in order that the works of God be manifested in him" (9:3b). Only an agent from God performs works of God.

The accusers depend on the man's witness because no other eyewitness comes forth. We infer that, before questioning the man directly, the Pharisees first confirmed the validity of a healing through interaction with the man's acquaintances.[15] Then his acquaintances can be defense witnesses because they knew the healed man in his former condition. The fact that he now sees implies a healing. Apparently the Pharisees do not regard the acquaintances as adequate witnesses, because they turn directly to the man for questioning. What they really want is a witness to the miracle worker's identity. This is something that the man's acquaintances cannot do. The formerly blind man was the only one present when the healing took place. So his testimony is crucial.[16]

We infer from 9:16 that the Pharisees' genuinely struggle over Jesus' identity. Some reasoned: "Surely Jesus is a sinner; after all, he broke the Sabbath." Others countered: "But how can he be a sinner since he is able to do such a wonderful thing?" Actually, the latter group of Pharisees said: "How can a man who is a sinner do such signs?" The plural "signs" lumps the blind man's healing with earlier signs that Jesus performed. They acknowledge a consistent witness based on Jesus' works (cf. 5:36), and so appear ready to accept the reliability of that witness in the juridical controversy. If there was no opposing faction, then the dispute with Jesus would have ended for this group of Pharisees.

The opposing faction, however, will win them over due to a paradox in the Pharisaical worldview. A miracle worker must be a holy man from God; but he cannot violate God's law. The mutual exclusivity of the two conditions highlights their dilemma.

Two possible solutions to the paradox arise: Jesus, though a miracle worker, is either a sinner or he is equal with God who alone works on the Sabbath (5:17). This is the ripple effect of Jesus performing the works of God, particularly on the Sabbath that confronts the world. He comes from God and is even equal with God.

---

15. The omission in the narrative is what Staley calls a "narrative gap" ("Stumbling in the Dark," 67).

16. The adverb "again" (9:15) signifies that the Pharisees put the same question ("how did he gain his sight?") to the healed man, as to his acquaintances earlier. The conjunction "therefore" links 9:15 back to 9:14 and explains why they were so adamant in questioning the man. A potential Sabbath violation awaits confirmation.

The Pharisees cannot accept him as equal with God. That leaves only one recourse—Jesus is a sinner. But there remains one problem. The healed blind man can undermine their case against Jesus. However, if he can be persuaded to label Jesus a sinner, then the Pharisees can claim victory in their dispute with Jesus. So they formulate a strategy. Their line of thinking runs thus: "We have this unresolved tension; something has got to give. Let's see if we can't get the man to cave in to our pressure. If we can, our problem is solved and we win."

We, the readers, wonder about the juridical outcome. Will the man successfully resist the pressure and prove to be a reliable witness? Or will he, like the lame man before him, crumble? Then what about our witness to the world for Jesus? Are we prepared to withstand the pressure should opposition become intense, in order to maintain our principles?

8

One Step Forward, One Step Back

> So they spoke to the blind man again, "What do you have to say about him since he opened your eyes?" He replied, "He is a prophet." The Jews did not believe that he was blind and gained his sight until they summoned his parents and asked them, "Is he your son whom you say was born blind? How then does he now see?" His parents answered, "We know that he is our son and that he was born blind. But how can he now see we don't know; nor do we know who opened his eyes. Ask him. He is old enough to speak for himself." His parents said these things because they feared the Jews, for the Jews agreed together that if anyone should confess him as Christ, he would be cast out of the synagogue. For this reason his parents said, "He is old enough. Ask him."
>
> —John 9:17–23

WE COME TO A critical juncture of the healed man's journey to full faith in Jesus. The man has not attained mature faith yet. Although he makes progress, he still faces an important step as his interrogators apply greater pressure on him to recant. We admire his steadfast refusal to succumb and his loyalty to the truth. However, as we will see, his grasp of the truth is still not fully developed, but what he understands he clings to with a tenacity that nurtures his maturing faith.

As we follow this juridical controversy between Jesus and his accusers, we note that Jesus is absent and the healed man speaks as his witness. The man may not be aware of his function, but he fulfills his role effectively. The accusers do not gain any advantage in the dispute. In fact, they lose ground. Amazingly, Jesus' case gains strength. Throughout the Gospel narrative Jesus is portrayed as being in command of all situations, particularly in his dispute with his detractors. He displays superior rhetorical skills. They cannot answer his countercharges nor dispute his logic. He makes them look foolish and defenseless. But in this critical portion of the juridical controversy (9:8–34), Jesus deliberately withdraws to let a man with less than adequate understanding and faith in him to become a potent weapon to further his case.

Through the example set by the healed blind man, we discover the power of an effective witness for Jesus. Jesus does not need to be present. The presence of a witness is sufficient. Not any witness however; but one who cannot be intimidated and who clings to the truth regardless of personal cost. Like the healed man, we too can become that kind of witness for Jesus.

Jesus counts on this man, and he comes through for the defense. The question of our readiness to be counted upon begs for an answer. What kind of witness will we be?

TURNCOAT?

The Pharisees divide over the healed man's testimony (9:16). Some are persuaded by Jesus' signs that he comes as a miracle-worker from God. But others stubbornly cite Jesus' Sabbath violation to brand him a sinner. They reach an impasse. The ultimate issue at stake is whether or not Jesus is equal with God, who alone works on the Sabbath (5:17). If he indeed performs a work of God on the Sabbath, then he is from God and even equal with God as he claims. But if no miracle occurs then he is merely a sinner and the man who claims healing is a fraud. The healed blind man becomes the linchpin in the dispute, a critical witness. So the Pharisees summon the man back for further questioning.[1]

We catch the drift of the Pharisees' interrogation of the healed man. They are not interested in his healing or even in how the healing is accomplished because they are persuaded that no healing actually took place (9:18).[2] Implicit is the fact that they do not know the man in his former

---

1. The inferential conjunction "so" or "therefore" that introduces 9:17 connects the verse with 9:16. Because of the division among the Pharisees (9:16), they approach the healed man a second time to help resolve the internal conflict among themselves (9:17).

2. Because of the intermingling in referring to the Pharisees and the Jews in this narrative, I too use the terms interchangeably. See Moloney, *Signs and Shadows*, 124, n. 31.

condition. But in their unbelief they tacitly dispute the claims of the man's acquaintances who have already testified to his former blindness (implied in 9:13 where the narrative explicitly states that "they brought the former blind man to the Pharisees"). The acquaintances know he was blind and recognize that a healing occurred. They too can be potential witnesses for Jesus. However, the Pharisees ignore them and, instead, focus their attention on the man himself. Their questioning deals exclusively with Jesus' identity. Their plan is character assassination. If they can undermine Jesus' credibility, his case falls and they win.

For the Pharisees, the man's acquaintances are of no value because they did not witness the alleged healing. Hence, they can offer no reliable assessment of Jesus. But the healed blind man can. So the Pharisees ask him, "What do you say concerning him since he opened your eyes?" They are hopeful that he will supply the necessary testimony in order to condemn Jesus. So they probe the man for his opinion about Jesus. They want the man to confirm their contention that Jesus is a charlatan. Will he become a turncoat?

But in reply, he states, "He is a prophet." As many commentators note, the man makes progress in his understanding of Jesus' true identity.[3] At this point we wonder whether or not the man discerns his inquisitors' intentions. This is the fourth question asked. The first two are by his acquaintances on "how" (9:10) and "where" (9:12), and the third question by the Pharisees also on "how" (9:15). The fourth question finally asks "who" with the demand for the man's assessment of Jesus (9:17). The Pharisees already know that Jesus is credited with the alleged healing.

Labeling Jesus a prophet reveals an inadequate understanding about Jesus. Recalling Nicodemus's similarly inadequate confession of Jesus as a teacher from God, we note that he ascribed Jesus' ability to perform signs to God empowering Jesus (3:2). This is probably the healed man's understanding as well: Jesus healed him because God empowered him.

However, Duke distinguishes between the sympathetic Pharisees who leave the scene and the Jews who stay and represent the hardened opposition against Jesus at 9:18 (*Irony in the Fourth Gospel*, 120). But the Pharisees are again mentioned in 9:40 when Jesus condemns them (9:41—10:18). Note also 12:42 ("nevertheless, however, even many of the leaders believed in him but because of the Pharisees they would not confess lest they be expelled from the synagogue"), which parallels 9:34, where the Jews expel the healed man.

3. See, for example, Hendricksen, *Commentary*, 2. 84; Witherington, *John's Wisdom*, 183; Lincoln, *Gospel according to Saint John*, 283; and Morris, *Gospel according to John*, 432.

The title of teacher, or prophet, from God grants the seal of approval to Jesus, though it is woefully short of the truth about Jesus. Yet, even this rather plebeian characterization is unacceptable for his inquisitors. But the healed blind man remains true to his convictions, as he understands them, for the time being.

A TALE OF TWO KINDS OF BELIEVERS

The healed man's characterization of Jesus before the accusers echoes that of Nicodemus's but with a sharp difference. Nicodemus confessed Jesus under the cover of night (3:2a), and so is one of the group of secret believers in Jesus (12:42) that includes Joseph of Arimathea (19:38).[4] The spiritual status of these secret believers is questionable and no overt judgment is pronounced about them. But the now seeing man is not one of them. As a result of his openness about Jesus, his status is quite clear in the end.

A dualistic motif threads through the narrative. Those who believe in Jesus divide into two categories: those who believe openly, and willingly face ostracism, and those who believe in secret, for fear of ostracism. Surprisingly, the disciples face no threats of ostracism within the confines of the narrative; rather they expect the world's hatred after Jesus' departure (15:18–21, 27), which lies beyond the end of the narrative. The difference between the disciples and the healed man is a matter of timing.

---

4. See Culpepper for an insightful discussion on Johannine secret believers (*Anatomy*, 135–36). According to Culpepper, these secret believers are not children of God (1:12). Joseph of Arimathea is identified as "a concealed disciple of Jesus" (19:38). The descriptive "concealed" is a perfect passive participle that, according to Fanning (*Verbal Aspect*, 416–18), "often emphasizes the *resulting state* and only implies the anterior occurrence" (p. 416). The italics is the author's. Because of his fear of the Jews, Joseph stays concealed with regard to his faith in Jesus. The verse gives equal emphasis to the anterior event (the past moment in which Joseph first became fearful) and the present resultant state (his concealed faith). Obviously, he is still fearful and there is no indication that his fear will dissipate in the foreseeable future. Hence, his faith continues to be hidden. The next verse (19:39) characterizes Nicodemus as "the one who came to him [Jesus] at night before" (19:39). As I mentioned in an earlier chapter, "night" symbolizes the darkness that marks the world's spiritual condition. Thus, the negative descriptions of both men condemn them, especially in view of a parallel in 12:42–43. Many of the Jewish rulers believed in Jesus, but they would not confess him openly for fear of the Pharisees. These secret believers did not want to be expelled from the synagogue. The narrator provides the damning reason: "For they loved the glory of men rather than the glory of God" (12:43). This reason recalls Jesus' indictment of the Jews in round one of the juridical controversy (5:41–44). The Jews cannot believe in Jesus and are devoid of the love for God precisely because they prefer the glory or praise of men rather than that from God.

The disciples' witness comes with the Spirit's advent; the man's witness is now. This Gospel correlates witnessing and suffering ostracism—the two are inseparable. In fact, one cannot be a witness of Jesus unless he willingly suffers for Jesus.

Belief in Jesus necessitates a corresponding shift in one's association. Either a person belongs to the world or he belongs to the realm above through a relationship with Jesus. Jesus invokes the proverbial principle "a servant is not greater than his master" (15:20; 13:16). As the world persecuted Jesus, it persecutes his servants because of Jesus' name (15:21).

Given the parallel circumstances of the disciples facing the world's wrath upon Jesus' departure to the Father, and the healed man facing Jesus' accusers in his absence, we observe that one of the Fourth Gospel's portrayals of the true believer is as a witness for Jesus only in Jesus' absence. A witness must stand alone to face the world; and if he refuses to stand firm, he fails to be a witness.

A witness, then, is one who willingly and publicly identifies with Jesus. By witnessing, a person confirms his identity and affiliation. He stands in Jesus' stead before the world. This association parallels the association the Son has with the Father in the world. Jesus stands in place of the Father during his foray in the world.

However, Jesus is never alone because the Father is ever with him. He affirms this truth when he states: "The one who sent me is with me. He has not left me alone because I always do the things that please him" (8:29). Later, in the company of his disciples, he adds: "Behold, the hour is coming and has come when each of you will be scattered to his own place and you will abandon me. But I am not alone because the Father is with me" (16:32).

Jesus hints at a union between the Father and himself (14:10–11, 20; 17:11, 21–23), first mentioned in the prologue (1:1). This most intimate of relationships is not hampered when Jesus descends to the world below with the Father remaining above. Even during his time in the world the union continues in force.

Jesus promises a similar union for the disciples in three forms: the Spirit abiding in them (14:16–17); Jesus abiding in them, and they in Jesus (14:20); and both the Father and Jesus taking their abode in them (14:23). He reinforces the relationship through the command expressed as an extended metaphor: they must abide in him in order to bear much fruit, just as branches must remain connected to the vine to be fruitful (15:1–8).

Consequently, even after Jesus' return to the Father, the disciples are not abandoned in the world as Jesus' witnesses. In fact, they cannot be effective witnesses unless they abide in him through obedience to his word. This promised union is predicated on Jesus' departure and the coming of the Spirit (16:7).

Then is the former blind man really alone, with Jesus absent during his interrogation? The answer must be addressed at several levels. On the physical level, the man is very much alone. Uncharacteristically, Jesus is absent. The man must fend for himself, with no allies from among his acquaintances. He cannot even count on his parents for support. The full weight of the juridical process seems to fall squarely on his shoulders alone. Yet, there is another level in this process. The man is a witness for another; he does not testify for himself. The controversy is not about him. The controversy is about Jesus. The process does not call for Jesus to speak for the man, but the man for Jesus. At this level the man is alone as an independent witness. He is not a puppet.

There is still another level, however, in which the man is not alone. Jesus makes a significant point when he states: "in order that the works of God may be manifested in him" (9:3). The term "works" is plural, signifying a multiplicity of workings in the man. There is the gaining of physical sight, so the man now sees. But there is another working within the man as he progresses in spiritual perception and insight about the light of the world. God works in the man. Neither momentary nor instantaneous, it is a prolonged process. During his interrogation, the man undergoes an inward process of change. At this level God is with him.

"CLUB" MEMBERSHIP

Fearing the world's ostracism we, the characters in the story and the readers of it, desire to remain associated with the world and to value the world's esteem (12:43). Seeking the approval of the one who sent him, Jesus models what his witnesses must seek—God's approval rather than the world's.

In 9:18 the Jews summon the healed man's parents as witnesses. They are secondary witnesses, in that they testify about their son's qualifications as a primary witness for the defense. They can testify only indirectly in behalf of Jesus. The narrative makes clear the rationale for their appearance: "the Jews did not believe that he was blind and gained his sight." The

Jews challenge the veracity of the man's story that he was miraculously healed. Obviously, if no healing took place, Jesus has no case. The crux of the matter centers in the healed man's congenital condition. Only his parents can verify that.

The Jews come straight to the point: "Is this man your son whom you say was born blind? So how can he now see?" (9:19). The first question presupposes that the parents offered an earlier affirmation of their son's congenital condition, which is not recorded in the narrative. The Jews ask the question again in preparation for the second question. Not able to deny the man's former blindness, the Jews prepare to examine the manner by which he gained his sight. They have already heard the man's brief explanation and that of his acquaintances. This is now the third time that the Jews want to hear the healing account. It appears that in having the story told several times, they may be looking for inconsistencies by which to expose possible fraud.[5]

His parents answer, "We know that he is our son and that he was born blind. But how can he now see we do not know; nor do we know who opened his eyes. Ask him. He is old enough to speak for himself." They are prepared to acknowledge their son and his congenital condition. But they avow ignorance of the manner by which their son gained his sight. In their avowal they go further than what was specifically asked of them. They also avow ignorance as to who facilitated the healing. They link the manner of healing and the identity of the healer together. Both aspects of the healing in their minds are inseparable. The identity of the healer is very much in the minds of the interrogators, as is evident in their questioning the man. But his parents are presumably not present until summoned. So they did not witness the interrogation of their son. Yet, it is probable that the ongoing juridical controversy between Jesus and his accusers is common knowledge.[6] Jesus performed signs before, and, as a result, many believed in him because of those signs (2:23). And because Jesus has "violated" the Sabbath before, the Jews persecute him (5:16),

---

5. Whereas Carson (*Gospel according to John*, 368) refers to the Jews' inquisition as an attempt to uncover a mistake, I believe that they are trying to establish a case for fraud. Although the man can be so charged, Jesus is really their target.

6. Lindars believes the parents can answer the Jews' first question and give only an opinion to the second question "because they were not witnesses of what had occurred" (*Gospel of John*, 346). Lindars is correct in what he states; but the parents are asked for an *informed* opinion. They too are given a chance to be a witness for Jesus.

seeking his death for alleged blasphemy (5:18). The multitude is divided in their opinion of Jesus (7:40–43).

The narrative provides a helpful glimpse into the parents' thoughts (9:22–23).[7] They fear the Jews who have the authority to cast out of the synagogue any persons who acknowledge Jesus as Christ. They know that their son gained his sight miraculously and that Jesus healed him. Their fear as members of the synagogue is tragically outweighed by their joy as parents. They fear expulsion to such an extent that they essentially disavow their son.[8] They abandon him to his interrogators. They know he faces certain expulsion and they refuse to be party to such a fate.

Here we see a certain dynamic. Fear is very powerful as a deterrent to being an effective witness. It can be an insurmountable barrier to overcome in identifying with Jesus. There is another dualism in the Fourth Gospel in the form of two "clubs" or communities.[9] Membership in the synagogue is tantamount to being numbered with the covenant people.[10]

---

7. Writers categorize the Johannine "asides" or narrative commentaries to which only the reader is privy and not the characters in the story. The most recent and helpful is Thatcher ("New Look at Asides," 428–39), who seeks to make the categorization more objective compared to Tenney who made the first systematic study ("Footnotes," 350–64) and O'Rourke ("Asides," 210–19). O'Rourke identifies 9:22–23 as an aside, whereas Thatcher accepts only 9:22; and Tenney completely disregards 9:22–23. Thatcher (p. 430) provides a working definition: "An aside is a direct statement that *tells* the reader something. Asides are never observable events, but are interpretive commentary on observable events, commentary that reveals information 'below the surface' of the action." The italics is the author's. I concur with O'Rourke that 9:22–23 is an aside.

8. Horbury, when reviewing the early evidence for the Jamnian benediction (Birkat Haminim) concludes that the benediction only "reinforced an earlier, more drastic exclusion of Christians," but did not in itself contain language to that effect ("Benediction of the *Minim*," 52). Horbury notes that exclusion meant losing membership rights, although Christians were still welcomed as potential proselytes (p. 53). The *minim* ("heretics") were not restricted to Christians, but included sinners and apostates from Israel and the Gentiles. But exactly what an expulsion entailed remains uncertain. As Hare points out, the data is "too scanty to provide a clear picture" (*Theme of Jewish Persecution*, 48). Hare goes on to write: "Nowhere else in the New Testament [outside of John], Apostolic Fathers, or non-Christian Jewish literature do we find evidence that the confession of Jesus as the Christ was defined as a crime punishable by formal exclusion from the synagogues of Jewry" (p. 55).

9. Köstenberger prefers "contrasts" rather than "dualism" to avoid mistaken association with Greek and Qumran dualism (*Theology of John's Gospel*, 277–78, n. 7). I use "club" in quotation marks to avoid the frequent connotation of an informal association with common interests often of a social nature.

10. For taking "synagogue" to connote a community of Jews with religious and sociopolitical overtones, see Horsley, "Synagogues in Galilee," 46–69; Kee, "Defining the

To be outside of the synagogue is to be outside of the covenant and, thereby, excluded from covenant blessings. The parents refuse to forsake membership in the covenant, which means more to them than does their bond with their son. They made their choice, and they will not budge. But in fearing exclusion from the Judaic community, they have excluded themselves from the community of Jesus.[11] Symbolically, the healed man's parents prefer darkness to the light.[12]

DANCING WITH THE STAR

The healed man, in contrast to his parents, shows no fear so far. But the Jews are not done with him yet. With his parents distancing themselves from him, we wonder whether he will remain steadfast. He has no ally from among his acquaintances and family, and Jesus is absent. He has taken a step forward in his dance of faith in identifying Jesus as a prophet publicly. His parents, on the other hand, have taken a step backward, distancing themselves from Jesus. They refuse to dance with him in refusing to confess him.

Significantly, the parents use the expression "we know" three times in their brief reply. In the first incidence, they affirm: "We know that this man is our son and that he was born blind" (9:20). But they quickly follow with two negative statements: "But how can he now see we do not know; nor do we know who opened his eyes" (9:21). Both Brown and Kysar note a correlation between the terms "know" and "believe" in the Fourth Gospel.[13] In the present situation, the parents refuse to "confess Christ"

First-Century," 7–26; and Scott, *Jewish Backgrounds*, 139–44, 155. For an emphasis on a communal organization, place of meeting, and institution of Judaism, see Sanders, *Judaism*, 197–202; Cohen who sees it as a "private association" in the western diaspora (*From the Maccabees*, 106–11); Sigal, *Judaism*, 96–98; and Gutmann, who cites "the Synagogue of Israel" as referring to "the entire Jewish community" (*Synagogue*, 18–26).

11. For a fuller discussion of the hypothesized emerging Johannine community, see Moloney "Excursus," 69–86. For regarding the threat of expulsion as a part of an intra-Jewish tension between members sharing a common familial background, see Klink, "Expulsion from the Synagogue?" 99–118. Klink's proposal counters the common opinion that 9:22 is an allusion to the Council of Jamnia and the Birkat Haminim, an official decree supposedly directed against Christians. This decree is at the heart of the two-level reading of the Fourth Gospel first put forth by Martyn, *History and Theology*, 35–98.

12. Brodie (*Gospel according to John*, 349) heads in the right direction with his assessment of the parents being "somewhat alien to the light." But he does not go far enough—the parents reject the light.

13. Brown, *Gospel According to John*, 512–14; and Kysar, *Maverick Gospel*, 90–95.

(9:22) publicly and, in that sense, refuse to know or acknowledge Jesus. They fail to believe in him by refusing to enter into a personal relationship with him and by rejecting any statements about him, including their own son's testimony about Jesus.

But their son, who is making progress in his perception of Jesus, grows in his knowing Jesus. At this point he associates Jesus' ability to grant him sight with the office of prophet. The Jews' policy of expulsion is evidently public knowledge. Because the man is part of the community associated with the synagogue, we assume that he is aware of this policy.[14] He must realize that the Jews have targeted Jesus—confessing him as Christ incurs automatic expulsion. The healed man is not quite prepared to make that confession, but he is approaching that danger zone.

He advances at least as far along in his understanding of Jesus as those Pharisees who are open to Jesus (9:16).[15] But the man has actually moved further in recognizing Jesus as a prophet, which none of the Pharisees is prepared to do. Whereas the Pharisees struggle with the tension between Jesus' alleged Sabbath violation and his performing miracles, the man has no such qualms. He apparently sees no paradox. Or, if he does, he does not let it bother him. For him the matter of Jesus' ability to heal supersedes any concern over Judaic legislation. Nor is he intimidated by the threat of expulsion that forces his parents to a cowered position of nonrecognition of Jesus.

Whereas Kysar limits his discussion to the Greek word *ginōskō* ("to know"), Brown also includes *oida* ("to know") in which there is some overlap semantically. However, both writers agree that "to know" stems from a relationship. Kysar goes on to distinguish three nuances: (1) personal allegiance to Jesus; (2) belief in Jesus' words; and (3) faith in statements about Jesus.

14. The fact that the Jews will cast the man out of the synagogue (9:34) implies that he is a member of the synagogue. Otherwise the act is meaningless.

15. The actual term is "signs." A more recent work on signs as central for recognition scenes of Jesus' identity is that of Culpepper ("Cognition in John," 251–60) which is based on Larsen's *Recognizing the Stranger*. Eventually the open Pharisees renege on their recognition of Jesus and move to non-recognition. They take a step forward but then take a step back. In doing so, they merge with their more resistant peers. I believe the fear that prevented the parents from moving forward is the same fear that forced the open Pharisees back in the fold—the fear of being expelled.

THE NEXT MOVE

As we continue our reading of this dance sequence, we search our hearts for any reticence toward recognizing Jesus publicly. There is an incongruity in identifying with the man. Whereas, up to this point, he has never recognized Jesus as Lord, or, in Johannine parlance, as the one sent from the Father above, we readers already have—and so call ourselves Christians. Yet, the challenge the healed man faces parallels the one we face. The world neither recognizes Jesus as personal Savior nor does it possess a full understanding of Jesus' identity, similar to the Pharisees' distorted perception of Jesus. Two recent publications in America document young people's perception of Jesus and Christians.[16] Both books are the result of surveys conducted among young people outside Christianity; and the common finding is that they have an inadequate view of Jesus and a negative opinion of Christians. And what of the perceptions of people living elsewhere in the world? In Asia, for example, there are competing religious beliefs and varying degrees of regard for Christianity, with significant hostility in some regions.[17] Our next move is to understand the perception of Jesus of those who are in our "world," the sphere where we live and serve. Without compromising our perception of Jesus, we can engage them in dialogue much like the healed man did with his interrogators.

Singapore, the country of my current residence, is an amalgam of people groups from Southeast Asia. Singapore is a city-state with a population just over five million. The majority are ethnic Chinese; although Malaysians and Indians comprise a sizeable portion of the population. The government's strategy for making this city-state competitive in the global market involves employing a large migrant workforce. Thus migrant workers, with dependents, comprise approximately a third

---

16. Kinnaman and Lyons, *Unchristian*; and Kimball, *They Like Jesus But Not the Church*. All three authors focus on young people between sixteen and twenty-nine years of age.

17. "Operation World: Asian Countries" divides Asia into eight regions: the Arab world (including North Africa), the Indo-Iranian bloc, the South Asian bloc (including India but excluding the country's northeast), the Turkic bloc (from southeast Europe to northeast Siberia, with most of Central Asia), the East Asian bloc (mainland China, Japan, and the Koreas), the Tibeto-Burman bloc (the Himalayas, Central Asia, northeast India, Myanmar, and parts of China), the Southeast Asian bloc (Indo-China, Thailand, and South China), and the Malay peoples (from Madagascar to Polynesia, including the Philippines, Indonesia, Brunei, and Malaysia).

of Singapore's total population. Because I am a US citizen, I am classified as a migrant worker. There are two categories of migrant workers: unskilled *foreign workers* and highly skilled *foreign talent*.[18] Workers of the first category predominantly come from China, Malaysia, Indonesia, Philippines, Sri Lanka, Myanmar, and India. The talent for the second category represents mainly the United States, Britain, France, Australia, Japan, and South Korea. The ethnic and cultural diversity presents both an opportunity and a challenge to dialogue with these people groups. Indeed, for Jesus' sake, we all must explore this opportunity and connect with those people in our spheres, whether or not they originate from our particular ethnic group.

Indonesian domestic workers (IDWs) working in Singapore represent one such opportunity for Christians. Concerned Christians spearhead fellowship-based ministries to these domestic workers (DWs) who are exclusively female. Although the ultimate goal is to bring them to Christ so that they can become "agents of change" to their own communities back home, many of them struggle with complex personal issues. They often go overseas for work, to Singapore for example, in order to run away from problems in Indonesia. And because they may have left marital or family problems behind, they are not mentally or psychologically prepared to work productively in a foreign culture—a place where they typically have little to no command of the local language. Because they represent unskilled, temporary labor they have little social status. If their employer is abusive or takes advantage of them, they have some legal recourse. But they must be willing to come forward and know how to contact available advocates. The agencies that facilitate their finding employment often deduct the first seven to nine months of their earnings as payment for placement.

Some years ago, a leading local newspaper estimated that 60 percent of the total Indonesian population in Singapore was DWs. So the challenge to minister to them is great. With perhaps fifty churches involved in IDW ministry, Christians are just scratching the surface. Presently the contact potential to IDWs is mainly limited to those serving in church members' households. But at least for this subgroup of IDWs, they have the opportunity to experience firsthand the Christian witness of their employers. Success depends on the nature of the witness.

18. See Yeoh "Singapore," lines 109–12.

A winsome witness invites a closer examination of Christ; by contrast a disillusioned witness repels.

A few churches offer education to help DWs acquire marketable skills so that they may find other kinds of work back home. One church ministers to DWs living in a shelter because of problems with their employers. There are seminars for employers, when the need arises, to enable them to understand the cultural differences in the hopes of reducing issues and tension. The underlying intent is to engage these migrant workers in dialogue, to enable them to perceive that Jesus is relevant.

There are multiple ways to bring a person closer to Jesus. But any approach requires striving to understand those in our "world," loving them unconditionally, and being innovative, if need be, in identifying potentially effective avenues to draw them step-by-step to Jesus. There are risks. For example, they may not reciprocate our overtures of kindness. We may not succeed; but we have to try.

The nature of our witness provides a clear indication of our faith movement, either moving closer to Jesus or further away. Like the healed blind man we can take a step forward when we stand true to our convictions about Jesus, even if our understanding of him is limited. Our forward movement confronts the world and compels people to review their assessment of Jesus. But any backpedalling on our part, when we succumb to the world's pressure to compromise, only reinforces people's tendency to regard Jesus as irrelevant.

9

The Facts and Nothing But

> Then they summoned a second time the man who was blind and said to him, "Give glory to God. We know that the man is a sinner." So he answered, "That he is a sinner I do not know. One thing I do know is that although I was blind I now see." Then they said to him, "What did he do to you? How did he open your eyes?" He answered them, "I told you already and you didn't listen. Why do you wish to hear my account again? You don't really want to become his disciples, do you?" And they reviled him and said, "You are that man's disciple; but we are Moses' disciples. We know that God spoke to Moses; but we do not know from whence this man has come."
>
> —John 9:24–29

When I was a child, I followed Jack Webb's Los Angeles police detective character, Sergeant Joe Friday, on the television series *Dragnet*. Sgt. Friday was a no-nonsense cop who is best known for his one-liner: "Just the facts Ma'am, nothing but the facts" (Friday's actual phrase varied slightly). We should all be like that. In the pursuit of truth, we should demand the facts and nothing but the facts. In tracing the fast-paced exchange between the healed blind man and his interlocutors, one thing differentiates the two parties—the man is interested in the facts and nothing else; but the Jews cling blindly to their presuppositions in spite of the facts laid out clearly before them.

THE MOMENT OF TRUTH

Recently I caught an episode of the television reality show *The Moment of Truth* in which contestants win money by truthfully answering questions that become progressively, more personally revealing. A young woman was in the hot seat of this particular airing. She was quizzed by the host while a short distance away sat her family and boyfriend, people who knew her best and who could verify the truthfulness of her replies. For $10,000 she was asked whether she was ever dissatisfied with her boyfriend's appearance. After a moment of struggle, in which she furtively stole glances at her boyfriend, she said yes. The grimace on the young man's face told me that perhaps this piece of information was news to him. When the contestant won the price money, the game show host offered her a chance at $25,000. At the urging of her mother, she opted to proceed. The next round of questions was even more personally intimate and uncomfortable. All of this was presented before both live and television audiences. In this round, the host asked, "Have you ever been unfaithful to your boyfriend?" After a moment of hesitation, during which she again looked at her boyfriend, she answered in the affirmative. I don't know who was more uncomfortable—the contestant or her boyfriend. It is amazing what people willingly endure for money.

The healed man in our narrative does not seek money or fame. Only one thing interests him—the truth about Jesus, apparently at any personal cost.[1] The Jews, on the other hand, also have one interest—safeguarding their traditions, which condemn Jesus as a sinner. He violated the Sabbath regulations and is thus a lawbreaker.[2] The central issue of this

---

1. Although the word for *truth* or its other forms is not in the current passage, concepts related to this word group is a major motif of the Fourth Gospel and is present in this narrative. See Hawkin, who cites de la Potterie's contention that John's truth mirrors apocalyptic and sapiential literature of the late biblical and post-biblical period featuring a moral "*revealed truth*" ("Johannine Concept of Truth," 3–13); Lindsay, who sees Jesus portrayed "as the complete embodiment of God's truth" ("What Is Truth?" 135, 137); Köstenberger, who discerns "a *personal, relational* concept that has its roots and origin in none other than God himself" (*Theology of John's Gospel*, 437–38); Kuyper who writes of "a relationship in life" ("Grace and Truth," 9); and Lincoln, who speaks of truth as judgment and verdict in a trial where the central issue is Jesus' identity (*Truth on Trial*, 222–31). I agree with Lincoln about the central issue, but I dispute his setting of a trial scene, except for Jesus' appearance before Pilate.

2. Sanders characterizes ancient Judaism as "orthopraxy," the emphasis on proper conduct in everyday life (*Judaism*, 190–95). Willful transgression of the Sabbath automatically incurs the death penalty (Num 15:30–36). The Sabbath was a day to abstain

conflict revolves around Jesus' identity. If Jesus is a mere man, then he can be charged with guilt, depending on the definition of work prohibited on the Sabbath.[3] Already in round one of Jesus' juridical controversy with the Jews, they persecute him for violating the Sabbath in healing the lame man (5:16). At that time Jesus answered: "My Father is working until now, also I am working" (5:17). They correctly understood him to be claiming equality with God as his Father (5:18). An implicit tandem exists between the Father and Jesus as the Son. Both work in unison within an intimacy that "what God does Jesus also does."[4] As God, Jesus can work on the Sabbath without violating Sabbath restrictions.

The truth portrays Jesus working together with the Father as the Father's agent in the world. The intentionality of working on the Sabbath highlights this relationship and Jesus' representation of the Father because the Sabbath serves as the vehicle by which Jesus showcases the Father's prerogatives. No man can presume on the Father's prerogatives. It would be blasphemous to do so. But if someone assumes those prerogatives without committing blasphemy, he must be more than a man.

This truth confronts both the healed blind man and the Jews. Their response drives the unfolding drama.

"from any form of work except what was necessary to preserve life" (Scott, *Jewish Backgrounds*, 253). Obviously, blindness is not life-threatening and so, according to the Jews, Jesus was not saving a life but doing prohibited work.

3. According to *m. Shab* 7.2., prohibited work includes "sowing, ploughing, reaping, grinding, kneading, baking, hunting a gazelle, writing two letters, erasing in order to write two letters, putting out a fire, lighting a fire." Attention to minutiae is legendary. For example, a total of four paragraphs were devoted to restrictions on writing two letters of the alphabet (*m. Shab* 12.3–6). The Pharisees passed on a growing body of oral tradition (*halakoth*) in the Second Temple period to succeeding generations, much of it preserved in the *Midrash halakah*, rabbinical commentaries. Collections of this tradition eventually ended up in the Mishnah. See Danby, *Mishnah*, xvii–xxiii. According to *m. Abot* 1.1., however, Moses received both the written and oral law. Thus, for the Pharisees the oral law equals the written law in authority. But the Sadducees recognized only the written law. Hence, Jesus' Sabbath conflict was with the Pharisaic party.

4. Barrett, *Gospel according to St. John*, 213. Carson (*Gospel according to John*, 247–49) makes the same point but provides a fuller discussion of the ancient writers' belief that God continued working on the Sabbath without violating the Sabbath. Carson carefully observes that Jesus is not claiming to be "*another* God," given his subordination to the Father (p. 250).

AN ACT OF DESPERATION

The healed blind man's parents provide no answer to the Jews' query "How can he now see?" (9:19). The answer is critical to Jesus' identity. To ascribe a sign to Jesus is tantamount to confessing Jesus as the Christ (9:22). Out of fear, the parents defer the answer to their son. Fading from the spotlight and, as a result, taking a step backward from full faith in Jesus, the parents disappear not to be heard from again. Their journey over, they recede into the darkness (1:5, 9–11). Their failure to testify for Jesus equates to a testimony against Jesus.

As the Jews return to the healed man a second time (9:24), they pursue an answer to their question (9:19). But they had already asked that question (9:15a) and received an answer (9:15b). And based on the man's answer, they followed up with "What do you have to say about him since he opened your eyes?" (9:17a). He responded with "He is a prophet" (9:17b). Obviously, then, the Jews are not looking for a repeat answer, for there would be no forward progress in their quest to condemn Jesus. Rather, they hope that the man will change his answer, and so clinch their case against Jesus.

They provide him with a lead, an aggressive cue in how he should respond when they state (9:24b): "Give glory to God. We know that the man is a sinner." Their presumptive opinion leaves no room for uncertainty. To differ is to go against the established position of religious authority, risking their ire. They give the man a chance to follow in his parents' footsteps on the path marked by intimidation and to recede into the darkness.

They do not ask but demand acquiescence with "Give glory to God."[5] To disagree with their assessment that Jesus is a sinner denies God the glory. This is an unveiled threat—denying God glory is to sin. To regard Jesus as anything but a sinner is to become a sinner. And sinners have no place in the synagogue community.

In stating "we know that the man is a sinner," the Jews have already passed judgment. They "know" in the sense of an "unassailable assumption."[6] The earlier division within their ranks (9:16) has now closed into a unified front of singular condemnation and coercion. No

---

5. Lincoln identifies the expression as "putting the witness under solemn oath" (*Gospel according to Saint John*, 285). The Jews demand that the man tell the truth. But their truth is that Jesus is a sinner. Barrett renders the expression as "admit the truth" (*Gospel according to St. John*, 300).

6. Ridderbos, *Gospel according to John*, 344, n. 283.

one it seems can withstand such pressure. The healed man's isolation both actual and threatened exacerbates the tension. His parents have already abandoned him and his neighbors offer no assistance. He stands alone before the company of Jews unified against Jesus. The threat of expulsion is palpable. Riveted on this drama, we the readers recognize the man's representative role—his situation and performance may mirror ours when we are confronted with the truth about Jesus. Although we do not know how we will react until tested, we can at least ponder the truth about Jesus and consider its importance.

The Jews' resorting to coercion unveils a desperate strategy to manipulate the man's answer into becoming favorable to their case.[7] There is no subtlety here. It is a power move in prodding him to change his opinion about Jesus from prophet (9:17) to sinner. This is nothing other than verbal arm-twisting.

POLITICALLY INCORRECT[8]

As the exchange between witness and interrogator moves quickly with each party giving brief but pointed responses, the tension escalates. The man proves politically inapt. He will not cooperate; and he will not back down. He states his convictions with simplicity and integrity. He offers no niceties and shows no diplomacy. If he offends his interrogators, so be it. He is, to use an American saying, a straight-shooter. Only the truth matters.

He answers (9:25): "That he is a sinner I do not know. One thing I do know is that although I was blind I now see."[9] The man reflects on his empirical data and draws some tentative conclusions.[10] He stands in

---

7. This brute force strategy worked on those Pharisees who earlier hesitated in calling Jesus a sinner (9:16). See Carson, *Gospel according to John*, 372–73. Morris notes the irony of the Jews' tact that brings about the unintended clarification for the man on his own position and understanding of Jesus (*Gospel according to John*, 436).

8. Whitters uses the same expression to describe the healed man ("Discipleship in John," 426).

9. Asiedu-Peprah, based on Burchard's article, "*Ei* nach einem Ausdruck," 73–82, favors rendering *whether* as *that* in "that he is a sinner I do not know" (*Johannine Sabbath Conflicts*, 138, n. 91). The particle normally introducing an *if* clause in a conditional statement is usually translated "if" or "whether," thereby allowing for the possibility of something—in the present case, of the possibility that Jesus is a sinner. However, the healed man is not giving ground to the Jews on their assessment of Jesus. He holds to his convictions based on his experience with Jesus. The man declines their view.

10. De la Potterie contrasts two verbs translated "to know" in the Fourth Gospel

sharp contrast to his interrogators who ignore the data because of their presuppositions. He is objective; they are subjective. They refuse to believe in Jesus. Not only is Jesus a mere man in their estimation, he is a sinner. They progress further backward in their faith journey. Their hardening resolve prods them to reject the evidence. They defy logic in their defiance of Jesus. The man, however, assesses the evidence logically and dispassionately. He remains unperturbed by their intimidation tactics. He says in effect, "I don't accept your evaluation of Jesus." The man may not fully understand Jesus' identity, but he holds on to the only thing he can be sure about—his personal experience. That he will not deny. He cannot deny the reality of his new sight. This leads to a growing insight that Jesus is no mere man—he is at least a prophet and certainly is no sinner.

THE RIGHT QUESTIONS

The healed man moves forward in his faith journey by refusing to cower before his detractors. His courage rests on the certainty that he, a man born blind, now sees. Alone without an ally, he remains firm in his conviction in the crucible of a fiery ordeal. Such steadfast valor prompts a number of questions. What convictions are nonnegotiable, for which I am willing to sacrifice all to retain? If others back away or refuse to confirm me, am I willing to stand alone in remaining true to my convictions? If I have not found something of great value to live by and stand up for, am I really living?

IT AIN'T OVER 'TIL IT'S OVER

When the then Baltimore Bullets team won their only National Basketball Association (NBA) companionship in 1978, the refrain, "It ain't over 'til the fat lady sings," characterized their persevering spirit.[11] The colloquialism captures a truth: in life, the final outcome is not determined until the process is over. This truth surfaces in the healed man's heated exchange with his interrogators. When it seems that an

---

("*oîda et ginōskō*," 713–17). The verb the man uses twice in 9:25 indicates a personal conviction that is part intuition and part unshakable faith. He may not have all the facts at his disposal yet, but he knows undeniably that he now sees. And that truth invalidates the Jews' claim about Jesus. The man will not be persuaded to side with the Jews. His conviction does not permit him to do so.

11. Yogi Berra, former New York Yankee hall of fame catcher, and known for his malapropisms, famously said in a similar vein, "It ain't over 'til it's over."

impasse has been reached, with neither antagonist yielding to the other, another sparring session begins.

The Jews again ask the man (9:26): "What did he do to you? How did he open your eyes?" They are not asking for new information. They already know his answer from before (9:15).[12] They may be trying to trap him with an inconsistency in his testimony.[13] More likely, their objective is to pressure him into changing his story—just a moment before they demand (9:24) "Give glory to God. We know that the man is a sinner." They employ an oath formula ("give glory to God") that usually precedes a call to confession or repentance.[14] The Jews demand that the healed man confess and repent for failing to acknowledge Jesus as a sinner.

But the man refuses to buckle. Instead, he goes on the offensive (9:27): "I told you already and you didn't listen. Why do you wish to hear my account again? You don't really want to become his disciples, do you?" He makes three counteraccusations. First, he accuses them of not listening. He has already made it clear what happened. The Jews' persistent and repetitious questioning indicts them for failing to accept the healed blind man's testimony. Second, he cross-examines the Jews with an accusatory *why* question that expresses suspicion of an ulterior motive. Third, his

---

12. They had also asked his parents the same question (9:19), but the parents pleaded ignorance (9:21).

13. Brown, *Gospel According to John*, 377; Hendricksen, *Commentary on the Gospel of John*, 2. 89; Morris, *Gospel according to John*, 437; and Ridderbos, *Gospel according to John*, 344–45. Staley, however, explains that because the man earlier gave only partial answers, by withholding critical information, his inquisitors press him to be more forthcoming ("Stumbling in the Dark," 68). But I believe Staley is overly harsh in labelling the man a "liar." It presupposes that the man is fully cognizant of what sensitive information is and what it is not. If, however, he grows steadily in understanding, he may not be aware of the implications of his answers in the earlier stages of the exchange. Additionally, his fuller account to his neighbors (9:11) no doubt were passed on by them to the Pharisees in his presence before the Pharisees queried him. The fact that his neighbors took him to the Pharisees (9:13) suggests that they did so.

14. Moloney, *Signs and Shadows*, 126. Moloney cites the following examples (also Brown, *Gospel According to John*, 374). The oath formula calls for confession in Josh 7:19 ("Joshua said to Achan, 'Give glory to the Lord the God of Israel today, and confess; and tell me what you have done. Do not hide it from me.'"), and 1 Esd 9:8 ("and now give confession, glory to the Lord the God of our fathers"), and repentance in Jer 13:15–16 ("Listen and give heed, do not be haughty, for the Lord has spoken. Give glory to the Lord your God, before He brings darkness and before your feet stumble on the dusky mountains, and while you are hoping for light He makes it into deep darkness, and turns it into gloom."). *m. Sanh* 6:2 cites Josh 7:19.

second question, phrased in anticipation of a negative response,[15] is really an accusation: "You really don't want to be his disciples because you reject him." The tables are turned; the momentum has shifted. The one interrogated becomes the interrogator.[16]

The Jews are caught in the web of their own making. They cannot refute the man. They can only revile him and say dismissively (9:28), "You are that man's disciple; but we are Moses' disciples."[17] The contrast between the two antagonists sharpens as the man moves steadily toward greater clarity and the Jews recede further into their self-delusion. He stands firm on what he knows from personal experience; they stubbornly cling to a knowledge based on a false premise. His logic and argument are forceful and irrefutable; they must resort to insult and verbal abuse.

But the Jews have spoken truthfully. The man is becoming Jesus' disciple.[18] They, on the other hand, condemn themselves by identifying with a Judaism that cannot accept that one greater than Moses is here.

The healed man has caught on to his interrogators' ploy.[19] He displays remarkable perception, a growing insight that begins to match his newfound physical sight. He perceives their lack of interest in what really happened. Since they cannot cover up what happened—the man's parents confirm the healing by acknowledging their son's congenital

---

15. Of the two possible negative particles in Greek, the man chooses the one that expresses the expectation of a negative answer to his question. His interrogators no doubt catch the point and feel the sharpness of the accusatory question as indicated by their verbal abuse (9:28).

16. This turning of the tables recalls Jesus' similar tact in 5:37-47 (Moloney, *Signs and Shadows*, 23-27). The tact confirms the man's role as Jesus' advocate and witness in the juridical process.

17. The verb "to revile" is contrasted with "to bless" in 1 Cor 4:12, and the noun form is likewise contrasted in 2 Pet 3:9. Those who revile are grouped with fornicators, covetous persons, and idolaters in 1 Cor 5:11 (another list is found in 1 Cor 6:10). Jesus resisted responding in kind when he was reviled (1 Pet 2:23). It is what the adversary would do if an unwary female believer slipped (1 Tim 5:14). And it is what Paul is accused of doing in insulting the high priest (Acts 23:4). In the NT, the term, as a verb or noun, describes a condemnable activity or trait that ought not to characterize the believer. All the variant readings from the Greek manuscripts concerning the conjunction at beginning of the verse consistently feature the verb "to revile." So it really does not matter which variant reading is favored because 9:28 depicts the Jews' reaction to the man in all variations.

18. Talbert notes that from the man's retort ("Do you too want to become his disciples?" 9:27), the expression "you too" is an implicit confession that Jesus is his master and he is Jesus' disciple (*Reading John*, 160).

19. Carson, *Gospel according to John*, 373.

condition—they condemn Jesus for Sabbath violation. They attempt to coerce the healed man into joining their accusation. He, in contrast to his parents, desiring only the undeniable truth, boldly and with forthrightness refuses to acquiesce.[20]

The dispute focuses on Jesus' identity. Unable to deny the healing, the accusers zero in on the healer's status—sinner, prophet, or man of God. Given the same set of evidence, one party concludes that Jesus is a sinner and the other party concludes the opposite. The differing presuppositions explain the irreconcilable conclusions. Steeped in the traditions of Moses, the Jews cannot accept the Sabbath declaration: "My Father is working until now also I am working" (5:17).

Jesus continues working on another Sabbath (9:14) and in doing so makes yet another declaration. He refuses to stop working because his Father continues to work. The Jews understand his claim. The dispute between Jesus and them remains unresolved. Jesus' absence in the current round of the juridical controversy causes the Jews to turn with a vengeance upon the healed blind man, the surrogate disputant in Jesus' stead. Their sole aim is to end the dispute by getting him to agree with their assessment of Jesus. Achieving that objective, they can claim victory. But as Jesus refused to deny himself in the first round (5:19–47), so the healed man refuses to deny Jesus in the current round. The controversy, therefore, continues.

MORE QUESTIONS

The issue emerging from the controversy between the Jews and the healed blind man concerns Jesus' identity, the same issue that dominated the earlier round.

Jesus' identity continues to be an issue today. I consider Oprah Winfrey's view of Jesus to be important because of her powerful influence with a daily television viewership that, at its height, reached twenty million.[21] Oprah publicly acknowledges her belief that Jesus is but one of many ways to God, and that he did not come to die for our sins.[22] Instead,

---

20. There is general consensus about the man's boldness in the face of such intense pressure. See, for example, Ridderbos, *Gospel according to John*, 345; Hendricksen, *Commentary*, 2. 88–89; and Lincoln, *Gospel according to Saint John*, 285.

21. "Oprah Winfrey Show: United States Viewership," line 1.

22. "Oprah Winfrey: Jesus Did Not Come To Die On The Cross," video clip.

Jesus came to show us how to attain "Christ consciousness." On January 1, 2008, Oprah launched a year long course entitled "A Course in Miracles" led by Marianne Williamson, a recognized New Age proponent, through the radio program "Oprah and Friends."[23] The teachings of this course reflect Oprah's beliefs. There are 365 lessons, one for each day of the year. The point of lesson 61, for example, is that each of us is to repeat to ourselves: "I am the light of the world."[24] God brings salvation through us. Lesson 271 teaches that God created Christ as his Son.[25] Warren Smith, a former student of this course, cites other teachings related to Jesus that are unscriptural.[26]

The Jews of Jesus' day were very influential and swayed many, including the healed man's parents, to deny Jesus' identity. But the man resisted the pressure and stood firm on the truth about Jesus. As he did so, his understanding and appreciation of Jesus grew. Circumstances do not seem to have changed much today, as those in power and influence have swayed millions to adopt a false understanding of Jesus' identity and their need for a Savior. The questions of the moment emerge. What is your understanding of Jesus? Is your position swayed by others, or are you standing firm and steady? What is the basis for your view on Jesus? Is it based on the absolute and uncompromising truth of the Scriptures, or is it relative truth in which each person has the prerogative to believe whatever he or she deems appropriate for himself or herself? Are you a seeker of truth? And what is truth? Does the truth draw you into the light that is Jesus, or does it propel you deeper into the recesses of darkness?

I am not blaming Oprah as the one person who is solely responsible for America's spiritual dilemma. To do so is to give her too much credit. Although she is influential, surveys reveal that many young people hold similar views about Jesus. I cite a 2009 survey of twelve hundred American Millennials born between 1980 and 1991.[27] In response to the statement "when he lived on earth, Jesus Christ was human and com-

---

23. "Miracle Times: It's Your Window to the Real World," lines 1–4.
24. "Course in Miracles: Lesson 61," lines 18–20, 32.
25. "Course in Miracles: Lesson 271.", line 1.
26. Warren Smith, "'Oprah and Friends' to Teach Course on New Age Christ," lines 21–29. The teachings include the following: there is no sin, the death of Christ is meaningless, trusting in the cross is an error, and the name Jesus Christ is a symbol that replaces the names of other gods.
27. Phillips, "LifeWay Research," lines 1–47.

mitted sins like other people," half of all respondents agreed strongly or somewhat strongly. To another statement, "believing in Jesus Christ is the only way to get to heaven," exactly half agreed and half disagreed.

A QUESTION OF ORIGINS

The Jews continue their smug assessment of Jesus (9:29): "We know that God spoke to Moses; but we do not know from whence this man has come." They challenge Jesus' professed origin that he comes from above (8:23). The Jews boast of knowing that God spoke to Moses, but they do not know about Jesus' claims. The verb "to know" connotes conviction or belief.[28] They believe in Moses but not in Jesus.

However, their avowal of Moses is tragic irony. They confess that God spoke to Moses. But they fail to understand that Moses spoke of Jesus. Earlier in the juridical controversy, Jesus declared (5:45–46): "Do not think that I accuse you before the Father. The one who accuses you is Moses, in whom you hope. For if you believe Moses, you would believe me, for he wrote concerning me." In actuality, the Jews know neither Moses nor Jesus. They have misappropriated the Scriptures in developing a worldview that excludes Jesus and God.

A motif emerges in this pericope. To know someone is to believe or to accept that person. Nicodemus said to Jesus: "Rabbi, we know that you have come from God as a teacher" (3:2a). He is convinced that Jesus comes from God because the signs substantiate that God is with him (3:2b). After many disciples abandoned Jesus because of his hard sayings, Peter confesses, "We have believed and know that you are the Holy One of God" (6:69).[29]

The significance of knowing and believing in Jesus becomes clear when we note Marianne M. Thompson's observation: "According to the Gospel, their [characters in the Gospel] only access to God is through Jesus . . . who speaks so that God is heard, and in whom they see the Father. God is known primarily through the agency of Jesus."[30] Jesus af-

---

28. See footnote 10 previously in this chapter.

29. The verb "to know" that Peter uses here connotes knowledge gained through a progressive process of learning or discovery. Over a period of becoming better acquainted with Jesus through his teachings and works, Peter has gained a familiarity that enables him to stay with Jesus when others leave Jesus. This knowledge undergirds Peter's faith in Jesus. See de la Potterie, "*oîda et ginōskō*," 725.

30. Thompson, "God's Voice," 188.

firms this relational truth before Philip (14:7, 9b): "If you [have come to] know me, you will [come to] know my Father also. And from now on you know him and see him. The one who has seen me has seen the Father." Knowing and accepting Jesus, then, implies knowing and accepting God who sent Jesus. Conversely, rejecting Jesus rejects God.

But, at least, we give the Jews credit for recognizing that Jesus' origin is critical to his identity when they declare: "We do not know from whence this man has come."[31] Jesus' origin distinguishes him from anyone else including Abraham and Moses, both revered by Jews (5:45–46; 6:31–32; 7:19, 22–23; 8:33, 39; 52–53, 56–58; 9:28–29); for only Jesus descended first before ascending back to the realm above (3:13; 6:62). Thus, Jesus proclaims (8:23): "You are from below; I am from above. You are of this world; I am not of this world." An important characterization of Jesus, then, is that he serves as "the link between heaven and earth."[32] He explains the Father (1:18). And because Jesus has come from the Father, Jesus alone knows the Father (7:28–29; 8:55; 10:15). Yet, those who believe in Jesus will come to know the Father also (14:7; 17:3, 26).

FINAL QUESTIONS

As the distance between the Jews and the healed man widens in the narrative, with which character do we more closely identify and align? The Jews represent the world, which has a distorted view of Jesus and his origin. The man stands firm and uncompromising in his conviction about Jesus. And his parents represent those who straddle the fence for a while before acquiescing to the pressures of the world. There is no common ground for the world and the healed man. Nor is there common ground for the man and his parents. Do our convictions distinguish us from the world so that there is no common ground? Or will the world *convert* us? Are we willing to stand alone as this man does?

The disciples will fully understand Jesus' teaching when the Holy Spirit teaches and guides them into all the truth (14:26; 16:12–15). Until then, they cannot attain mature faith with Jesus still present.[33] Only upon

---

31. For a fuller discussion on Jesus' origin and its significance for the Fourth Gospel, see Borgen, "God's Agent," 137–48; Meeks, "Man from Heaven," 44–72; and van der Merwe, "Towards a Theological Understanding," 339–59.

32. Koester, *Symbolism in the Fourth Gospel*, 41.

33. Grayston surveys all known occurrences of Paraclete in the extant Greek literature between the fourth-century BCE and third-century CE, the patristic usage to

his departure and the Spirit's advent will they grasp the truth. The sense of a "not yet until a later time" is similarly conveyed in Jesus' statement to Peter: "Where I am going you are not able to follow now, but you will follow later" (13:36). The chronology in the disciples' journey toward deeper faith and understanding is event-driven. Jesus must depart first. Then the Spirit comes and indwells the disciples. At that point they will understand.

We wonder then whether all Johannine believers must proceed through this chronology. Because the presence of Mary, Martha, and Lazarus is not implied in John 13–16 in any way, Jesus' promise of the Spirit may or may not apply to them. The narrative does not designate them explicitly as Jesus' disciples. There is, however, an insightful sequence. After Lazarus's death, Martha greets Jesus (11:21–22): "Lord, if you had been here, my brother would not have died. But even now I know that whatever you should ask of God, God will grant to you." She seems to hope that Jesus can raise her brother from the dead with a prayer, right then and there. But when Jesus replies, "your brother will rise" (11:23), Martha simply affirms: "I know that he will be raised in the resurrection in the last day" (11:24). Her hope is eschatological not immediate, typical of Jewish beliefs at that time.[34] Hence, Martha does not voice a conviction that differs significantly from that of any devout Jew of her time. She has no "illusions" of a miracle and resigns herself to the natural course of

---

the fourth-century CE, and early rabbinic occurrences. He concludes that the term most often means supporter, sponsor, or helper, with no legal or judicial connotations ("Meaning of *Paraklētos*," 67–82). Contra Liddell and Scott, *Greek-English Lexicon*, 1313. Grayston differentiates the Paraclete from the Spirit of Truth as two distinct persons. But Grayston wrote from a source-critical perspective. Typical of that time period, Segovia, for example, takes a redaction-critical approach to the Farewell Discourse in seeing at least two distinct discourses ("John 15:18—16:4a?" 210–30 and "Structure," 471–93). But he later shifts to a literary-rhetorical study in *Farewell*. My approach mirrors more closely that of Segovia's later work. As a result, I see the Paraclete, the Spirit of Truth, and the Holy Spirit as referring to the same person with different but complementary roles.

34. In Second Temple Judaism, belief in an eschatological resurrection was prevalent. See, for example, 2 Macc 7:9 ("in his last breath he said, 'You an avenging angel may remove us from the present life, but the king of the world will raise us who die in behalf of his laws unto eternal life'"); 1 En 51:1–2 ("In those days, Sheol will return all the deposits which she had received and hell will give back all that which it owes. And he shall choose the righteous and the holy ones from among them, for the day when they shall be selected and saved has arrived," translated by Isaac in *Pseudepigrapha*, 1:36–37); *Pss. Sol.* 3:12; 14:1–3; 2 Esd 7:32; *T. Jud.* 25:4; and *T. Benj.* 10:6–9. See also early second-century (100–132 CE) *2 Bar.* 50:2–3.

events. Her disappointment at Jesus' absence while her brother was dying does not mitigate her faith, although inadequate, in Jesus.[35] Immediately following his self-declaration that he is the resurrection and the life, Jesus asks, "Do you believe this?" (11:25-26). It is a probing question that exposes Martha's insufficient understanding when she answers: "Yes, Lord. I believe that you are the Christ, the Son of God who comes into the world" (11:27). She assigns accepted Judaic terminology in ascribing Jesus' identity. Jesus is the Christ and the Son of God, terms that echo Nathaniel's confession (1:49). And like Nathaniel, Martha does not go far enough in her confession.[36]

Even though her brother has died, she intimates that she still believes in his future resurrection because she believes in Jesus. Jesus confirms her inadequate faith when he tells her, "Did I not tell you that if you believe you would see the glory of God?" (11:40). Jesus already intends to raise her brother from the dead (11:11). He does not say to her, "If you believe you would see your brother live again." Rather, she will behold God himself if she has faith.[37]

Kysar provides an important insight into Johannine signs and their ability to invoke faith.[38] For a sign to stimulate growth in one's faith, a certain amount of faith must be already present that predisposes a person to perceive God. Martha's existing faith prepares her to perceive God in Jesus raising her brother from the dead. The right perception increases resident faith toward mature faith. Mature faith does not require signs to believe. The narrative never indicates that Martha progresses in faith with her brother's resurrection. Then it seems that Martha, like the disciples who also witness Lazarus's resurrection, does not attain mature faith at

---

35. Moloney provides a cogent case for regarding Martha's faith as inadequate (*Signs and Shadows*, 160-62). In particular, he highlights her saying "I have believed that you are the Christ" (11:27). The expression "I have believed" is in a form that conveys "*her long-held convictions*" (the italics is the author's, p. 162). So Jesus' self-declaration (11:25-26) does not affect Martha. Her existing faith and understanding do not grow. Contra to Moloney is Schneiders ("Death in the Community," 53) and other authors she cites.

36. See Moloney, *Belief in the Word*, 72-73.

37. Jesus' conditional statement in 11:40 is of a form that denotes an expectation based on a concrete situation at the present time (BDF, §371, 373). But there is a degree of tentativeness assigned to Martha's faith as a so-called third class conditional (Porter, *Idioms of the Greek*, 262). The tentativeness asks, "Will she believe?" For understanding "the glory of God" as connoting God's presence, see Moloney, *Belief in the Word*, 55-57.

38. Kysar, *John: Maverick Gospel*, 84-86.

the present time. She, like all the others, must wait for the Spirit's advent before achieving full faith.

Thus, I would make a preliminary modification to Kysar's diagram by inserting the Holy Spirit into the process of maturing faith in the following manner:[39]

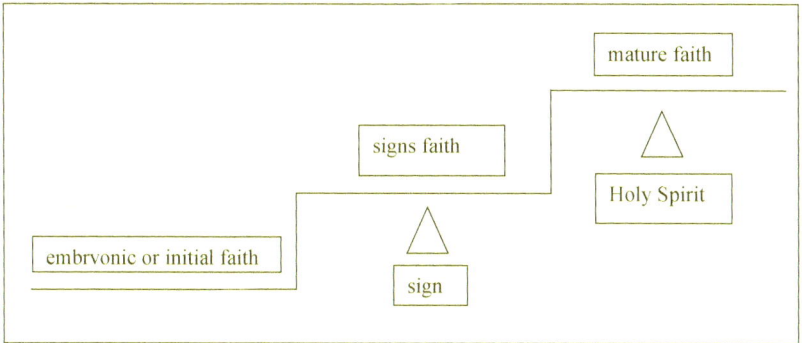

Figure 1. Process of Maturing Faith

Is the now sighted man's path to full faith defined by a different trajectory than that of Martha and the disciples? At the beginning of the blind man's story, Jesus takes the initiative by declaring, "When I am in the world, I am the light of the world" (9:5), anointing the man's eyes (9:6), and instructing him to go wash (9:7a). The man's obedience (9:7b) indicates openness or embryonic faith. Then he experiences the sign of receiving sight.

The sign is indispensable to the man's journey. But so is the Spirit whose advent postdates the Gospel timeline. According to the modified diagram above, no one can attain mature faith until the Spirit comes. A person can make significant progress but will not complete the process within the confines of the story time of the Gospel.

I realize that such a conclusion stands at variance to the estimate of those who view Jesus' mother and the sighted man as representatives of laudable faith.[40] But I believe the man to be a positive example of faith,

---

39. Ibid., 85. A final version of this diagram is presented in the last chapter upon completion of our study of 9:1—10:21.

40. See, for example, McHugh (*Mother of Jesus*, 403) and Moloney (*Belief in the Word*, 84) who lauds Mary's faith. And for a similar assessment of the sighted man's faith, see Lincoln, *John*, 287. Lieu demurs at assessing Mary's faith in 2:1–11 because "faith is the response to Jesus' act, not that which prompts the request" ("Mother of the Son," 64). However, in a parallel scene the royal official also makes a request of Jesus (4:46–49). The

just not of mature faith. More precisely, he is "a model of what it means to grow in genuine faith."[41] The present narrative highlights this process of growth, which we emulate in our pursuit of growth.

---

narrative states that the official believes Jesus' word when Jesus tells him that his son lives (4:50). And upon confirmation of the healing he and his household believe (4:53). Stages of faith development are delineated: the official has initial or, to use Kysar's terminology, embryonic faith when he comes to Jesus requesting healing for his son (4:47), then a faith that believes Jesus' word before the healing (4:50), and a reaffirmation of that faith after the healing (4:53). See also Carson, *John*, 239.

41. Howard, "Significance of Minor Characters," 75.

10

The Lecture

> The man answered them, "Indeed, in this it is amazing that you do not know from whence he came, and yet he opened my eyes. We know that God does not listen to sinners; but if someone is a God-fearer and does his will, God listens to him. From ages past it has not been heard that someone has opened the eyes of a person born blind. If this man was not from God, he would not be able to do anything." They answered him, "You have been born entirely in sins, and do you teach us?" Then they cast him out.
>
> —John 9:30–34

As I read the healed blind man's response to the Jews' avowed ignorance of Jesus' origin, I recall the feeling I had in the pit of my stomach when I faced my father's monologue for some infraction of the household rules. Normally, Dad was more a man of action than a wordsmith. But he could become quite eloquent and expansive in his lectures that often lasted an hour or so. Sometimes, as I endured his verbal rebuke, I found myself preferring corporeal punishment—painful yes, but quick. These lectures were like slow torture, figuratively speaking.

In this pericope, the man utters the longest speech thus far. Only Jesus will deliver a longer one (9:41—10:18). We wonder if the Jews experience that feeling in the pit of their stomachs as the man berates them without interruption. Impatient, they concur on his punishment—excommunication.

THE STARE DOWN

The man expresses amazement or, more likely, mock amazement bordering on scorn: "Indeed, in this it is amazing that you do not know from whence he came, and yet he opened my eyes."[1] The undeniable evidence of his healing clearly supports his contention that Jesus cannot be a sinner but one righteous before God (9:31). Yet, the Jews deduce that Jesus is a sinner. Incredulous at their willful disregard of the evidence and distorted logic, the man discerns something seriously awry.

We can almost picture the man wagging his finger at his interrogators. Scolding them for their irrational opposition to Jesus, he lectures them on the basics of logic and history. Everyone present would have been grounded in the fundamentals. We can almost detect exasperation in his tone. Perhaps he looks upon them sternly, disapprovingly. The gift of sight and growing insight permits him to do so. Dare we say it? It seems that the man stares down his opponents as he steadily gains the upper hand.

THE LESSON

The healed man's logic is impeccable.[2] "We know that God does not listen to sinners; but if someone is a God-fearer and does his will, God listens to him" (9:31). Two kinds of people exist—those to whom God listens and those to whom God does not. Fearing God and doing his will differentiates the two. If someone does not fear God, and so refuses to do his will, he is a sinner. Although the Jews demur on Jesus' origins (9:29), the man bypasses the issue of origins, perhaps a philosophical matter at this point, and keeps to the verifiable and concrete. Jesus healed, proving that God heard and enabled him. Because God clearly listened to Jesus, he must fear God and does God's will. He cannot be a sinner, as the Jews accuse. With undeniable evidence the conclusion is inescapable.

---

1. Robertson translates the first part of the verse as "why, just in this" to convey the man's scorn toward his interrogators (*Grammar*, 1190). The conjunction normally translated "for" assumes an emphatic nuance "indeed" here. See Dana and Mantey, *Manual Grammar*, 243–44. Similarly, BDF, §452.3.2. The man's first spoken conjunction "and" that introduces the following "he opened my eyes" should be rendered "and yet" to convey a contrastive sense. See Zerwick, *Biblical Greek*, §455.b.α.

2. Carson, however, cautions that the man's argument is not foolproof, in that occult powers can mimic divine power to a certain extent; hence, the healing "does not *prove* that Jesus is a righteous man" (*Gospel according to John*, 375).

The allusion to God hearing and enabling a person to do the extraordinary recalls OT incidences of prophets and leaders who wrought some great deliverance or healing when God heard their prayer. Battling the Amorites, Joshua called on the Lord to stop the sun's progression; and the biblical account (Josh 10:14) notes: "There has never been a day like it before or since, a day when the Lord listened to a man. Surely the Lord was fighting for Israel." In contrast to the false prophets' protracted and futile beseeching of Baal, Elijah prayed one short prayer and God sent fire from heaven by which the Lord manifested himself as God and vindicated Elijah as his servant before the people (1 Kgs 18:22–39). Elisha, the man of God (1 Kgs 4:25), prayed to the Lord before resuscitating the Shunammite's dead son back to life (2 Kgs 4:32–35).

At the very least, then, Jesus ought to be numbered among the men of God from Israel's past. The underlying assumption views miraculous healings to be within the realm of prophets and holy men. The religious authorities, argues the healed man, ought to discern and recognize a man of God when they see his works. And standing before the Jews the healed blind man presents himself as a work of God (9:3).

LANGUAGE OF DISPUTATION

Consistent with his standing in Jesus' stead in the juridical controversy with the Jews, the healed man employs Jesus' verbal tactic in disputing with his opponents. They claim (9:29), "We do not know from whence this man [Jesus] came." In his rebuttal, the man answers (9:30), "Indeed, in this it is amazing that you do not know from whence he came." He reiterates their disavowal word for word in the exact same word order ("we [you] do not know from whence he came"). This echoing technique mirrors Jesus' response to the Pharisees.[3] They challenge Jesus (8:13), "You testify concerning yourself; your testimony is not true." Jesus answers (8:14a): "Even if I testify concerning myself, my witness is true." Jesus

---

3. I regard Jesus' disputation with the Pharisees and the Jews in 8:12–59 to be an extension of round one of the juridical controversy spawned by his healing of the lame man (5:1–15). Jesus' reference to that Sabbath healing in 7:21–23 ties 7:14–52 to round one. And 8:12 continues where 7:52 leaves off. The overarching context is the Feast of Tabernacles. Round two begins with the second Sabbath healing of the blind man. The pericope of the woman caught in adultery (7:53—8:11) is generally regarded as spurious. Lincoln, for example, moves directly from 7:52 to 8:12 in his commentary without mention of the intervening passage (*Gospel according to Saint John*, 260). The early Greek manuscripts for the most part omit it. See Metzger, *Textual Commentary*, 187–89.

repeats their words, except for word order, contrasting their negative charge with his positive affirmation. With this technique Jesus expresses the exact opposite. The healed man, however, uses the technique for a different effect. Whereas Jesus contradicts his opponents' charge, the man taunts his inquisitors.

The healed blind man continues (9:30b–31a): "you do not know from whence he came, and yet he opened my eyes. We know that God does not listen to sinners." Here the man recalls Jesus' earlier reference to the witness of the works the Father had given him to do, substantiating that the Father had sent him (5:36). The man addresses this very issue with his interlocutors. In answer to their confessed ignorance of Jesus' origin, he cites his own healing. His inference is clear—undeniably Jesus must be from God because the healing is undeniable. In his allegation, the man places the Jews outside of Orthodox Judaism. This is an ironic twist of fortunes. Arrogant defenders of orthodoxy, as Moses' disciples (9:28) boasting "we know that God has spoken to Moses" (9:29),[4] the Jews find themselves outside with one simple but devastatingly effective put down. The "we" in "we know that God does not listen to sinners" is a corporate "we" encompassing every devout Jew who clings to Moses and the Scriptures (cf. 5:45–47). Thus, every devout Jew knows that God does not listen to sinners but he does listen to those who fear him.[5] In accusing Jesus, the Jews directly contradict their own tradition—for God must have listened to Jesus because he healed the blind man. Thus, the man effectively places them outside of mainstream Judaism.

Ironically, he does to them theologically what they will do to him ecclesiologically (9:34). The greater irony, however, is that the Jews condemn themselves with their own words. The man simply takes advantage of their gaffe. He outwits them; but their pride and smugness make them vulnerable.

Tactically, the healed man utilizes another of Jesus' techniques of disputation. In exposing the Jews' bogus claim to be Moses' disciples, the man follows Jesus in uncovering their empty boast that Abraham is

---

4. In their boast, the Jews add the superfluous "we" for added emphasis in "we know." The Greek verb features an embedded subject and does not need a separate pronoun subject "we" in order to function syntactically. The addition of the pronoun expresses their smug confidence.

5. Ridderbos cites *b. Ber.* 6b, "everyone in whom the fear of God is present, that person's words are heard" (*Gospel according to John*, 346, n. 291).

their father (8:33, 39a). Jesus rebukes them (8:39b–41a): "If you are the children of Abraham, you would do the works of Abraham. But now you seek to kill me, a man who has spoken to you the truth which I heard from God. This Abraham did not do. You do the works of your father." Exemplifying unbelief, they distance themselves from Abraham's faith. Jesus infers that their deeds reveal their true lineage. As true descendants of Abraham, they should do what he did. Abraham rejoiced in anticipation of Jesus' advent (8:56); but they seek his death. Jesus points to his opponents' murderous intent in condemning them and disputing their claim of Abrahamic parentage.[6]

The healed man mirrors this tact by exposing the Jews' false claim to be Mosaic disciples. The man contends that Jesus must be from God. However, the man stops short of identifying his opponents' father as the devil himself (8:44).

In one additional manner the man echoes Jesus in this disputation. Earlier, Jesus entered into an extended discourse in rebuking the Jews (5:19–47), and in the process succeeded in reversing the direction of accusation back against them (5:37–47). The man employs the same tactic through a more concise "discourse" (9:30–33). But it is long enough for the Jews to become indignant with an icy "and do you teach us?" (9:34). The syntax of their indignation reveals a deep offense at this turning of the tables. Their emphatic "you" is a verbal jabbing of the finger into the man's face. He, a former blind beggar, teaches them, the interpreters of the law. The gesture is tantamount to saying, "How dare you teach or lecture us! Who do you think you are?" In the present tense, the verb "teach" conveys the sting they feel so sharply at the moment, a feeling that lingers for a long time. They feel desperate in having no effective reply to his "teaching." It was the same desperate feeling earlier when Jesus effectively silenced them in John 5. The man in this round has done to them what Jesus did earlier. The result is the same—the light of the truth reveals them to be in the dark.

In following Jesus' tactics in his disputation with the Jews, the healed man proves to be apt and an able surrogate for Jesus in this juridical controversy. Jesus gains a further advantage, even though largely absent, and his disputants lose ground in this round. The man has the upper hand

---

6. Jesus repeats this tact in 8:41b–42 when they claim God as their father.

when he stands firmly on the side of truth. The Jews, on the other hand, slip badly because of uncertain footing when they deny the truth.

THE CRUX OF THE DISPUTATION

The central motif of John 1–12 focuses on Jesus' mission as revealer, identity as the one sent by the Father, and origin as from the realm above.[7] If he is from above, then he is not of this world and he is the Son of God. This motif and irony further links the healed man with Jesus in this protracted juridical controversy.[8] The particular brand of irony threading this disputation makes "false claims of knowledge" specifically about Jesus' origin. Because Jesus has earthly parents, the Jews posit that he cannot be the living bread from heaven (6:42). With a known origin he thereby contradicts the apocalyptic expectation of Christ's unknown presence and origin (7:27). Besides, Jesus hails from Galilee and not Bethlehem (7:41–42). No prophet has ever come from Galilee, thus disqualifying him (7:52). Then in the present round, the Jews reverse themselves saying that his origin is unknown (9:29), which is an ironic twist from 7:27. Although correct to an extent in that Jesus has earthly parents and originated from Galilee, the Jews fail to grasp that Jesus transcends their smug estimation of him. Even though the earthly circumstances surrounding his background are true, he is much more than what those circumstances appear to dictate. In particular, he is from above, and all that he says about himself is true—he has been sent to reveal God to the world and God is his Father.

In the disputation, the Jews fall prey to the irony of false knowledge. They think they know, and they are smugly confident in this false knowledge. Their nescience sharpens the irony—incognizance to their deep entrenchment in the dark appalls the healed man. His logic brings their ignorance to light. They cannot refute him and hence resort to

---

7. Schnelle entitles this section "the ministry of the revealer in the world" (*History and Theology*, 483–84). Jesus reveals himself as sent by the Father from above; so too Matera, *New Testament Christology*, 215. Jesus "ushers in the messianic age" as the new object of worship, source of life, bread from heaven, and light of the world (p. 220–24). Moloney concludes that the earthly Jesus reveals God to the world in the context of his relationship with God (*Johannine Son of Man*, 208–20). Jesus' unique origin defines his identity as the only begotten Son of God.

8. Duke, *Irony in the Fourth Gospel*, 64–69. My subsequent discussion on the irony found in the ongoing disputation between Jesus and the healed man with their opponents draws from Duke's observations.

strong-arm tactics, first in reviling him (9:28) and then in casting him out of the synagogue (9:34).

The irony peaks when they label Jesus a sinner (9:24) and likewise dismiss the man with "you have been born entirely in sins" (9:34). They lump Jesus and the man together as sinners. Ironically, they are half correct. The disputation forges a strong link between Jesus and the man. He describes his relationship with Jesus as one between master and disciple, "you don't really want to become his disciples too, do you?" (9:27). The truth about Jesus' origins, to which the Jews remain stubbornly blind, implies that the man is saved from his sins in contrast to his opponents (9:41). Ironically, in falsely accusing Jesus and the man as sinners, they themselves are tragically blind to their own sin.

The connection between Jesus and the man goes further whereby, perhaps as a consequence of being Jesus' disciple, the man assumes Jesus' role as disputant. Although Jesus is noticeably absent, his absence is hardly missed because the man steps in as an able witness for the defense. He, like Jesus, proves to be apt at turning the plaintiffs into defendants by effective counterpunching. No doubt the amazement expressed by the Jews toward Jesus ("how does this man know the writings since he is unlearned" 7:15) is likewise felt about the man. Neither one possesses the recognized authority to teach, derived from taking the traditional path to becoming a respected teacher.[9] Yet both manage to confound their opponents.

IRREFUTABLE LOGIC

Another affinity the healed man shares with Jesus is irrefutable logic. He states a truism (9:31): "We know that God does not listen to sinners, but if someone is a God-fearing person and does His will, then He listens to him." The argument is impeccable:[10]

---

9. Moloney, *Signs and Shadows*, 75–76. Moloney bases his discussion on Pancaro, *Law in the Fourth Gospel*. The rabbinical teachers frequently referenced in the Mishnah enforce the contention for the traditional recognition of a teacher. Note the list of teachers in appendix 3 of Danby, *Mishnah*, 799–800.

10. Hendricksen constructs a syllogism (*Commentary*, 2:82–83): "Major Premise: Only people who are from God can open the eyes of those born blind, *in order that by doing this they may display the works of God*. Minor Premise: This man, Jesus, *with that purpose in mind*, has opened the eyes of one born blind. Conclusion: This man is from God." The italics are Hendricksen's and function interpretatively.

1. A miraculous healing is possible only by God's power.

2. The human agent God employs must be God-fearing and righteous.

3. Jesus performed a miraculous healing.

4. Therefore, Jesus must be righteous and God's agent.

The healed man's opponents cannot deny or dispute the power of his argument. His thought process leads him to this conclusion: Jesus must be God's agent. It is a necessary process that enables him to have faith in Jesus. The process must be accomplished in Jesus' absence, symbolic of faith—the conviction of things not seen.

The man continues by particularizing the miracle of his healing (9:32): "It is unheard of that someone can give sight to a person born blind." This is no ordinary miracle. It then follows that Jesus is no ordinary miracle worker. Jesus stands head and shoulders above all the prophets and holy men of the past. He is unique and far superior.

The man continues yet further (9:33): "If this man was not from God, he would not be able to do anything." The NT features different kinds of conditional statements. This particular conditional statement presumes something contrary to reality from the perspective of the speaker in the "if statement" (protasis): "If this man was not from God." For the sake of argument, the man states something he believes to be untrue: "Let's just suppose for the moment that Jesus was not from God." He believes Jesus is from God but argues as if Jesus is not, in order to show the falsity of the premise by the absurdity of the conclusion. The conclusion or apodosis logically follows: "He would not be able to do anything." But in truth Jesus did do something noteworthy. Hence, Jesus must be from God and is not a sinner.

The man uses first positive logic (9:31) and now negative logic (9:33). Argued both positively and negatively the man can draw but one conclusion: Jesus is from God, hence the answer to the question "from whence has he come?" implied by the Jews' disavowal "we don't know from whence he came" (9:29). Essentially, he rebukes them for their professed ignorance. He accuses them of blatant rejection of the evidence and of the accompanying logical and inescapable inference. He accuses them thus: "You deliberately reject the evidence of my healing and deny that Jesus must be from God even though he granted me sight." In effect, he chides them.

His logic is irrefutable and their pride insufferable. They reject the man, as they have rejected Jesus, by casting him out (9:34). Whereas Jesus' rejection will result in his crucifixion, the man suffers the fate of a *persona non grata*. However, that fate strikes fear in others, including his own parents and many of the leaders (12:42–43).

INTELLIGENT FAITH

The healed man represents every person who must traverse the path toward greater faith. Christian faith is not blind faith, but intelligent faith. With the mind we must think sanctified logic. Right thoughts lead to right convictions and to faith in the proper object or, in our case, in the proper person. God provides the stimulus (in the case of the blind man, his healing) that triggers our quest for truth, a quest that compels us to embark on a journey. But it is a journey fraught with danger that threatens to derail us from our destination.

For the man, his opponents symbolize danger. They represent the darkness that threatens to blind one to the truth, the light that is Jesus. The man reaches his destination because he accepts the logic of his mind as he ponders reality (in his case, his healing). Unlike his opponents, he is not encumbered by presuppositions that blind him to what he experiences. Presuppositions are the prewiring of the mind to think in certain prescribed ways. The man's reality leads to but one conclusion. In accepting that conclusion, he confirms his faith. In rejecting that conclusion, his opponents' faith never materializes and they remain trapped in their delusion and blindness. The man moves from sight to insight that leads to faith. His opponents move from sight to blindness that leads to judgment.

The healed man prompts us to examine ourselves in order that we discover the presuppositions that may color our perspective of Jesus. Our sanctified thought process conditioned by Scripture, personal experience, and the experiences of others refines our faith. The pressure from others who may hold a different perspective of Jesus threatens to derail us. Our convictions hang in the balance.

EXCLUSION

We read a story about exclusion. The whole Fourth Gospel is a story of mutual exclusion. Two realms, the one above and the one below, have no common bond. A person cannot belong to both realms at the same time, although he may exist in one and belong to the other, as the disciples experienced (15:19; 17:11, 14–16).

The prologue encapsulates the irony that encompasses the entire Fourth Gospel. "And the light shines in the darkness but the darkness did not accept it" (1:5). "He was in the world, and the world was made through him, but the world did not acknowledge him. He came to his own and his own did not receive him" (1:10–11). God visited the world in the person of his Son Jesus. This is the irony of the Fourth Gospel—Jesus entered into the world, but the world did not recognize God in Jesus. The world should have but did not. The visitation invites—it is a divine overture toward inclusion. But in rejecting the invitation, the world excluded itself from the realm above. This is the tragedy of the Fourth Gospel.

The healed man's opponents cannot rebut his logic. There is no effective counter-argument. They can do only one thing to preserve their smug religiosity, rejection. The Jews do not simply reject the former blind man. In rejecting him they have rejected Jesus who is more than a man. Their hardened heart manifests arrogance in being judgmental and condemnatory. Irony asks, "Who is the real sinner? Who needs to be taught? Who is being cast out, and being cast out from what?" The Jews and Pharisees, stuck in the dark, still in their sin, exclude themselves from the light of the world. In braving excommunication, the now sighted man is free from bondage of fear, of Mosaic traditions, of blindness. He is free from the world to become part of the realm above.

Again, we ponder about our affiliation and profession of faith. The Fourth Gospel presents a choice—either we associate with the world in a manner that excludes us from God and what he offers, or we associate with the realm above that excludes us from being identified with the world and places us in an adversarial relationship with it. We must count the cost and make a decision. Rejecting certain cherished presuppositions requires clarity of thought and courage. The break must be clean and final. There cannot be a straddling of the fence.

11

Commencement

> Jesus heard that they had cast him out and, having found him, he said, "Do you believe in the Son of Man?" He answered, "And who is he, sir, that I may believe in him?" Jesus said to him, "You both see him and he is the one speaking with you." And he said, "Lord, I believe." And he worshipped him.
>
> —John 9:35–38

AT A RECENT COMMENCEMENT, I sat with fellow faculty on stage. We faced the graduates seated at the front and the general audience behind them and to the side. Throughout the proceedings I kept scanning the faces of former students. Each face recalled a story or two. I wondered what thoughts transpired behind those faces and what emotions welled within their breasts. Some were beginning their first pastorate and others would continue where they left off on the missions field. And a few were going to explore in earnest what God had in store for them. As we all know, commencement means both a beginning and an end.

That is the significance I find as we arrive at this juncture of the narrative of a blind man given sight. In a brief interlude in round two of the juridical controversy between Jesus and his opponents, the Jews are momentarily off stage. This leaves Jesus and the healed blind man alone. The man weathered a terrifying tempest of a disputation and triumphed, his role as witness for the defense successful. Now he begins a life of worship as part of an exclusive community not associated with the world.

But the man is not quite at the end of his faith journey. He still does not know Jesus in the fullest sense; he needs one more step. For this, Jesus finally reappears. At this point, we should reexamine the significance of Jesus' absence before proceeding further.

JESUS, WHERE ARE YOU?

Throughout round two of Jesus' juridical controversy with his opponents Jesus is absent. When he sends the blind man off to the Pool of Siloam, he disappears, leaving the man alone. As soon as the blind man gains sight, he plunges into a controversy not of his choosing. Jesus took the initiative by noticing him and anointing him with mud. Unlike other incidences involving the blind, the man does not beseech Jesus for healing. Rather, Jesus chooses him, a significant detail that speaks of election.

As the man returns from washing his eyes, now able to see for the first time in his life, his acquaintances mob him and besiege him with questions. Without his consent they take him to the Pharisees who submit him to immediate interrogation. Significantly, the narrative makes no mention of his reaction to the quick succession of events. We do not know if he is surprised, overwhelmed, or resentful. The only clues center on the verbal exchanges. The man answers in an honest and straightforward manner to questions put to him. He shows no emotion.

His characterization in 9:1–7 is that of an "agent" limited in function to a plot device that facilitates the story's movement. Things happen to him. Jesus simply designates him as the location where God manifests his works (9:3). He is a conversation piece that prompts the disciples' theological inquiry (9:2). However, he does comply with Jesus' directive by going to the pool to wash his eyes. Only with the query of his acquaintances does he have his first speaking part (9:9–12). In this first cross-examination the man morphs into a type, a character possessing one distinguishable quality or trait. He experienced a work of God through receiving his sight. He affirms to those who knew him in his prior condition that he is still the same person, but one who now sees. Hence, he is characterized as one who has been healed by Jesus and given the opportunity to relate in concise terms how he gained his sight. He credits a man called Jesus. But when asked about Jesus' whereabouts, he pleads ignorance (9:12). His role, though significant, is quite limited—a witness to what Jesus has done to him.

Taken to the Pharisees for a second series of questions (9:13–17), the man's role takes on added complexity because Jesus worked on the

Sabbath (9:14). The man is now party to a perceived Sabbath violation and the tension instantly escalates, with him in the middle of the juridical controversy between Jesus and his opponents. The man's character is progressing toward becoming a full-fledged or rounded character, but incrementally. With Jesus absent, the narrative centers on the man. He subsumes Jesus' role in the disputation. His responses to the questions require thought and care. He must now think quickly on his feet. He has no allies and, it seems, the whole world has ganged up on him. Will he wilt and fold? Or will he stand firm? His poise is telling. As the proceedings advance, we see that he has backbone, a resolve to tell his story as he experienced it; and he wants to be sure that the truth about what happened and Jesus' identity remain uncompromised, at least to the best of his current understanding. And we detect a progressive advancement in his understanding of Jesus' identity. The man grows and, as a result, gives more mature answers about Jesus. We watch the man assume the qualities of a person of faith and insight, of courage and steadfastness. He is someone who Jesus entrusted the major responsibility of representing him in a life-and-death struggle with representatives of the unbelieving community who will eventually crucify the Son of Man.

What kind of person would Jesus choose to shoulder such a crucial role as witness and disputant? The narrative does not answer. We must infer through our reading and reflection.

We must infer the reason for Jesus' absence in all of this. Taking our cue from 2:24–25 ("But Jesus did not entrust himself to them [who believed on his name because they saw his signs] because he knew all things, and because he did not need for anyone to testify concerning man, for he knew what was in man"), we read "he saw a man blind from birth" (9:1) as more than physically noticing a blind man by the wayside. Jesus reads the man, has insight into his congenital condition, and discerns his character; and from his character Jesus assesses his potential for faith.[1] This potential

---

1. Some may take issue with the idea that God's activities appear contingent and not sovereign. I believe in God's absolute sovereignty and do not mean to imply anything less. I also believe that the blind man and every man is made by God (1:3, 10). I further believe that 3:16 implies that the "world" is all-inclusive of those who believe and those who do not, as 1:11 intimates about his "own" who reject him. My interpretation of Jesus reading the man's potential is based on and consistent with the overall thrust and message of the Gospel: "These are written in order that you may believe that Jesus is the Christ the Son of God, and that by believing you may have life in his name" (20:31). Jesus intentionally sets the stage through the healing to permit the man and his interlocutors

Kysar calls embryonic faith (see chapter 9). But Jesus also knows that for his faith to develop and mature, he has to undergo an intense process that will challenge and stretch him. In short, he has to be tested as by fire. In order for the fire of interrogation to be fully directed at the man, Jesus has to step out of the line of fire even though he is still the main impetus for the disputation. "Faith is the assurance of things hoped for, the conviction of things not seen" (Heb 11:1). Hence, with Jesus absent and so unseen, the man must slog his way through toward keener insight and assurance. In so doing, he progresses from perceiving Jesus as a mere man to being the object of worship.

NEXT STEP

Although he is cast out of the synagogue, the now seeing man is triumphant. He defeats his opponents in round two of Jesus' disputation with the Jews. Ironically he beats them at their own game: he utilizes their Scriptures and tradition to prove that Jesus must be from God and is not a sinner.[2] At the same time, his understanding of Jesus matures. Jesus is greater than any of the prophets and holy men of old, in that he has done something none of them ever accomplished—granting sight to a person congenitally blind (9:32). The man acknowledges Jesus as master and sees himself as his disciple (9:27). He confesses that Jesus is a God-fearer and does the will of God (9:31). Jesus has proven, in convincing fashion, to be one who comes from God (9:33). In this confession, the man backs down from no one and does not keep silent. He willingly pays the price others fear to pay.

However, he still lacks something. Apparently he cannot progress further in his faith journey without Jesus' presence. So Jesus reappears after hearing that the man is casted out and looks for him (9:35). Jesus' reappearance and actions tell me that he understands the juridical process well. Being cast out implies that the man does not cave into the intense pressure and intimidation of the Jews, and that he professes Jesus in faith. The man willingly pays the price of rejection and separation from the

---

to react in their respective ways so that their faith or unbelief surfaces. This is consistent with Jesus' pronouncement: "For judgment I have come into this world, in order that those who do not see may see and those who see may become blind" (9:39).

2. See Duke's treatment of this pericope as a "sustained narrative irony" (*Irony in the Fourth Gospel*, 117–26).

community rooted in the world. He denies the world and so is ready for the next step.

The narrative indicates that Jesus looks for the man and finds him. The man does not look for Jesus.[3] What is the man thinking, and what emotions does he harbor? The narrative is silent about whether he feels ostracized, left out in the cold, isolated, and abandoned. We cannot tell if he regrets his stand or ponders his next move, or what life has in store for him. He cannot return to begging, for he is no longer blind. Does he wonder about Jesus and repeat to himself the question posed to him earlier (9:12): "Where is he?" And does his earlier answer ("I don't know") return to haunt him? No narrative marker tells us how much time transpires between 9:34 and 9:35. We do not know for how long the man has been cast out before Jesus finds him. News of his censorship no doubt propagates quickly. It would not take long for Jesus to hear of developments. Evidently Jesus does not delay—once he hears about the man he begins his search for him.[4]

Curiously, Jesus does not introduce himself to the man although the man has never seen him before, being blind the first time they "met." But Jesus comes straight to the point: "Do you believe in the Son of Man?"[5] The question presupposes that the man understands the connotation of the title.[6] Belief in Jesus as the Son of Man is the next step after professing

---

3. Barrett notes that the man "has not yet understood what has taken place, or come to faith in Jesus. Jesus therefore, taking the initiative, as he must, *finds* the man" (*Gospel according to St. John*, 302). Brown likens Jesus' search for the man to Wisdom in search of those worthy of her in Wis 6:16 (*Gospel According to John*, 375).

4. The syntax in 9:35 of the finite verb ("Jesus heard") followed by the conjunction "and" introducing the circumstantial participle ("having found him") suggests a sequence of actions.

5. A number of ancient Greek manuscripts, including the Majority text, feature "God" in place of "Man." However, two early papyri, one ca. 200 CE and the other third-century, and two fourth-century majuscules considered by many to be of the first order in importance, support "Man." Moreover, a basic tenet of what scholars call Transcriptional Probabilities, the perceived habits of ancient scribes copying manuscripts, is that the more difficult of two alternative readings is to be preferred as the more likely original reading. See Metzger, *Textual Commentary*, 11*–13* (pagination in Metzger's introduction), 194. Thus, it is deemed improbable for a scribe to alter an original and expected "Son of God" to the more difficult to explain "Son of Man," given the scribal tendency to simplify the text. A confession of Jesus would be more naturally expressed as "Son of God" rather than as "Son of Man." Then "Son of Man" is the preferred (harder) reading.

6. For an exposition of the title in 9:35, see Moloney, *Johannine Son of Man*, 149–59. My discussion draws from Moloney's insights. See also Lincoln, *Truth on Trial*, 102–4.

his heavenly origin (9:33). Jesus desires the man to continue in his faith development. With this title as a high point of the narrative thus far, some other points of data from the immediate context serve to help the reader come to a better grasp of the title's significance. Jesus initially pronounces that in the man the works of God will be manifested (9:3), followed by the self-designation "I am the light of the world" (9:5). With the overarching gospel theme of Jesus being sent to reveal the Father and give life (3:16), we understand Jesus' light as revelation and life (1:4). The title Son of Man signifies Jesus as the revelation of God on earth through his works (in the present situation the healing of the blind man) and his words (most recently 9:5). But there is more in view of the contrasting paths the man and his opponents traverse as they move in opposite directions in their belief in Jesus. Jesus declares that for judgment he has come into the world (9:39). Earlier, 3:18 specifies the particular concept of judgment according to this gospel: "The one who believes in him is not judged; but the one who does not believe is judged already because he does not believe in the name of the only begotten Son of God."

The healed man affirms his readiness to believe in the Son of Man with a question (9:36): "And who is he, sir, that I may believe in him?"[7] In contrast to the Samaritan woman who simply expresses the general expectation of a Messiah, the man asks "who?" He does not ask the "where" question of his acquaintances (9:12), the "how" question of his interrogators (9:15, 19, 26), or even the "what sort of fellow is he" question (9:17). The man is solely interested in the identity of the object of his faith. Ready to believe, he must believe in the right person.[8]

Jesus answers, "You both see him and he is the one speaking with you" (9:37). The first part of the answer seems more of an acknowledgement. The man perceives Jesus in a progressively clearer manner during the exchange with the interrogators. The reference is not to physical sight but to a faith-empowered insight. The verb "to see" is the same that

---

Lincoln regards Jesus as judge in this disputation; however, Moloney is closer to the Gospel's portrayal of judgment as based on a person's faith response to Jesus.

7. Carson characterizes him as being eager to believe (*Gospel according to John*, 376).

8. Morris makes an overly fine semantic distinction between the different tenses of the same verb "believe" in 9:35-36 (*Gospel according to John*, 440, n. 52). He interprets Jesus as asking, "Do you habitually believe?" and the man as answering "that I may come to believe." The context disallows Morris's rendering of the question. The man is only now coming to a fuller faith after a difficult process.

was used with respect to Jesus seeing the man blind from birth (9:1) and perceiving him to be the venue by which the works of God may be manifested (9:3). The tense of the verb here suggests a characterization of the man by Jesus.[9] Jesus pronounces approvingly, "You see me with faith."

The second part of Jesus' answer ("he is the one speaking with you") recalls similar words to the Samaritan woman ("I am he, the one speaking to you" 4:26). In fact, there may be a parallelism between the two responses. The corresponding parts would be the following:

"I am he" (4:26b) / "you see him" (9:37b)

"the one speaking to you" (4:26c) / "the one speaking with you is he" (9:37c)[10]

The first pair of corresponding clauses refers to Jesus in his person as the expected Messiah in the first incidence; and as the light, the revelation of God, in the second. The pair refers to the same person who was sent from above. The second pair employs the same verb "to speak."[11] This pair of self-identifications marks the end of the dialogue Jesus fosters with the Samaritan woman and the brief exchange with the healed man. The woman goes back to her townspeople to tell them about Jesus, and many of them believe in Jesus because of her testimony (4:28–30, 39). The man, on the other hand, confesses, "Lord, I believe" (9:38a). In both situations, belief has tangible results: the woman becomes an effective witness and the man becomes a worshipper. The theme of worship also marks the woman's exchange with Jesus (4:20–24). Indeed, Jesus teaches the woman that "the Father seeks such who worship him [true worshippers will

---

9. The perfect tense can convey the state of affairs—the man sees Jesus for who he really is by faith. Porter advocates a stative aspect (*Verbal Aspect*, 245–70). McKay states: "the ancient Greek perfect expresses the state or condition of the subject of the verb, as the result of a prior action, but most often with comparatively little reference to that action itself" ("On the Perfect,"296). Fanning finds inherent in the perfect: "Aktionsart-feature of stative situation, the tense-feature of anteriority, and the aspect of summary viewpoint concerning the occurrence" (*Verbal Aspect*, 119–20). The anterior action resulting in the man's faith is 9:1–34. Campbell dismisses the stative aspect in favor of the imperfective for the perfect tense (*Basics of Verbal Aspect*, 46–51).

10. I follow the Greek word order in 9:37c literally in order to highlight the parallelism.

11. In fact, the verb appears as a substantive participle with the article in both incidences. However, to the Samaritan woman Jesus conveys the indirect object "to you" by using the second person pronoun in the dative case, but to the man he uses a prepositional phrase "with you." There is the addition of an explicit subject and verb in answering the man ("is he" as shown in the text above).

worship the Father in spirit and truth]" (4:23).¹² Then he, in the Father's stead, seeks the healed man and manifests himself to him that he may believe and worship him (9:38).

The trajectory of growing faith leads to beholding the revelation of Jesus as the Son of Man.¹³ And belief in the Son of Man leads to worshipping him as Lord in the full Christological sense.¹⁴ If the healed man's true worship of Jesus as the Son of Man is representative, as I believe that to be the case, then true worship ought to be the end point of our trajectory in our growth in insight and understanding of Jesus.¹⁵ But as we saw earlier (chap. 9), none of the disciples, including the man, receives the Spirit yet according to the narrative (16:13).

IT'S YOUR MOVE

We too must arrive at the place the healed blind man now stands. Jesus finds him and declares: "You both see him and he is the one who is speaking with you." If we see Jesus in faith and hear his words through the words of this story, our response should be to worship Jesus in spirit and truth. We have new life and a new identity.

The purpose of manifesting the works of God in the blind man is that he may come to faith, and worship Jesus as the Son of Man, the revelation of God in the world as the light. The objective of Jesus' mission in the world is to form a community of believers who acknowledge him through true worship. Getting to that place of worship may require undergoing an

---

12. Lee suggests a possible hendiadys in which "in spirit and truth" is equivalent to "in the Spirit of truth" or the Holy Spirit ("Spirit of Truth," 280). A chiasm formed with the two occurrences of "in spirit and truth" (4:23, 24) sandwiching "God is spirit" signifies that the divine Spirit forms the center of true worship. Lee's observation that the gospel's teaching on worship is concentrated in the woman's dialogue with Jesus (pp. 278–82) provides the rationale for referring to that episode as the backdrop for examining the healed man's worship.

13. Both the Samaritan woman and healed blind man reach corresponding intermediary stages of faith when each regards Jesus as a prophet in response to a demonstration of supernatural insight (4:19) or healing (9:17).

14. The vocative "Lord" by which the man addresses Jesus in 9:38 is made with full understanding. The same vocative in 9:36 connotes merely polite etiquette ("sir") since it precedes Jesus' self-declaration (9:37).

15. Lee sees 4:23 rivaling 20:30–31 as the expressed purpose of the gospel ("Spirit of Truth," 280 n. 10).

ordeal that tests our mettle but refines the purity of our faith and clarifies our vision of Jesus.[16]

The Feast of Tabernacles frames the narrative context for the blind man's story and hence of his worshipping Jesus (7:2—10:21). A major motif of the Fourth Gospel is the relationship between Jesus and the feasts of the Jews. The Johannine portrayal is of Jesus coming into the world to fulfill the expectations and replace the various symbols of the feasts that commemorate God's faithfulness to his people over the course of their national history.[17]

Of particular importance is the symbolic significance of the Feast of Tabernacles. Ruberstein writes: "Sukkot, more than any other festival, was associated with the temple, not with eschatology. When the prophet pictured worship in an ideal temple, he naturally pictured it in terms of the most important and popular cultic observance: the autumnal festival. The temple is the key eschatological concept, while Sukkot is associated with eschatology as a reflex of its association with the temple."[18]

Eschatological expectations associated with the temple would naturally transfer to the rites of the feast.[19] Jesus apparently identifies with two

---

16. For regarding Jesus as the locus of worship, see Matera, *New Testament Christology*, 220–21; and Lee, "Spirit of Truth," 282–87. As Hoskins explains in discussing 4:20–24, true worship is not a matter of physical location but of belief in Jesus and receiving the Spirit (*Jesus as the Fulfilment*, 135–46).

17. Brown, *Gospel According to John*, 201–4; and Koester, *Dwelling of God*, 102–8. For other scholars advocating a replacement theme, see Koester's list (ibid., 105, n. 15). Hoskins's typological study reveals that the temple and the major feasts have their fulfillment and replacement in Jesus (*Jesus as the Fulfillment*, 160–81). Hoskins gives a definition: "Typology may be defined as the study which traces parallels or correspondences between incidents recorded in the Old Testament and their counterparts in the New Testament such that the latter can be seen to resemble the former in notable respects and yet to go beyond them" (p. 19). He continues: "the Old Testament type prefigures and predicts its goal, the New Testament antitype" (p. 22). Specifically, the antitype replaces the type because the antitype fulfills major aspects of the type and surpasses it (pp. 22–23). Hence, the temple and its rites are OT types finding fulfillment in Jesus the antitype.

18. Rubenstein, "Sukkot," 187. Sukkot is the plural of Sukkah or booth/tabernacle, which, according to the Mishnah, were to be built for temporary residences during the feast (*m. Sukk.* 1.1—2.9) in accordance to Lev 23:34–43.

19. The eschatological expectations were probably messianic, in view of the singing of the *Hallel* during the Feast of Tabernacles (*m. Sukk.* 4.8), which incorporates Pss 113—118 (Finkelstein, "Origin of the Hallel," 319–37). For a messianic understanding of Ps 118, see Kaiser, *Messiah*, 100–3; Howard and Rosenthal, *Feasts*, 139. John 12:13 depicts the multitude citing Ps 118:25–26 as Jesus entered Jerusalem; and Luke 20:17 has Jesus repeating Ps 118:22 in identifying himself as the rejected cornerstone. Additional

rites, the water libation and light, when he offers living water (7:37–38) and declares himself to be the light of the world (8:12; 9:5).[20] Earlier, Jesus had intimated that his body was the temple (2:19, 21). The Jews misunderstood his reference to be the temple building (2:20).[21] Only after the resurrection do the disciples finally understand the import of Jesus' declaration (2:22). In proclaiming himself to be the new temple during the Feast of Tabernacles, Jesus positions himself to become the object of the celebrants' hopes and expectations. Instead of coming to the temple during the feast to offer thanksgiving and praise to God, they are to come to him as the new temple to worship. That is exactly what the healed blind man has done. Instead of going to the temple, he worships before Jesus.

As God works in our lives, we look for a transformation similar to what the man underwent. So we ask, Is my worship transformational, or is it affected by the trappings of "church"? If we critique the preacher, we may fail to apply the message. If the praise songs do not suit our taste, we may become inhibited in our praise. The perceived lukewarmness of fellow worshippers may distract us. These concerns lead to a central question: Is Jesus really the focus of our worship to such an extent and purity that nothing external to us dissuades us from our devotion? But at the same time, the church is the temple of God in which the Holy Spirit dwells (1 Cor 3:16–17; 2 Cor 6:16; Eph 2:21).[22] Hence, a corporate

---

allusions appear in Matt 21:9, 42; 23:39; Mark 11:9–10; 12:10–11; Luke 13:35; 19:38.

20. *m. Sukk.* 4.9 specifies the water libation; and *m. Sukk.* 5.2–3 addresses the provision of light during the festival. But Hoskins is cautious in associating Jesus' declaration to be the light of the world with the light in the temple given the tentative nature of the Scriptural evidence (*Jesus as the Fulfillment*, 169–70).

21. Jesus' use of "temple" in 2:19 may be *double entendre*, a literary device conveying a double meaning with a darker shade in the second meaning. The Jews challenge him for a sign (2:18). He counter-challenges: destroy "this temple," which he will raise in three days (2:19). They are astounded, recalling that the building required forty-six years to complete. But "this" points to his own body. Jesus chooses not to explain. But the narrator does in 2:21. Thus the reader understands; but the characters do not. The second meaning of Jesus' body being destroyed anticipates the crucifixion, the darker shade of meaning. Here the rhetorical device of a narrative aside (2:21) enables the reader to be inside of God's plan and, at the same time, keeps the characters in the story outside of God's plan. With this privileged information the reader does not make wrong conclusions in the reading.

22. Traditionally, people have regarded 1 Cor 3:16–17 and 2 Cor 6:16 as applicable to individual believers in terms of purity and holiness. But the temple language in these passages refers to the community of believers as the temple. See, for example, Draper, "Tip of an Ice-berg," 57–65; and Taylor, "Kingdom," 188–90.

dimension informs our worship. But if the church is much less than perfect, can we still worship effectively? Instead of licking his wounds and nursing grudges for being kicked out, the healed man moves forward in faith and worships.

Vigilantly, we examine the clarity of our vision of Jesus and of our hearing his voice. Are we knowing him better and is our faith maturing? We may not have encountered a miracle. But miracles constitute a very small part of the story. The heated exchange between the man and his interrogators dominates. More importantly, however, Jesus' pronouncement (9:3–5) governs the proceedings and gives meaning to the story. Belief in Jesus' words leads to genuine faith. Signs alone form an insufficient foundation for growth in insight and appreciation of Jesus' identity, as the lame man in John 5 demonstrates. And, of course, the Pharisees and Jews reject the miracle of the blind man gaining his sight.

So we read this story to draw closer to Jesus with greater faith so that our worship may be in spirit and in truth.

12

Judgment Day

And Jesus said, "For judgment I have come into this world, in order that those who do not see may see and those who see may become blind." Those of the Pharisees who were with him heard these things and said to him, "We too are not blind are we?" Jesus answered them, "If you were blind, you would have no sin. But now you say, 'We see.' Your sin remains. Truly, truly I say to you, the one who does not enter into the fold of the sheep through the gate but climbs over by another way is a thief and robber. But the one who enters through the gate is a shepherd of the sheep. The gatekeeper opens to this one; and the sheep hears his voice and he calls his own sheep by name and leads them out. When he takes all that are his out, he goes before them and the sheep follow him because they know his voice. But they will certainly not follow a stranger but will flee from him because they are not familiar with the voice of strangers." Jesus spoke this figure of speech to them. But they did not understand what he was saying to them. So Jesus spoke again, "Truly, truly I say to you that I am the gate of the sheep. All who came before me are thieves and robbers. But the sheep did not listen to them. I am the gate. If anyone enters through me, he will be saved and will enter and go out and will find pasture. The thief does not come except to steal and kill and destroy. I have come that they may have life and have it abundantly. I am the good shepherd. The good shepherd lays down his life for the sheep. The hired hand indeed since he is not a shepherd, the sheep not being his, sees the wolf coming and abandons the sheep and flees. And the wolf snatches and scatters them, because he is a hired hand and does not care about the sheep. I am the good shepherd, and

I know my own and my own know me, just as the Father knows me and I know the Father. And I lay down my life for the sheep. And I have other sheep that are not of this fold. And it is necessary for me to lead them, and they will hear my voice and become one flock with one shepherd. For this reason the Father loves me because I lay down my life in order that I may take it up again. No one takes it from me, but I lay it down on my own. I have authority to lay it down and I have authority to take it up again. I received this command from my Father." Again a schism arose among the Jews because of these words. Now many of them were saying, "He is demonized and insane. Why do you listen to him?" Others were saying, "These words are not those of a demonized person. A demon can't open the eyes of the blind can he?"

—John 9:39—10:21

FOR THE JUDEO-CHRISTIAN FAITH, judgment day marks an inevitable finality in which God executes judgment on the wicked and ushers in a new age for the righteous. We don't quite have that finality in the present narrative, but the sense of finality prevails as Jesus concludes the blind man's story with a judgment discourse. As I observed in chapter 4, Jesus' words in the form of two pronouncements and a discourse define this story. John 9–10 is a hybrid pronouncement story that features an inquiry pronouncement (9:3–5) by which Jesus answers the disciples' question about the man born blind (9:2) and a commendation pronouncement (9:39) in which Jesus commends the healed man for his spiritual perception. Jesus concludes with a discourse that declares judgment against the Pharisees (9:41—10:18). The verdict "your sin remains" (9:41) ominously nails the metaphorical coffin shut without the possibility of reprieve.

RACING TOWARD FATE

A tremendous amount of movement flows in the story of the healed blind man. However, the only physical movement takes place when Jesus walks by the blind man and stops, applies mud to his eyes, and directs him to go wash at the Pool of Siloam. The man returns seeing, and his acquaintances immediately accost him. In short order, they lead him to the Pharisees for interrogation. The only other physical movement occurs when the Jews summon the man's parents and then the man again for a second round of interrogation. The real movement, however, takes place in the man's mind and heart as he wrestles with the reality of his healing and its implication for understanding Jesus' identity. He rides a bullet train speeding him ever closer to his fate. He has no time to catch his breath, no time to pause and reflect. He must think on the fly and do it clearly under pressure. And at the critical juncture when his fate hangs in the balance, he makes the right decision in standing up for Jesus.

Tragically we detect no movement of growing perception and faith on the part of his interrogators; they remain obstinately stationary in their unbelief and condemnation of Jesus. The only possible movement on their part, if we can call it that, is when they grow indignant enough to cast the healed man out. They too hurl rapidly to their destiny. Ironically they seal their own fate in casting the man out of their community. In doing so, they have shut themselves out of the community that Jesus is forming, and about which he will discuss in his judgment discourse (9:41—10:18).

As we read this account, our imagination goes on high alert. The drama of this story engages our minds and our souls. Having been clued by the prologue (1:1–18), we know that Jesus is the preexistent Son who was ever with the Father, who participated in creation, and who is sent into the world as the light so that those who believe in him may have life.[1] But the characters in the story have no access to the prologue and so do not have our vantage point with regard to Jesus. They have to make the most of their encounter with him with little or no prior knowledge about him. That makes the healed blind man so much more remarkable in his mental and spiritual journey to full realization of Jesus' identity and to his relationship with Jesus. He easily wins our admiration, and we feel compelled to enter into his thought world. We strive to follow his logic and reach agreement with his conclusion. We witness how he transforms before our very eyes from a nearly ignorable plot device as a former blind beggar who suddenly becomes the center of everyone's attention to, finally, a full-bodied hero who single-handedly holds at bay innumerable villains, and then vanquishes the overwhelming odds with hardly a scratch. In the end we stand to applaud and cheer. And all the while we are invited to step into the man's shoes, become him, replicate that change within him in our hearts as we return to our world and see things a lot clearer.

---

1. For a helpful discussion of the Christology in the prologue, see, for example, Kim, "Literary and Theological Significance," 421–35; Carter, "Prologue and John's Gospel," 35–58; and Brown, "Prologue of the Gospel of John," 429–39.

The pace of this story speeds us along with a sense of urgency. Because the man has no time to catch his breath, we too feel pushed to reach a decision about Jesus and our relationship with him. No time to waste. Decision time approaches fast, for our fate looms before us.

Whenever we encounter Jesus, it is, in his words, judgment time. No one can remain neutral. Every character in the story is for or against him. And so every reader of the story will likewise move in one direction or the other, and must decide what impact Jesus will have in his or her life. Our decision judges us, because it exposes our true selves. We cannot drag our feet to delay the inevitable. Indecision spells doom, as the healed man's parents discover. For the Pharisees and the Jews, judgment day is now; their fate is sealed with Jesus' indictment (9:41—10:18). What will be our fate?

PAT ON THE BACK OR SLAP IN THE FACE?

When the now seeing man worships Jesus as the Son of Man, the light of the world, Jesus pronounces a commendation (9:39). However, this commendation is not purely positive but a hybrid.[2] A mixture of commendation and condemnation pour forth when he states, "For judgment I have come into this world, in order that those who do not see may see and those who see may become blind."

This pronouncement addresses two audiences. In a sequential reading of this story, we the readers are aware of only the man's presence when Jesus utters these words. After he speaks, however, the narrative informs us that some Pharisees hear Jesus' pronouncement (9:40a).

In declaring that he comes for judgment, Jesus does not proclaim himself as judge per se, as 3:17 makes clear: "For God did not send the Son into the world in order to judge the world, but in order that the world may be saved through him." He assesses no one's merit. Rather, his presence invokes judgment in that an individual's inward faith or unbelief emerges upon encountering Jesus. The Fourth Gospel (3:18–21) explains:

> The one who believes in him is not judged. But the one who does not believe is judged already because he does not believe in the name of the only begotten Son of God. Now this is judgment,

---

2. Tannehill notes that most commendation stories in the Synoptic Gospels, the purview of his study, are hybrid ("Varieties," 105). I extrapolate his useful findings for the Fourth Gospel.

that the light came into the world and people loved the darkness more than the light for their works are evil. For everyone who does evil deeds hates the light and does not come to the light, lest his works are exposed. But the one who does the truth comes to the light in order that his works may be manifested because they are done in God.

Jesus employs two metaphors with two mutually exclusive referents (9:39). Those who see and those who do not see refer to two kinds of people. Two levels of meaning, physical sight and spiritual perception, differentiate these two groups. Jesus formulates an antithetical parallelism: "those who do not see may see" contrasts with "those who see may become blind." The healed man who could not see physically but has now gained physical sight, belongs in the first group. At the same time the healed blind man demonstrates spiritual perception to the truth about Jesus. The Pharisees and Jews who have physical sight and continue to have physical sight but prove to be spiritually obtuse represent the second group.[3]

However, as the preceding exchange reveals, the parallelism suggests another contrast: the smug knowledge of the Jews and the honesty of the man in admitting to the limits of his knowledge.[4] The Jews confidently declare, "We know that this man is a sinner" (9:24), to which the man replies, "That he is a sinner I do not know. One thing I know, that although I was blind I now see" (9:25). Again they boast, "We know that God spoke to Moses" (9:29a). Their subsequent avowal that they do not know Jesus' origin (9:29b), however, is not an admission of ignorance but a rejection of Jesus. Hence, their "knowledge" of Jesus has blinded them. But the man's openness to the evidence (the fact of his healing) and willingness to acknowledge his own limitations (not knowing Jesus' location or his real identity) enables him to see.

Everyone has the potential to go in either direction, leading to contrasting conditions. We can become the man, gaining spiritual perception and faith, or we can become the Jews, growing steadily blinder and

---

3. The expression "those who see may become blind" utilizes the verb "become" rather than "to be," a stative verb. The expression indicates a change: they lose the capacity to see. The Jews had the same opportunity as the healed blind man to see Jesus; but in rejecting the evidence, they made themselves blind to the truth.

4. Moloney, *Signs and Shadows*, 125–26.

hardened in unbelief. One is exonerated, the other condemned. Will we be patted on our backs or slapped in the face?

SMACK DOWN

What is the difference between a slap and a smack down?[5] A slap stings and insults. A smack down, well, let's just say the objective is to crush—nothing subtle. That is what Jesus does when he enters into a judgment discourse directed at the Pharisees (9:41—10:18). He smacks them down hard.

To use a cliché—the straw that broke the camel's back—the final little show of arrogance that triggers Jesus' discourse occurs when the Pharisees ask (9:40), "We too are not blind are we?" Their question begins with a negative particle (not evident in English) that indicates their expectation of a negative response to their query. In effect, they say, "Of course we're not blind. What you just stated (9:39) doesn't apply to us. We're not the ones who are going to become blind." They reject Jesus' indictment. The referent of "those who do not see may see" is obviously the healed blind man. Everyone, including the Pharisees, understands that correlation. Rather, the referent of "those who see may become blind" is debatable. Their disputation with Jesus continues unabated.

The second linguistic clue to their arrogance is the use of "too" (actually the conjunction often translated "and"). The Pharisees imply that Jesus talks about someone else becoming blind and not them, and ask for assurance that he does not intend to include them as well. "Guilty?" they ask. "You're saying someone is guilty? Oh, by the way, you're not going to implicate us too, are you?"

With that little nudge, the floodgates open wide. Jesus begins with a hypothetical case for the sake of argument (9:41b): "If you were blind, you would have no sin." He introduces an added nuance in continuing the metaphor. Obtaining forgiveness is conditioned on whether one is blind or not. If the Pharisees acknowledge their blindness, they are forgiven. The prologue explains the symbolism of blindness: "And the light shines in the darkness but the darkness did not accept it" (1:5). As the light of the world Jesus comes to offer the world life (1:4). He is the greater gift that

---

5. SmackDown is a World Wrestling Entertainment (WWE) event featuring professional wrestlers.

surpasses the gift of the law (1:16–17).[6] The law was a light to the people in its time.[7] Jesus is now the greater light that replaces the light of the law. But the Jews and the Pharisees distance themselves from the light that is Jesus by clinging to Moses and rejecting Jesus (9:28–29). They stubbornly prefer the fading light of the law. In that sense, they are tragically blind to Jesus as the true light. Hence, they remain in their sin.

Jesus continues (9:41cd): "But now you say, 'We see.' Your sin remains." They boast of a sight dependent on the light of the law. They reject Jesus' assessment that they are blind, desperately in need of the light he alone offers. The exchange repeats an earlier proclamation (8:31–32): "If you remain in my word, you are truly my disciples. And you will know the truth, and the truth will liberate you." The Jews' arrogant rejoinder (8:33) sounds familiar: "We are the seed of Abraham and have never been enslaved by anyone. How can you say, 'You will become free'?" Enslaved and needing his liberation, they reject his offer in denying their need. Jesus then states (8:34, 36): "Truly, truly I say to you that everyone who commits sin is a slave of sin. So if the Son should liberate you, you will certainly be free." Earlier they denied their enslavement to sin and their need for Jesus' liberation. Now they again dispute Jesus' claim that they are blind and need Jesus' light. Thus, throughout this disputation the Jews and Pharisees make no headway and are deeply entrenched in their sin and blindness. They leave Jesus no recourse but to condemn them as he now embarks on his judgment discourse.

---

6. Edwards argues cogently for interpreting the last phrase in 1:16 as "grace instead of grace," that is, "a grace in place of or instead of a grace" in which the gift of the law is replaced by the gift of Jesus Christ (1:17) ("Xapin," 3–15). This rendering contrasts, for example, with "grace upon grace" according to the NASB, which seems to suggest a piling on of more grace on top of previous grace. But such a rendering forces a foreign idea on the preposition that usually means "instead of." Moloney improves on Edwards' word choice with "a gift in place of a gift" to signify the replacement of one gift with another gift (*Belief in the Word*, 46–48).

7. Edwards, "Xapin," 9; and Barrett, *Gospel according to St. John*, 304.

SLAMMING THE DOOR IN YOUR FACE

Jesus' discourse (9:41—10:18),[8] according to classical rhetorical speech species, is an invective speech where the speaker condemns his audience.[9] This discourse, according to general consensus, articulates Jesus' polemic against his audience because of their hardened resistance.[10] The collection of terms—thieves, robbers, and hired hands—convey a decidedly negative connotation.[11] Jesus makes no appeal to change one's perspective, conviction, or judgment. Purely condemnatory, he is most explicit when he declares, "Your sin remains" (9:41d). Ironically, those who condemn Jesus as a sinner (9:24) are themselves mired in sin, without the possibility of forgiveness.[12]

Structurally, the discourse begins with an explicit condemnation of the audience remaining in their sin (9:41). An enigmatic figure of speech (10:1–5) follows with a narrative aside (10:6). Then Jesus resumes with the metaphors of the gate (10:7–10) and the good shepherd (10:11–18). The bulk of the discourse (10:7–18) explains 10:1–5 and introduces explicit references to the crucifixion.

---

8. Talbert finds a major break between John 9 and John 10 (*Reading John*, 143, 162–64). But Hendricksen (*Commentary*, 2. 97–98) and Quasten ("Parable," 1–12) see a connection between 10:1–21 and John 9. Narratologically, Du Rand regards John 5–10 to be a literary unit ("Syntactical," 94–115). Asiedu-Peprah discerns that the second Sabbath conflict maps over 9:1—10:21 (*Johannine Sabbath Conflicts*, 117–20). Of particular importance is the bracketing effect of 10:21 that alludes back to the blind man's healing

9. Kennedy, *New Testament Interpretation*, 74. The invective is the negative form of the epideictic speech that seeks to persuade an audience of a particular point of view (pp. 19–20).

10. For the thieves, robbers, and hired hands, writers propose different referents. Regardless of the referents' identity, however, the polemical nature of the discourse is clear. For a list of possible referents and their proponents, see Soo Hoo, *Pedagogy of the Johannine Jesus*, 150, n. 210.

11. The first term is used "of a thief as a figure for something sudden, surprising, unexpected"; and the second points to a "robber, highwayman, bandit" or "revolutionary, insurrectionist" (BDAG, 547, 594). The idea of suddenness makes the first term a NT metaphor of the advent of the messianic age (Preisker, "*kleptō, kleptēs*," 3:754–56). Rengstorf suggests a possible allusion by the second term to those who attempt to usher in the kingdom violently ("*lēstēs*," 4:257–62).

12. Ridderbos poignantly states (*Gospel according to John*, 351): "If it does not become an object of forgiveness, it remains the object of judgment. It is not sin as such; it is the repudiation of grace that makes a person a lost being." Barrett labels such blindness incurable (*Gospel according to St. John*, 304). He and Brown (*Gospel According to John*, 376) liken the sin to the sin unto death (1 John 5:16).

Although 10:6 clearly marks 10:1–5 as a *paroimia*, a figure of speech, there is uncertainty as to what that entails.[13] Apparently the overriding thrust is enigma or mystery. Hence, Jesus' audience does not understand, because he uses enigmatic language. The question that immediately arises is whether Jesus is intentionally masking the meaning. He may be excluding them from entering the inner circle of those who are privy to Jesus' teaching by hiding the meaning from them. We recall Jesus' riddle (8:21): "I am going away and you will seek me, but you will die in your sin. Where I am going, you cannot come."[14] Puzzled, the Jews are incredulous at the prospect of Jesus' possible suicide (8:22). They do not understand that Jesus is alluding to his return to the Father.

The conjunction introducing 10:7 can be translated "so," "therefore," "consequently," "accordingly," or "then."[15] In response to their inability to ascertain his meaning, Jesus resumes with a fuller explanation in an effort to clarify (10:7–18).

An Enigma and Its Effect (10:1–6)

Jesus begins with a contrast between two referents, the shepherd of the sheep and everyone else. The manner by which each enters into the sheepfold contrasts the two. The shepherd passes through the gate, but anyone else uses any other means. Anyone not the shepherd is a thief and

---

13. Carlston explains that a parable and allegory "are not the same kind of phenomenon; parable is a [species] while allegory is simply a literary mode that may appear, in a variety of ways, in various [species] (parables, speeches, poems, epics, novels, etc.)" ("Parable and Allegory Revisited," 240). Blomberg agrees and observes that parables use allegory when two or more levels of meaning are intended (*Interpreting the Parables*, 29–69). De la Potterie cautions: "*Paroimia* is not simply synonymous with *parabolā*. The fact that John employs only the first of these two terms and the Synoptics the second hints that they must not be equivalent. The LXX translates the same Hebrew word *māšāl* with the two terms. However, *paroimia* seems to place the emphasis on the idea of enigma, secret, mystery." ("Le Bon Pasteur," 2:932). I translated the preceding quote originally in French. With de la Potterie's lead, I regard the term to signify an enigma or mystery that Jesus' audience fails to grasp.

14. Thatcher defines a riddle as "a concise, interrogative unit of language that intentionally and at once conceals and reveals its referent with a single set of signs" (*Riddles of Jesus*, 179). The blurring of referents forces the audience to possess special knowledge, either cultural or ideological, in order to understand. The rhetorical effect is to include or exclude the audience from the group who has the requisite knowledge. The prologue of this Fourth Gospel gives the requisite knowledge. Because of the resultant confusion of the Jews (8:22), 8:21 is a riddle.

15. BDAG, 736–37.

robber. The two latter terms are synonymous.[16] The main idea is stealth and theft, implying that the sheep will suffer some consequence including possible loss of life.

The rhetorical intent is characterization. Jesus portrays two extremes of character—the legitimate shepherd responsible for the sheep and recognized as such by the gatekeeper (10:3), and others not recognized by the gatekeeper and so not permitted into the sheepfold. Not granted normal access, the thief must seek another means of entry by stealth in order to escape detection by the gatekeeper.

Jesus' figure of speech delineates two kinds of recognition—both the gatekeeper and sheep recognize the shepherd. The sheep recognize the shepherd's voice when he calls them by name (10:3). How the gatekeeper recognizes the shepherd remains uncertain, possibly by voice or visual recognition, or both. It really does not matter because the inference is clear—the gatekeeper recognizes the shepherd when he comes.

Jesus contrasts the two referents, the shepherd and the thief, further by the manner in which the sheep respond to each. The sheep follow the shepherd when he takes them out of the sheepfold because they recognize his voice (10:4). The shepherd's characterization takes on two additional traits. First, because his relationship with the sheep is based on familiarity and trust, we can infer that he is trustworthy and relational, as demonstrated through long-term caring for the sheep. He relates to the sheep individually in view of the fact that he calls them by name. They know him well enough to follow without any qualm. Second, he is a leader—he goes before them as he takes them out. As the leader he determines the direction and destination of their foray. He guides. This presumes that he knows what the sheep need and how to meet that need.

On the other hand, the characterization of the thief is one with whom the sheep are unfamiliar, implying a lack of a prior relationship. Instead of following him, they flee from him (10:5). The thief has not invested any time previously to become familiar with the sheep, and they with him. His chief characteristic is that he is a stranger.[17] He has no interest in the sheep's welfare. If anything, he harbors hostile and selfish motives toward them.

---

16. Carson, *Gospel according to John*, 381.

17. BDAG, 47–48. The term in 10:5 basically means "a stranger." But the idea can extend beyond simply being someone unfamiliar to being false with the attendant implication of being an enemy or hostile.

Jesus carefully portrays the two referents as complete opposites with no common traits shared. This picture prepares both the audience within the story and us, the readers, to infer that anyone else is a bad shepherd, at best, or simply a thief in contrast to Jesus' self-designation as the good shepherd (10:11, 14).

So far Jesus makes no correlation between anyone in his audience with the thief and stranger. He has only identified himself in his discourse. He paints a familiar yet timeless pastoral scene. Proverbial and yet, because it follows immediately after 9:41, an intentional barb emerges, designed to prick the conscience and to condemn.

His audience, presumably the Pharisees and the Jews, are mystified (10:6).[18] Undoubtedly they understand the general drift of Jesus' judgment discourse. But given the sharp indictment for sin (9:41), they struggle with applying this truth in the context of the juridical controversy. It sounds crazy as far as they are concerned (10:20). They wonder, "What has this got to do with us? Why is he talking about a shepherd and sheep? What is his point?"

We try to fathom why Jesus intentionally confuses his audience. Dodd offers a possible explanation in his definition of a parable: "At its simplest the parable is a metaphor or simile drawn from nature or common life, arresting the hearer by its vividness or strangeness, and leaving the mind in sufficient doubt about its precise application to tease it into active thought."[19] Although Dodd's definition is confined to parables, Jesus' enigmatic figure of speech shares significant aspects of a parable which, being vivid and strange, causes confusion and uncertainty as to its application. The objective is not to mystify but to stimulate active thought.

In this continuation of round two of the juridical controversy, Jesus presents his case to his disputants. The understood objective of each disputant is to persuade the other of the legitimacy of his position; and if he succeeds the controversy ends.[20] Persuasion involves three

---

18. The pronouns "to them" twice and "they" in 10:6 have no immediate referent except the Pharisees as the closest candidate (9:40). The next closest is the Jews (9:22; 10:19). Probably both comprise the audience given that the Jews split in their reaction to "these words" (10:19) referring to what Jesus just said (9:41—10:18).

19. Dodd, *Parables of the Kingdom*, 16.

20. Asiedu-Peprah, *Johannine Sabbath Conflicts*, 16–18. The other way of termination is if the accused admits to the charges submitted by the accuser.

aspects—*ethos*, *pathos*, and *logos*.[21] Ethos refers to the speaker's credibility as a respectable character. Pathos pertains to the audience's emotional reaction to the speech. And logos deals with the logical argumentation of the discourse. Jesus' character has been a point of contention since John 5, and is the focus of the juridical controversy. Jesus continues to address his identity, as 10:7–18 will show,[22] and has no trouble evoking an emotional reaction. His opponents are so incensed that they seek to kill him (7:19). It is not, however, the reaction he desires. The sign of healing the man born blind should have triggered a mental process designed to reach a certain conclusion. The sign serves as a data point from which a person ought to conclude inductively that Jesus comes from God. The healed man reaches that conclusion. Tragically, the Jews and Pharisees do not, even though they have the added advantage of the earlier sign of the lame man's healing (5:5–9) and Jesus' argument based on irrefutable witnesses (5:32–47). Ironically the healed blind man draws the correct conclusion with less information. The nature of their failure stems not from logos but ethos. They refuse to believe the truth about Jesus' identity in spite of irrefutable logic.

Jesus' use of a figure of speech (10:1–5) depends largely on inference. He presumes his audience's familiarity with the shepherd and sheep imagery derived from the OT.[23] Jesus likely has his audience recall God's indictment against the unfaithful shepherds of Israel who took advantage of the sheep which, as a consequence, were abused, scattered, and plundered (Ezek 34:2–10). These false shepherds correspond with the thief and robber (10:1), and the stranger (10:5). Jesus pushes for a further identification of the true shepherd with God himself (Ezek 34:11–16) and David (Ezek 34:23–24). Hence, Jesus' opponents should make the ready inference that they, the spiritual leaders of Israel, have failed as shepherds. But they are blind to the truth (9:39–40) and Jesus exacerbates that weakness with an enigma (10:1–6).

The audience's composition is uncertain, perhaps only the Pharisees and the Jews.[24] If the healed blind man and even the disciples are present,

---

21. Kennedy, *New Testament Interpretation*, 15–16.

22. Smith, *John*, 202–3.

23. Nielsen, "Old Testament Imagery in John," 66–82, especially 76–80.

24. Smith believes the disciples have long ago faded from the scene (*John*, 203). The healed blind man also seems to have gone away after worshipping Jesus. He and the disciples have no active role throughout Jesus' discourse. But that is an argument from silence.

they too hear the discourse. Their reception would of course be different, because they most probably see themselves as sheep. If they recall the OT imagery, they may identify God or possibly a Davidic king as being their shepherd. Until they hear Jesus' declaration in 10:11, they may not regard Jesus as a shepherd.

Certainly we the readers are "present" and must acknowledge that we cannot remain neutral, impervious to Jesus' words. Spurred by the *paroimia*, we make inferences about the referents of the shepherd, sheep, and thief and stranger metaphors. From the prologue we know that Jesus is the preexistent Son, ever at the Father's bosom sent as light into the world to offer life. Perhaps we infer that Jesus is our shepherd even before 10:11. As sheep, we strain to hear his voice as he calls our names. We may even be eager to follow his lead. But we scan the horizon for possible thieves and strangers, ever ready to flee.

Portal (10:7–10)

Jesus resumes his discourse ("therefore Jesus again said" 10:7).[25] The self-declarative "I am" appears four times in this portion of the discourse. The first pair has the predicate "gate" (10:7, 9) and the second pair "good shepherd" (10:11, 14). Ball makes an insightful observation about each pair: "The first occurrences of each 'I am' saying in John 10 contrast Jesus with imposters. The second occurrence of each *egō eimi* ['I am'] saying is in terms of Jesus' relationship with his sheep and the benefits he gives them."[26] However, I would not consider the hired hand (10:12) an imposter because he cannot be expected to sacrifice for the sheep as the shepherd would. Yet, the idea of contrast is present.

Because Jesus immediately speaks of judgment (9:39) as the man worships (9:38), it is possible that the man and also the disciples are present during the subsequent discourse.

25. Instead of "again" a few papyri and Greek manuscripts feature "to them," a personal pronoun in the dative case. Other manuscripts including the majority from the Middle Ages support "to them" as a prepositional phrase. Only two papyri, the reading of one being somewhat uncertain, and a major fourth-century manuscript read "again." Hence, the attestation for "again" is shaky. The alternatives lessen the idea of continuation. However, the solemn "amen, amen" serves to tie 10:7 with the preceding. See Moloney, *Signs and Shadows*, 133.

26. Ball, *'I Am' in John's Gospel*, 95.

Character of the Disputants

At this point of the discourse, we have enough data to take a closer look at Jesus' disputants. The characterization of Jesus' audience, according to some writers, is limited to a "type" that possesses one distinguishable trait, that of misunderstanding[27] or unbelief.[28] As foils they would merely serve as plot devices. In the preceding exchange with the healed blind man, they had a more active role than in the current discourse where they are passive listeners. In fact, they dictate the juridical proceedings by summoning the healed man's parents (9:18) and the man a second time (9:24). I disagree with the assessment that there is not much in the way of character development for the Jews and Pharisees. There is a certain complexity to their portrait. I think that there is some change in them as they gradually become more hardened in their opposition to Jesus—in contrast to the healed blind man as he grows in his understanding and faith. In the second round of the juridical controversy, their irrational condemnation of Jesus, based on their interpretation of the law and utter disregard for the evidence of the healing, highlights their blindness even more clearly than before. Yet Jesus does not change his prognosis against them over the course of the controversy—"You will die in your sins" (8:21, 24) compared with "Your sin remains" (9:41). And they do not change in their resolve to kill Jesus over the course of their hardening (5:18; 7:19; 10:31; 11:51, 53).

The clearest characterization of Jesus' disputants comes from Jesus himself when he describes them. They are from the world below (8:23), and are murderers and liars in accord with their lineage (8:44). They have become blind and their sin remains (9:39, 41). Yet much of Jesus' characterization is by inference. In the present discourse, he does not identify the referents of his allegories—thief and robber (10:1), stranger (10:5), and hired hand (10:12). But because he addresses them as the intended audience, we the readers infer the correlation even if they themselves do not (cf. 9:40).

So what can we infer about the character of Jesus' dogged disputants? Give them credit; they are tenacious, conceding not an inch in the face of Jesus' and the healed man's irrefutable logic and argumentation.

---

27. Ibid., 96.
28. Culpepper, *Anatomy*, 126.

They have a logic all their own, derived from their law[29] (see 8:17; 10:34); that is, from their worldview. As false shepherds, in contrast to Jesus as the good shepherd, they plunder the sheep and are destructive (cf. Ezek 34:2–10). They harbor no genuine concern for the sheep's well-being. They are hostile strangers who do not know the sheep nor do the sheep know or follow them. Characterized by stealth and interested only in personal profit (inferred from the thief and hired hand metaphors), they flee at the first hint of danger. They rule by intimidation and fear (9:22). They are characterized by evil deeds, preferring the cloak of darkness and shunning the exposure of light (3:19–20). Jesus comes to give life, but they prefer death by way of preferring the bondage of sin (8:32, 34).

As we read this discourse, the Ezekiel imagery comes to mind and, by inference, we think of Jesus' disputants as shepherds, though delinquent in their duties. Their character becomes less flat and more round as we proceed in our reading of this juridical controversy. Irony taints their self-characterization when they smugly claim to be Moses' disciples (9:28), that Abraham is their father (8:33, 39), and that even God is their Father (8:41). Tragically, they neither understand nor are they willing to admit that Moses accuses them (5:45), that they have rejected God's witness of Jesus (5:37–38, 43), and that they have failed to obey the law that Moses gave them (7:19). There is also the inference that they themselves know that they are false shepherds in Jesus' *paroimia*, because of the manner by which they seek access to the sheep (10:3).[30] Thus, they are characterized by ulterior motives with regard to the sheep.

An interesting thought emerges when we note Jesus' identification of their father the devil (8:44). Tracing the use of the term "devil" and the related term "slander" in the OT, one uncovers the basic idea of accusation

---

29. I designate this term in the lowercase to distinguish it from the law as given by Moses, which actually testifies for Jesus (5:39) and which the Jews do not keep (7:19). Instead, the "law" connotes their interpretation of the law as Jesus makes clear by designating it "your law" (8:17; 10:34).

30. Carson supposes that the gatekeeper is a hired undershepherd (*Gospel according to John*, 382). Ridderbos regards a major function of the gatekeeper to be recognizing the shepherd as the rightful owner of the sheep (*Gospel according to John*, 355). By implication, no one else has rightful access through the gate. Hence, the only possible access is by illegitimate means. In the *paroimia*, the thief does not even bother using the gate, knowing as he does that the gatekeeper would not grant him entry. Thus, Jesus infers that his disputants know that they are not legitimate shepherds.

(usually false).[31] The related term "Satan" in the OT signifies *enemy* or *adversary*.[32] In Num 22:22, the angel (or messenger) of the Lord stood in Balaam's way as an adversary (satan) to oppose him on his mission. In the NT, the two terms "devil" and "Satan" appear to be interchangeable.[33] Again, the idea is accuser and adversary. The prevailing impression from scriptural usage pictures the devil as primarily opposing God, God's agenda, and God's people. Portrayed similarly in the Fourth Gospel, the Jews and Pharisees prove to be the true children of the devil. By this I mean they represent the chief opposition to Jesus in his mission and, in the juridical controversy, are Jesus' accusers.[34] They charge him with being unqualified to teach (7:15), a false witness about himself (8:13), demonized (8:48, 52; 10:20 depicts a divided assessment), a mere man (inferred in 8:57; 9:29), and a sinner (9:24).

During Jesus' absence for much of the second round of the juridical controversy, they oppose the healed blind man (9:24–34). There is a distinct difference between the two sessions they have with the man within round two. In the first session (9:15–18), they merely question the man, and in the end they do not believe that he qualifies as a witness for Jesus because they do not believe that he was formerly blind (9:18). But in the second session they change tactics by becoming adversarial (9:24–34). No longer able to deny the validity of the sign because of the parents' testimony (9:19–21), they are more aggressive. They place the man under a solemn oath to tell the truth—"give glory to God" (9:24b). But the truth must conform to their truth—"we know that this man is a sinner" (9:24c). In this second session, the man comes into his own as Jesus' surrogate in the juridical controversy. As the disputants had opposed Jesus earlier, so they now oppose the man who stands in Jesus' stead. They become the

---

31. In the LXX, Num 22:32; Prov 6:24; Sir 19:15; 26:5; 28:9; 38:17; 51:2, 6 for the noun "slander" (*diabolā*). 1 Chr 21:1; Esth 7:4; 1 Macc 1:36; Ps 108:6; Job 1:6–7, 9, 12; 2:1–4, 7; Wis 2:24; Zech 3:1–2 for *diabolos* or "devil." See Foerster on the OT use of the terms in "*diabolos*. Linguistic," 2:72–73. BDAG, 226–27.

32. Von Rad, "*diabolos*. The OT View of Satan," 2:73–75. BDAG, 916–17.

33. Foerster, "*diabolos*. The NT View of Satan," 2:79–81.

34. In the context of the ongoing juridical controversy, the Jews and the Pharisees oppose Jesus. However, in terms of Jesus' mission in the world, he, as the Son of Man, must be lifted up, that is be crucified, in order that everyone who believes in him may be saved (3:14–15). Then Jesus' juridical opponents unwittingly serve to facilitate his fulfilling his mission when they terminate the juridical controversy by referring him to Pilate for trial and subsequent condemnation (18:28–32).

man's adversary but, instead of hurling complaints against him, they still direct their accusations at Jesus. The healed man witnesses for Jesus and effectively rebuffs the charges.

The Jews and Pharisees are Jesus' adversary and accuse him falsely; thus, they are characterized as the devil incarnate, although the narrative offers no explicit statement to that effect. Rather, we infer this characterization from the circumstantial evidence. They are true to the character of their father, the devil, in their murderous intent and blasphemous slander of the one sent to reveal the Father above. They evolve into something more than merely a plot device. They represent the world in its hatred and persecution of Jesus (15:18–20). If Jesus calls Judas a devil because he will betray Jesus (6:70–71), we may safely infer that Judas's accomplices are devils (18:2–12).[35] Moreover, they are the ones who accuse Jesus before Pilate (18:28–30; 19:7, 12) and demand that he be crucified (19:15). In a cosmic sense, the devil is the personality behind the human opposition.[36] When Jesus forecasts that "the ruler of the world is coming" (14:30), the next movement in the narrative is the coming of the representatives of the chief priests and Pharisees led by Judas (18:2–12).

Characterization of Jesus as the Gate

As noted earlier, the first pair of "I am" declarations allude to Jesus as the gate of the sheepfold. The gate would probably be what Culpepper labels as an impersonal peripheral symbol.[37] "A symbol is an image, an action, or a person that is understood to have transcendent significance. In Johannine terms, symbols span the chasm between what is 'from above' and what is 'from below' without collapsing the distinction."[38] A core symbol, in contrast to a peripheral or supporting symbol, occurs more frequently and is found in more critical passages and carries the major

---

35. Strictly speaking the Jews, chief priests, and Pharisees do not personally arrest Jesus but their representatives. However, they are the authority behind the arrest.

36. The devil enters Judas (13:27) and the narrative states: "Therefore Jesus said to him, 'What you do, do quickly.'" The ambiguity of the pronoun "to him" creates uncertainty as to the identity of Jesus' addressee—Judas or Satan. Although Morris (*Gospel according to John*, 557) and Brown (*Gospel According to John*, 575) regard the antecedent as Judas, I think Satan can just as likely be the referent. Then the devil is portrayed as the operative principle residing within humans to prompt them in their opposition of Jesus.

37. Culpepper, *Anatomy*, 189.

38. Koester, *Symbolism in the Fourth Gospel*, 4.

responsibility of characterizing Jesus.[39] Culpepper identifies three core symbols—light, water, and bread.[40] Each may feature supporting symbols that help develop the core symbol more fully. There is some uncertainty as to whether the gate is a core or supporting symbol. On the one hand, the idea of access is also conveyed by Jesus' proclamation: "I am the way and the truth and the life" (14:6). This statement refers to Jesus being the access to the Father.[41] The disciples come to the Father through Jesus (14:2–7). However, the gate imagery appears to be overshadowed by the shepherd imagery (10:11–18).[42] Moreover, the entering into and going out of the fold (10:9) do not quite correspond to going to and staying in the Father's house (14:2–3; cf. 17:24). Hence, the image of the gate is probably a supporting symbol.

With Jesus as the gate, the sheep are to pass through in order to be saved and find pasture (10:9). They come into possession of abundant life (10:10). The benefits associated with this imagery raises a question as to which core symbol the gate supports—the light, the prevailing symbol of the context ("I am the light of the world" in 8:12 and 9:5, substantiated by the blind man's healing and the blindness of the Jews and Pharisees in 9:1–41) or the bread, with the attendant idea of sustenance for life (prominent in 6:5–70 and highlighted in 10:9).[43] The immediate context of 9:1—10:21 gives the nod to the light imagery. Then, the supporting gate symbol illustrates the healed blind man having access to Jesus, the object

---

39. Culpepper, *Anatomy*, 189. He provides a good discussion on symbolism (ibid., 180–98). For a book length treatment, refer to Koester's *Symbolism in the Fourth Gospel*.

40. Ibid. Koester adds the vine as a core symbol (ibid., 5).

41. Smith, *John*, 268–69.

42. Bruce, *Gospel of John*, 225. It seems a bit puzzling to have two seemingly unrelated symbols, the gate and shepherd, together. Perhaps it is wise to accept the mixing of different symbols even if an explanation is not readily apparent (Smith, *John*, 205–6). Carson simply notes that both have the same referent and leaves it at that (*Gospel according to John*, 384). However, Barrett opts for Christology as the unifying theme for the different images (*Gospel according to St. John*, 308).

43. The core symbols of light and bread are not mutually exclusive. Both have the same referent in Jesus and are designed to invoke faith in him or provoke unbelief (Painter, "Johannine Symbols," 31, 34–35). Both connote life (1:4; 6:33, 40, 47; 8:12) and a transcendence beyond the manna and the temple rite of light. Both are revelatory. Yet the symbols are not interchangeable—they have different functions (ibid., 36). Bread points to Jesus' flesh (Koester, *Symbolism in the Fourth Gospel*, 257–62). Light invites those in darkness to come to the light to be transformed and transfer association (Morris, *Gospel according to John*, 389–90).

of his worship (9:38). His sins are forgiven (cf. 9:41), and he represents those who come to the light in order for their deeds to be manifested (3:21). He is the sheep who hears Jesus' voice ("And you both see him and he is the one who speaks with you," 9:37).

The contrast with the thief (10:10) repeats 10:1. But earlier it is between the shepherd and thief; whereas later it is between the gate and the thief. The bases of the contrasts also differ—familiarity or lack of (10:3–5) versus benefits or dire consequences (10:10).

Thus, the thrust of Jesus' characterization as the gate portrays him as the means for obtaining the benefits he offers the sheep. The sheep on their part must recognize Jesus as their shepherd and pass through him. He alone is so characterized; for all his predecessors are thieves (10:8).

Good Shepherd (10:11–18)

Like the image of the gate, the good shepherd is a supporting symbol for the core symbol of the light. The second pair of "I am" declarations divides 10:11–18 into two subsections (10:11–13 and 10:14–18).[44] The concept of the shepherd laying down his life for the sheep dominates both subsections and defines what Jesus means by "good."[45]

In 10:11b, Jesus essentially defines what he means by "good shepherd" when he states: "The good shepherd lays down his life for the sheep." The proverbial statement expresses a universal truth. He infers that he will sacrifice himself for the sake of the sheep when he declares, "I am the good shepherd" (10:11a).[46] Interestingly, Jesus does not indicate directly his willingness for self-sacrifice. The audience must infer it. Jesus

---

44. Moloney suggests an alternative division of 10:7–13 and 10:14–18 based on Jesus' contrast with others as the gate and good shepherd (*Signs and Shadows*, 130). Brown separates the symbols and sections the verses thus: 10:7–10 (gate explanation), 10:11–16 (shepherd explanation), and 10:17–18 (laying down his life) (*Gospel According to John*, 393–99). However, I preserve the linguistic feature of the "I am" pairs following Ball, *'I Am' in John's Gospel*, 94.

45. Neyrey favors "noble" based on Greco-Roman concepts of honor and shame where the sacrificial death for the benefit of others was regarded a virtue ("Noble Shepherd," 267–91). But for a Jewish background, see Davies, "Reflections," 43–64. And the Johannine pattern of adjectives used in complementary distribution argues for "good" rather than "noble" (Gignac, "Use of Verbal Variety," 192).

46. Lindars treats the definite article generically and so translates the declaration "I am a good shepherd" in order to recognize the connotation of "good" as "ideal" (*Gospel of John*, 360–61).

employs a syllogism: (1) major premise: the good shepherd lays down his life for the sheep; (2) minor premise: Jesus is the good shepherd; (3) conclusion: Jesus lays down his life for the sheep. This syllogistic arrangement invokes thought on the part of the audience, who easily draws the proper conclusion. Here for the first time in the juridical controversy since the bread discourse (6:50–58) Jesus mentions his death. He intimates his approaching death not as demise (implying that his adversaries succeed in their murderous intentions, 5:18; 7:19; 8:59) but as a willing sacrifice characteristic of the good shepherd.[47] Following immediately upon his expressed mission ("I came that they have life and have it abundantly," 10:10b), Jesus signals the means by which he will accomplish his mission. He has come to give his sheep life abundantly by the laying down of his own life as the good shepherd.

A major rhetorical aspect of this discourse is inference, thereby engaging the audience in mental activity in order to connect the dots. Led to make their own conclusions, they would be more likely to accept the truth value of what has just been said, especially if the dots are viable. No one will challenge the proverb concerning the good shepherd. If they can accept Jesus' self-identification as the good shepherd, accepting the rest of the logic easily follows. Again, the crux of the discourse and the entire juridical controversy is Jesus' identity (the most important dot). Logos is made to serve ethos.

Then Jesus contrasts himself with the hired hand (10:12–13). Jesus' tactic is to portray himself positively and to tint that portrait with contrasting, negative elements. Positively, he is the good shepherd who goes through the gate of the sheepfold (10:2) and lays down his life for the sheep (10:11). He knows the sheep by name and they recognize his voice and follow him (10:3–4). Negatively, the contrast with the thief and stranger heightens the fact that Jesus does not come to steal and is not a stranger to the sheep. They trust him and he leads them. Not being the hired hand signifies that he cares for the sheep and will protect them from wolves, perhaps representing danger.

---

47. Some writers regard this self-sacrifice as an expression of love for the sheep. See Hendricksen, *Commentary*, 2. 112; Morris, *Gospel according to John*, 455; Barrett, *Gospel according to St. John*, 312. Although Jesus will teach about the greatest expression of love through laying down one's life for another (15:13), he does not mention love in the present discourse. It does not imply, however, that love is completely absent from the picture of the good shepherd; but rather that Jesus emphasizes obedience to the Father ("this commandment I received from my Father" 10:18). See Lindars, *Gospel of John*, 363.

Again by inference he condemns those who came before him, in the present situation his disputants, the Jews and the Pharisees, given the context of the juridical controversy. This concluding discourse commences with a specific indictment of sin against them (9:41) and follows with a totally negative portrayal of their character.

Then in 10:14a Jesus repeats the self-identification "I am the good shepherd" in order to infer intimate relationships. These relationships are characterized by a mutuality of familiarity. Jesus knows his own and they know him (10:14b). The relationship between the Father and Jesus (10:15a) functions as the pattern and basis for this mutuality of familiarity.[48] The mutuality with the Father prompts Jesus to lay down his life for the sheep (10:15b), a tacit reference to the Father's authority and the Son's submission. Twice Jesus characterizes his being the good shepherd with laying down his life for the sheep (10:11b, 15b).

The verbs "to know" and "to lay down" are in the present tense, suggesting emphasis. Jesus highlights the intimacy he enjoys with his flock and the sacrifice he will make for them. There may also be the connotation of an ongoing process of laying one's life down. Jesus may be continually sacrificial in shepherding his sheep, or be conscientiously heading to the cross during this juridical controversy. In an insightful study, O'Day examines the order or temporal sequence of the Farewell Discourse (John 13–17) and finds a shifting temporal landscape in which the crucifixion/resurrection/ascension is regarded sometimes as a past event and at other times as imminent or as yet future.[49] O'Day's findings apply to 10:15 where Jesus' death is future in narrative sequence but is viewed as a present reality.[50] Here Jesus connects his being the good shepherd with his impending death.

---

48. Carson correctly views the Father-Son intimacy as the grounds by which the shepherd-sheep intimacy is possible (*Gospel according to John*, 387). This perspective is consistent with Jesus' refrain that he can do nothing apart from the Father (5:19–21, 26–27, 30; 6:38–40; 7:16; 8:28–29, 40, 42).

49. O'Day, "I Have Overcome," 153–66.

50. O'Day's terminology renders 10:15 as an internal prolepsis, a future event fulfilled within the confines of the narrative, in contrast to an external prolepsis regarding a future event located beyond the end of the narrative in John 21 (ibid., 154–55). She cites Culpepper for his more complex categorization of temporal sequence (*Anatomy*, 54–70). Both O'Day ("I Have Overcome," 154) and Culpepper (*Anatomy*, 63) see 10:15 as proleptic.

The emphasis on Jesus' death (10:11, 15, 17, 18 twice) in this discourse, which is within round two of the juridical controversy, suggests that in some sense his death is judgmental. Not only does his death result in life for his sheep (10:10–11, 14), but it has repercussions for his disputants. When Jesus announces the arrival of his hour of glorification (12:23), an allusion to his death (cf. 12:24–25),[51] there is a corresponding pronouncement of judgment upon the world and the ruler of the world (12:31).

The reference to other sheep (10:16) may be an allusion to Gentile believers.[52] The future tense "they will hear" and "they will become" that look beyond the Fourth Gospel's story line support that possible identification.[53] This anticipation gives credence to the familiar 3:16 in which "world" assumes universal significance. The reference to one flock and one shepherd appears to point to the formation of a new community in which there is "neither Jew or Greek."[54] This, then, is Jesus' ultimate objective as shepherd. The indictment against his audience may be twofold—condemnation for failing to be good shepherds and exclusion from the new flock or community.

Jesus then highlights the means for accomplishing his objective of forming the new community—laying down his life in order that he may take it back again (10:17)—the crucifixion and resurrection. Because he fulfills his objective, the Father loves him. He is ever pleasing to the Father who sent him (8:29). The negative connotation is that in opposing him his disputants are really opposing the Father; for in opposing his work they oppose the Father's purpose for sending the Son. Here then is a strong indictment. But do the disputants understand the indictment; can they?

---

51. Moloney, *Signs and Shadows*, 188; and Lincoln, *Gospel according to Saint John*, 349. Carson includes Jesus' resurrection and exaltation (ascension) (*Gospel according to John*, 437).

52. Ibid., 388; Barrett, *Gospel according to St. John*, 312; Brown, *Gospel According to John*, 396; and Morris, *Gospel according to John*, 455. Later Brown seems to have changed positions by positing the merging of the Johannine Christians with a high Christology and the church of the apostles ("Other Sheep Not of This Fold," 5–22). But his view is highly speculative as he himself admits.

53. There is no explicit time idea embedded in the future tense of Greek as there would be in English. Rather, the tense expresses expectation or intention. See Porter, *Verbal Aspect*, 404–17. Jesus intends to gather all the sheep into one flock.

54. Bruce, *Gospel of John*, 228.

Earlier Jesus posed a riddle (8:21): "I am going and you will seek me, but you will die in your sins. Where I am going, you cannot go." The Jews replied (8:22b), "He is not going to kill himself is he?" Looking back, a number of thoughts emerge from the vantage point of the shepherd discourse. First, Jesus is already anticipating his death, and that is not surprising because the cross is central to his mission. Second, he speaks metaphorically about his death in his "going." Ironically, the Jews come close to understanding what Jesus meant. He will die, but he will not be a helpless victim because he will lay down his life. He will not commit suicide as they infer. In the present discourse Jesus speaks plainly about his death. Why does he shift from figurative language to direct speech? A possible reason is that he embeds his explicit reference to his death within the shepherd symbol. Otherwise there would be a metaphor within a symbol, thereby making it quite confusing. The significance of the shepherd characterization is his laying down his life for the sheep. It is not a potential, merely a willingness to die.[55] Jesus' death substantiates his identification as the good shepherd.[56] In 8:21, through the use of a riddle, Jesus excludes the Jews from the inner circle of those who understand and accept his identity. In the present incidence, Jesus uses clear language to identify himself in his role as shepherd. Third, in saying that the Jews cannot go where he is going (8:21), Jesus alludes to their failure as shepherds. They are thieves, strangers, or hired hands, but not shepherds. They will not lay their lives down for the sheep; he will. Fourth, ironically they will die in their sins (8:21); but he will die for the sheep. The contrast is complete when he declares, "that I may take it [his life] again" (10:17c). Although he dies, yet he will live. Their fate, however, is irreversible.

In 10:18 Jesus emphasizes the authority he received from the Father to lay down his life on his own terms and to reclaim it again. This is the

---

55. In commenting about 10:11, Carson notes that the laying down of one's life for the sheep "means no more than that he is prepared to do so" in the metaphorical world (*Gospel according to John*, 386). However, there is no contingency in 10:11. There is no "he lays down his life if necessary." It is a matter-of-fact statement: "the good shepherd lays down his life for the sheep." The implication is clear—the good shepherd *will* lay his life down.

56. Larsen writes that the "I am" statements are token-telling events compared to signs that are token-showing (*Recognizing the Stranger*, 148). In saying "I am the good shepherd," Jesus presupposes a previously defined identity familiar to his audience, which is based on imagery from Jewish tradition infused with innovation to describe his thematic role (pp. 149–50).

other aspect of his being the good shepherd. The reference to "this commandment I received from my Father" points to the Father's will and purpose for which Jesus is sent into the world.[57] Jesus' authority is the Father's commissioning. In the exercise of that authority, Jesus shows himself obedient.

Jesus' rhetorical intent becomes clear as he affirms his relationship with the Father. Jesus defines his identity by his relationship with the Father. Thus, anyone opposing Jesus opposes the Father. In this way, Jesus places his disputants outside of the Father's will and purpose. Through the use of repetition Jesus makes his point emphatically. The negative statement "no one takes it from me" is repeated positively with "I lay it down of myself" and "I have authority to lay it down." And 10:18 repeats 10:17 but adds the concept of authority and the Father's commandment. The idea of death and resurrection originates with the Father. Jesus obediently complies as the Father's agent. Then 10:18 functions to explain 10:15a ("the Father knows me and I know the Father"). The mutuality of knowing one another is seen in the Father making known his will to Jesus and Jesus obeying the Father's will. The mutuality of knowing found in the Father-Son relationship serves as the grounds for the shepherd-sheep relationship, and so the shepherd makes known his will to the sheep and they obey.

In light of the contrast between the good shepherd and hired hand in 10:11–13, 10:14–18, Jesus infers that the contrast extends to knowing and obeying the Father and not knowing nor obeying. Thus, 10:11–18 further defines Jesus' identity and condemns his disputants. And because his identity is the crux of the entire dispute, 10:11–18 is polemical.

Aftermath (10:19–21)

Jesus' discourse immediately spawns a schism among the Jews (10:19), recalling the earlier schism among the Pharisees over Jesus' signs (9:16). Hence, both signs and Jesus' words have a similar effect—demanding a decision about him and his claims. Many demonize him (10:20). But others do not, saying that his words do not reflect demonization because he healed a blind man (10:21). They grant Jesus' words credibility because of the sign. Although opinion about Jesus is divided, there will be a closing

---

57. Bruce, *Gospel of John*, 229.

of ranks, as before. Soon the Jews will present a united front against Jesus, as did the Pharisees (cf. 12:42–43).

As readers, we expect the juridical controversy to continue unabated until the trial before Pilate (18:28—19:16). The disputation increased in intensity as it entered round two, with the second Sabbath healing and conflict. Both disputants remain adamant in their respective positions, with neither willing to concede anything to the other. Jesus indicts his opponents with a condemnatory discourse (9:41—10:18). His sign and words provoke a division among his disputants, but only temporarily.

We know that Jesus will prove faithful in completing his mission, for he is the good shepherd who lays down his life for the sheep. He has the authority to do so and the authority to retrieve his life. He will obey to the very end. For this reason the Father loves him.

As his sheep, we can have full confidence in our shepherd. Although this concluding discourse is polemical in its address to Jesus' opponents, it nonetheless conveys assurance and hope to his sheep who hear these same words. As we conclude our reading of 9:1—10:21, we ask reflective questions. Do I hear and recognize Jesus' voice and follow his lead? Have I full assurance of receiving his blessings? Do I discern the dissenting voices of false shepherds and do not follow them? What does Jesus' death and resurrection mean to me and in what tangible ways do they apply?

In the concluding chapter that follows, we will explore the implications of these questions and also the symbolism of the blind man who gains his sight.

13

End of One Story, Beginning of Another

In previous chapters we traced the story of a man born blind and followed his progress to spiritual insight, which was prompted by his receiving of physical sight. His journey coincides with the largest portion of narrative in the Fourth Gospel that features Jesus' absence. With the benefit of hindsight we realize that the man has to navigate through some treacherous waters alone in order to deepen his understanding of and faith in the one who healed him. The man's story is part of a larger story of Jesus' juridical controversy with the Jews and, at other times, with the Pharisees. The point of contention is Jesus' identity. He claims to have been sent from above by the Father. They dispute his claim. We place the two loci of this controversy at two Sabbath healings. By the time Jesus brings the blind man into the controversy, the Jews are already seeking to kill Jesus for blasphemy and an earlier Sabbath violation: healing the lame man. Healing the blind man on another Sabbath exacerbates the existing disputation that remains unresolved until the cross.

In the disputation, Jesus always maneuvers into a superior position through irrefutable argumentation, augmented by undeniable signs. Jesus' absence at a critical juncture of the juridical controversy thrusts the healed blind man to the forefront of the dispute, directly into the path of Jesus' opponents. The healed blind man functions as a witness at first, but his role evolves into that of a disputant. He manages to hold his inquisitors at bay and moreover succeeds in gaining the upper hand, much like Jesus had done earlier. Hence, we sense that the man serves as Jesus' surrogate in the disputation. The opponents charge Jesus as a sinner. But the man proves that Jesus must be from God.

THE MEASURE OF A MAN

The story's characterization of the healed blind man captures our interest and stirs our imagination. He begins life as a colorless agent, merely a plot device. Simply introduced as congenitally blind, he serves as a prop for the disciples' question about retributive justice: who sinned that he was born blind, this man or his parents? Answering in the negative, Jesus quickly elevates the blind man to being a platform on which the works of God may be manifested. The blind man is still an agent, but one who spurs our anticipation of something wonderful. When the man returns from washing his eyes of the mud Jesus applied, he sees—thereby stunning all who knew him before.

The now seeing man progresses upward along a continuum of characterization, and in so doing becomes a type. He witnesses Jesus' ability to heal and testifies matter-of-factly. He offers no embellishments, only the truth. His acquaintances and later the Pharisees question him about the sign. He answers to the best of his ability, although he is hampered by a limited understanding of Jesus' identity. But as the exchanges continue, his appreciation of Jesus grows—regarding him first as a man, then as a prophet, and finally as someone who comes from God to perform something no one else in history has ever done. In spite of the intense pressure from his interlocutors to deny both his healing and Jesus, the man refuses to budge. He will not compromise on his perspective on the truth. So the character of this man is measured by the degree of his transparency. He has no hidden agenda. Simply and straightforwardly, he answers people's questions.

As the exchanges continue, his character evolves further toward being full-fledged or rounded. His portrait acquires complexity. We grow in our appreciation of his integrity and courage. He will not back down even if others, including his parents, do. We realize too that he is a reflective sort who capably weighs the evidence and draws logical conclusions. He knows history, insofar that he recognizes he is unique: he knows that he is the first congenitally blind person to gain sight. And he realizes that this makes Jesus very special, probably greater than all the prophets of old. We also acknowledge that the healed man has astute perception into his inquisitors' agenda; and his ability to parry effectively in verbal sword play gains our admiration. His mental agility is unhampered by theological presuppositions, something that encumbers his disputants. He can be sarcastic, and he taunts them for their baseless accusations against Jesus. In the end, we find that Jesus' gambit of disappearing and leaving the man to face his interlocutors alone accomplishes two things—the man grows in spiritual perception and he effectively represents Jesus in the juridical controversy. As a talking sign, he embodies Jesus' declaration "I am the light of the world" in that he transforms from blindness to sight, thereby becoming a sign to Jesus' sign. Because no one else witnessed his healing, he testifies to the fact of the sign, and so in a sense becomes a second sign. Jesus pronounced a plurality of signs to be accomplished in the man. There is the external healing of the physical eyes to see the things in the world. There is the internal healing of the spiritual eyes to see in a new way Jesus who is from above. When people see him and hear his story, Jesus' signs (plural) confront them.

The man's portrait is paradoxical. For the purpose of telling the story of Jesus and his juridical controversy with his accusers, the man's portrait effectively fulfills its appointed role. But as readers conditioned by modern analytical studies into a person's psyche, we are left dissatisfied. We want more. There are gaps in his portrait—no physical descriptions and mannerisms are given. Surely he possesses other virtues or even vices, we think. Born blind, we surmise that he is uneducated; and, being a beggar, he probably lived at the periphery of society. Most likely he is a loner—who would befriend him? His parents are still living; but what kind of family life and dynamic do they share? The parents virtually abandon him during the disputation; so we suppose that perhaps they don't really love him. Or we suspect that their fear of being cast out of the synagogue outweighs any allegiance they may harbor for their son. Understandably, he may be upset with or bitter toward them. If he is, it does not affect his performance as a disputant in Jesus' stead. But we still ask, why him? Other than his congenital blindness, what does Jesus discern in him that would make him not only a witness but an effective disputant? We infer that Jesus knows what is in man and, in the case of the blind man, Jesus sees potential.

Perhaps, in the overall scheme of things, it does not matter how we answer all these questions. Simply, the example set by the healed blind man teaches us that the important thing is to fulfill the role Jesus has thrust us into. Complete your designated mission. Speak up for Jesus.

Grow in your faith. Gain spiritual depth and perception through the experiences of your life, both pleasant and painful.

But there is more. There are certain irreducible elements in character that we can take away from this incomplete portrait of the healed blind man. Everything else is relative and somewhat secondary. One character irreducibility requires us to reflect on our life experiences and continually challenge ourselves by asking, what can I affirm or learn about Jesus from this or that? Our growth in faith and understanding is both experiential and mental. Faith is not just a matter of the heart; it also involves the mind. Reminiscent of an investigative reporter, the healed man gathers all the available evidence, shifts and analyzes, weeds out extraneous data, and synthesizes and draws logical conclusions. He carefully and resolutely bases his convictions on those conclusions. Tough-minded and uncompromising, he resists sentimentality, personal preferences, and the lobbying of others for some pet ideology. With a passion for the truth, he permits only Scripture and sanctified reasoning to shape his worldview in properly processing his experiences. In sum, he is a critical thinker. Only when he accomplishes all of this can he assure the validity of his faith. Similarly, we must be hard-nosed disciples pursuing the contemplative life, giving careful thought as we refine our personal ideology.

Another irreducible element reveals that the testing of our faith may be a juridical controversy. A familiar axiom states that although we live in the world, we ought not to compromise our truth convictions because of the world's take on the truth. There will be ideological clashes between two parties—I and the world. We intentionally think *I* because that mirrors the healed blind man's situation—just two participants, he and his disputants. No one else becomes his ally in his hour of testing. Even Jesus, it seems, desists. The collective, a faceless mass of opposition, operates as one. The healed man is forced to formulate his own convictions alone, given only the available evidence. He does not confer first with his friends (if he has any) to see what they believe before he determines what he believes. He comes to his own conclusions and stands firm by them before the collective. The juridical controversy is *I against the world* (represented by the Jews and Pharisees).

Yet another irreducible element instructs: whatever my starting point (in a real sense everyone starts at the same point), I am not so handicapped that I cannot be ennobled. There is no place for self-pity. Woe is me. I come from a dysfunctional family. God did not endow me with gifts of intellect or athletic prowess or natural wit and charm, or any of a host of other "blessings." The former blind beggar shows us that our perceived lack need not deter us if we do not allow it to do so. The blind man's spiritual condition at the start reflects our starting condition—darkness; that is, a deficiency in spiritual life and vitality, and alienation from God. The good news is that we do not need to remain lost in the void. The gaps in the narrative's portrayal of the blind man invites us to caricaturise him any way we want. He can be loquacious or laconic, dignified or zany, laudable for good habits or deplorable for bad, sanguine or melancholic. In brief, he can be anyone or everyone. He can be us; we can be him. We all have a starting point and we all have potential to become what God wants us to become.

A fourth irreducible element reminds us that we are sheep, and that Jesus is our good shepherd. Jesus has already laid his life down for us, and he has taken it back and now lives. We can hear and recognize his voice. He leads; we follow. Others may be thieves, strangers, or the hired hand. We don't follow them. The shepherd-sheep imagery is deeply relational, mirrored by and grounded in the relationship between the Father and the Son. There is to be a mutuality of knowing our shepherd as he knows us. As the healed blind man demonstrates, our relational knowledge ought to be ever growing and our perception of Jesus ever clarifying.

THE JOURNEY

Movement gives any story its edge. There has to be plot development. The healed blind man functions as a reference point by which we detect movement. He is moving. There are two primary indicators that demonstrate this movement. An internal indicator measures his development in his spiritual perception and insight as he grows in his understanding of Jesus' identity. His interlocutors personify a relatively stationary external indicator as they remain static in their grasp of Jesus' identity. The man passes them by on his way to enlightenment. They, on the other hand, if possible, are moving away from Jesus, deeper into darkness.

As we trace the man's movement, we trace his journey of faith as well as the change in the vitality of his spiritual condition. Our study of this man becomes a quest, not a literary one but a personal one. His story invites us to evaluate our journey. What is the state of our faith and our spiritual health? Are we moving closer to Jesus?

The man symbolizes the prevailing human condition in the world. Born blind, he dwells in darkness—helpless to remedy his situation on his own. He begs, and whatever others give only helps him survive in his condition. Nothing changes until Jesus takes the initiative and enters into his life. The man cannot see Jesus, indicative of his blindness. Jesus speaks and the man hears his voice. But the man does not recognize Jesus—not yet. Before the man moves forward, we must understand something about his condition. God is not punishing him for either his or his parents' sin. Rather, he is a candidate for the works of God to be manifested, and thereby showcases the truth that Jesus is the light of the world. He will glorify Jesus. There is no place for a victim mentality—God is not out to get him; God is not angry with him.

Next, Jesus anoints the man's sightless eyes with mud and instructs him to go wash in the pool of Siloam (literally meaning "sent one"). Anointing speaks of authority and divine prerogative. The man obeys, but how he manages to reach the pool while still blind befuddles us. The story gap leaves us guessing for possible solutions. He goes alone without someone leading him there, obedient and determined. He may stumble or even get a little lost, but he gets there.

Movement happens when Jesus enters and does something to a person. More importantly, Jesus speaks. His words and action start the process. He points to the man as being the venue for a God-event and declares, "I am the light of the world." Then the person responds. Either he takes the pronouncement as a cruel taunt—you're the light of the world and I'm blind, yeah right—or he embraces hope for perhaps the first time in his life. His immediate compliance informs us of his initial decision about Jesus.

Upon receiving his sight, the healed blind man becomes a witness of a sign. His acquaintances, no doubt shocked when they meet him, wonder whether it is really him. He assures them that he's the same beggar they all know. But now he sees. Naturally they pry him with questions. He tells them what he knows and has experienced. That is all he can do. He does not go beyond his grasp of the truth.

We may wonder about their reaction to the healing. The narrative glosses over that aspect. Perhaps the man jumps joyfully, celebrating and praising God. His acquaintances may join in. All we know is what the story depicts. The crowd ask, is it really you; and how? The man simply answers. The exchange certifies that a miraculous healing actually occurred. They can testify to his former condition; he can testify to how it happened. Everyone is a witness. The plot moves all of them into their respective roles.

In a seemingly innocuous move, they take him to the Pharisees. Informed by the narrative that Jesus heals him on the Sabbath, we suspect ulterior motives, given the confrontation the Jews had with Jesus in a previous Sabbath healing of the lame man. The story omits the rationale for bringing the now seeing man to the religious authorities. We surmise that this action resumes the juridical controversy. Having fulfilled their role, the man's acquaintances cease to be active (whether they remain or depart is unimportant).

In his first session with the Pharisees, he answers their questions as he had done for his acquaintances earlier. He is still a witness to a sign. But the juridical controversy intensifies because of a perceived second Sabbath violation. The Jews do not believe the man's story. Sceptical, they summon the man's parents who affirm his former condition. Unable to deny the fact of the healing, they summon the man a second time. This time they play hardball and demand on oath that he agree that Jesus is a sinner. At this juncture the man transcends his role as witness and becomes a disputant in Jesus' defense. No longer does he simply provide facts to their query. He meets their accusations head-on when he states undeniable evidence to expose their charges as groundless. Jesus healed his congenital blindness, a first-of-its-kind accomplishment in Jewish history. The man counters their professed ignorance of Jesus' origin with a taunt and perhaps a sneer: "How can you not know Jesus' origin since he healed me? He is obviously from God or else he can do nothing." The man's logic and argument prove irrefutable. His opponents raise no effective counter and are thus reduced to hurling verbal abuse and kicking him out of the synagogue. However, he is no martyr. Getting kicked out is the best thing that can happen to him. They do him a favor. No longer shackled to the synagogue and the attendant Judaism that is ill prepared to believe in Jesus, the man freely forges new relationships and enters into a new community.

Progressively the man advances in his understanding of Jesus' identity through this arduous process. The man actually needs the interaction with the Pharisees and Jews to grow. He seems to sense a new relationship forming with Jesus; he is becoming a disciple. The Jews and Pharisees confirm it overtly: "You are a disciple of that man." Beyond the point of turning back, the healed blind man seizes the moment to teach them. Imagine, a former beggar, uneducated in matters of the law, lecturing the religious leadership on Jewish ideology. He has definitely come a long way, even surpassing their understanding of the law, which he recognizes as pointing to Jesus.

But there is yet a further step he must take after being cast out. Jesus finds him and asks, "Do you believe in the Son of Man?" The man answers with a question of his own, "Who is he, sir, that I may believe in him?" Although the man professes Jesus, he does not know him by face. Jesus' subsequent answer delineates two aspects of recognition—sight and voice. The man sees Jesus and hears him speak. The title Son of Man signifies the revelation of God in Jesus. To see and hear Jesus is tantamount to seeing and hearing God. Hence, this step is recognition of the person of Jesus. Upon taking this step in faith, the man worships him. And in worshipping Jesus, the healed man worships God.

The man now fades from the narrative with no further role to assume. But is that the end of his story? Previously in chapter 9, I adapted Kysar's diagram that maps a person's progression from embryonic or initial faith to mature faith. There may be the experience of a sign along the way, as in the case of the healed blind man, that nurtures a sign-based faith; or there may be none. But everyone, including the healed blind man, must receive the Spirit in order to attain mature faith. With a less than mature faith, he still recognizes and worships Jesus. But what he yet lacks, the Spirit of truth provides. The Spirit guides the disciples into all the truth (16:13) by receiving from Jesus all that the Father has first given to him and then giving it to the disciples (16:14–15).

In his shepherd discourse, Jesus speaks of leading the sheep out of the fold and of leading other sheep in. He does so in order to form one flock with him as their shepherd. He also speaks of being the gate through which the sheep find pasture and obtain life abundantly. From Jesus' very words we infer that the healed blind man and all the disciples, including those like Mary, Martha, and Lazarus who are not explicitly called disciples, come together to form one flock. This flock will receive the Spirit when Jesus returns to the Father (cf. 14:16–17; 16:5–7). The Spirit's advent paves the way for the disciples to understand all the truth Jesus intends for them to receive (16:13). But until the Spirit comes, they cannot absorb all the truth (16:12). Hence, the disciples cannot attain mature faith until the Spirit's advent and ministry to them, located beyond the story line.

End of One Story, Beginning of Another   173

So the now seeing man awaits mature faith when he fades from the juridical controversy. He receives three faith-boosters along the way—the sign of his gaining sight, the interaction with the Jews and Pharisees, and the second meeting and worship of Jesus. The interaction with the religious leaders, though grievous, clarifies the man's understanding about Jesus and his relationship with Jesus. The man now awaits a fourth faith-booster in the person of the Holy Spirit as the following diagram depicts.

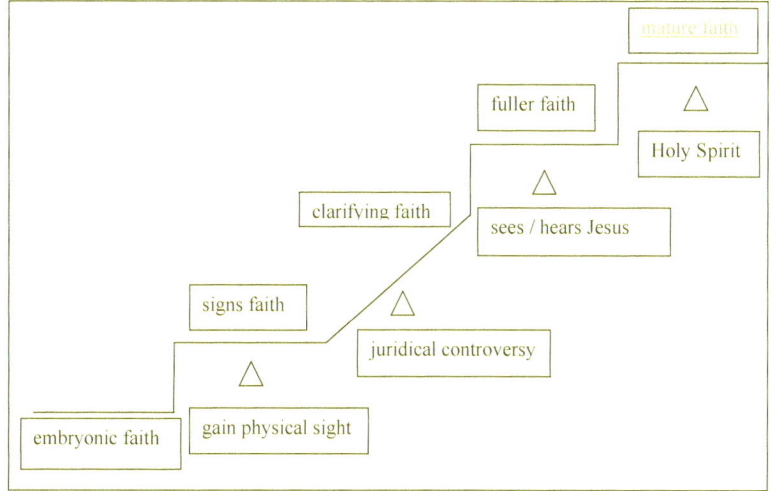

Figure 2. Healed Man's Faith Trajectory

He shows embryonic or initial faith when he obeys Jesus' instruction to go wash his eyes at the pool of Siloam. Jesus perceives this faith as he walks by and "sees a man blind from birth" (9:1). Upon gaining physical sight the man soon becomes a witness with a signs-based faith. Through the course of his interaction with the religious authorities, he gradually deepens in faith with regard to Jesus' identity and origin. The sloped line labelled "clarifying faith" in this diagram serves to portray the man's gradual advance from witness to disputant. He then acquires fuller faith upon seeing and hearing Jesus, and expresses that faith in worship. The final step of mature faith, however, awaits Jesus' departure and return to the Father, and the subsequent advent of the Spirit of truth. The diagram, then, maps the healed man's trajectory toward mature faith based on the Johannine depiction of faith.

Not everyone, of course, follows the man's exact path. There are parallels though. What marks the healed blind man's uniqueness in this

Fourth Gospel is his role in the juridical controversy. No other disciple faces such opposition within the confines of the story. However, they too will face the world's hatred and suffer persecution in the future (15:18–27). We learn of persecution's effectiveness in spurring growth from the man's example. So we understand the divine purpose for our facing the world's confrontation.

In reviewing the man's journey, we become better prepared to embark on our trajectory toward mature faith. Born in the world of darkness, we too are blind in that we do not know Jesus and are alienated from God. God takes the initiative and inserts himself in our lives to begin the journey. He did that with me. The Lord prompted a coworker to witness to me for Jesus.

We in turn can be a witness if we look at a person, see a potential sheep, and introduce him or her to the light of the world. There may not be a God-experience akin to a Johannine sign, but everyone can see and hear Jesus. The good shepherd calls each sheep by name and the sheep recognizes his voice. A person may encounter Jesus through the Scriptures. He once said (5:39), "You search the Scriptures because you think that you may have eternal life by them. And they bear witness concerning me." Later he added (6:63b): "The words which I have spoken to you are spirit and life." Jesus' words are "the product of the life-giving Spirit" and when the words are "rightly understood and absorbed, generate life."[1]

Because we live in the post-ascension period, the Spirit comes and guides us into all the truth; so we can grow to mature faith now. We do not need to wait for the Spirit. We become part of the one flock under the one shepherd. The immediate implication is that we are no longer "of the world," and we will experience the world's hatred and may even be persecuted (15:18–21). But we are to hearken to Jesus' final words to the disciples before his arrest (16:33): "I have spoken these things to you in order that you may have peace in me. In the world you have tribulation. But take courage, I have overcome the world."

---

1. Carson, *Gospel according to John*, 302. He cites 5:24, "Truly, truly I say to you, 'The one who hears my word and believes in the one who sent me has eternal life and he does not go into judgment, but he has passed out of death into life.'"

Bibliography

Alter, Robert. *The Art of Biblical Narrative*. New York: Basic Books, 1981.
"Are Singapore teachers overworked?" No pages. Online: http://sgforums.com/forums/2297/topics/399658?page=1.
Ashton, John. "The Identity and Function of the ΊΟΥΔΑΙΟΙ in the Fourth Gospel." *NovT* 27 (1985) 40–75.
———. *Understanding the Fourth Gospel*. Oxford: Clarendon, 1991.
Asiedu-Peprah, Martin. *Johannine Sabbath Conflicts as Juridical Controversy*. Tübingen, Ger.: Mohr Siebeck, 2001.
Bach, Alice. "Signs of the Flesh: Observations on Characterization in the Bible." *Semeia* 63 (1993) 61–79.
Ball, David M. *'I Am' in John's Gospel: Literary Function, Background and Theological Implications*. JSNTSup 124. Sheffield, UK: Sheffield Academic Press, 1996.
Barrett, C. K. *The Gospel according to St. John: An Introduction with Commentary and Notes on the Greek Text*. Reprint ed. London: Society for Promoting Christian Knowledge, 1970.
Barthes, Roland. *S/Z: An Essay*. Translated by Richard Miller. New York: Hill & Wang, 1974.
Bauer, Walter, W. F. Arndt, and F. W. Gingrich. *A Greek-English Lexicon of the New Testament and Other Early Christian Literature*. Revised and edited by F. W. Danker. Third ed. Chicago: University of Chicago Press, 2000.
Beck, David R. "The Narrative Function of Anonymity in Fourth Gospel Characterization." *Semeia* 63 (1993) 143–58.
Berlin, Adele. *Poetics and Interpretation of Biblical Narrative*. Reprint ed. Winona Lake, IN: Eisenbrauns, 1994.
Black, C. Clifton. "'The Words That You Gave to Me I Have Given to Them': The Grandeur of Johannine Rhetoric." In *Exploring the Gospel of John: In Honor of D. Moody Smith*, 220–39. Louisville, KY: Westminster John Knox, 1996.
Blass, F., A. Debrunner, and Robert W. Funk. *A Greek Grammar of the New Testament and Other Early Christian Literature*. Reprint ed. Chicago: University of Chicago Press, 1974.
Blofeld, John. *I Ching: The Book of Change*. London: George Allen & Unwin, 1976.
Blomberg, Craig L. *The Historical Reliability of John's Gospel*. Leicester, UK: InterVarsity, 2001.
———. *Interpreting the Parables*. Downers Grove, IL: InterVarsity, 1990.

Borgen, Peder. "God's Agent in the Fourth Gospel." In *Religions in Antiquity: Essays in Memory of Erwin Ramsdell Goodenough*, 137–48. Edited by Jacob Neusner, Studies in the History of Religions 14. Leiden, Neth.: E. J. Brill, 1968.

Braille Works. "Famous People with Visual Impairments." No pages. Online: http://www.brailleworks.com/Resources/FamousPeoplewithVisualImpairments.aspx.

Brodie, Thomas L. *The Gospel According to John: A Literary and Theological Commentary*. Oxford: Oxford University Press, 1993.

Brown, Raymond E. *The Community of the Beloved Disciple*. New York: Paulist, 1979.

———. *The Gospel According to John: Introduction, Translation, and Notes*. AB 29, 29A. Garden City, NY: Doubleday, 1966, 1970.

———. *An Introduction to the New Testament*. New York: Doubleday, 1996.

———. "'Other Sheep Not of This Fold': The Johannine Perspective on Christian Diversity in the Late First Century." *JBL* 97 (1978) 5–22.

———. "The Prologue of the Gospel of John." *RevExp* 62 (1965) 429–39.

Bruce, F. F. *The Gospel of John: Introduction, Exposition and Notes*. Reprint ed. Grand Rapids, MI: Eerdmans, 1984.

Burchard, C. "*Ei* nach einem Ausdruck des Wissens oder Nichtwissens: Joh 9:25; Act 19:2; 1Cor 1:16; 7:16." *ZNW* 52 (1961) 73–82.

Burnett, Fred W. "Characterization and Reader Construction of Characters in the Gospels." *Semeia* 63 (1993) 3–78.

Campbell, Constantine R. *Basics of Verbal Aspect in Biblical Greek*. Grand Rapids, MI: Zondervan, 2008.

Carlston, Charles E. "Parable and Allegory Revisited: An Interpretive Review." *CBQ* 43 (1981) 228–42.

Carson, D. A., Douglas J. Moo, and Leon Morris. *An Introduction to the New Testament*. Grand Rapids, MI: Zondervan, 1992.

Carson, Donald A. *The Gospel according to John*. Grand Rapids, MI: Eerdmans, 1991.

Carter, Warren. "The Prologue and John's Gospel: Function, Symbol, and the Definitive Word," *JSNT* 39 (1990) 35–58.

Charlesworth, James H. "Introduction for the General Reader." In *Apocalyptic Literature and Testaments*, xxi–xxxiv. In *The Old Testament Pseudepigrapha* 1. Edited by James H. Charlesworth. Garden City, NY: Doubleday, 1983.

Chatman, Seymour. *Story and Discourse: Narrative Structure in Fiction and Film*. Ithaca, NY: Cornell University Press, 1978.

Clines, David J. A. "The Shape and Argument of the Book of Job." In *Sitting with Job: Selected Studies on the Book of Job*, 125–39. Edited by Roy B. Zuck. Grand Rapids, MI: Baker Book House, 1992.

Cohen, Shaye J. D. *From the Maccabees to the Mishnah*. Second ed. Louisville, KY: Westminster John Knox, 2006.

Collins, John J. *The Scepter and the Star: The Messiahs of the Dead Sea Scrolls and Other Ancient Literature*. New York: Doubleday, 1995.

Collins, Raymond F. "From John to the Beloved Disciple." *Int* 49 (1995) 359–69.

———. "The Representative Figures of the Fourth Gospel." *DRev* 94 (1976) 26–46, 118–32.

———. *These Things Have Been Written: Studies on the Fourth Gospel*. Louvain, Bel.: Peeters, 1990.

Coogan, Michael D. *The Old Testament: A Historical and Literary Introduction to the Hebrew Scriptures*. Oxford: Oxford University Press, 2006.

Cook, Michael J. "The Gospel of John and the Jews." *RevExp* 84 (1987) 259–71.
"A Course in Miracles: Lesson 61: I am the light of the world." No pages. Online: http://acim.org/Lessons/lesson.html?lesson=61.
"A Course in Miracles: Lesson 271. Section 6. What is the Christ?" No pages. Online: http://acim.org/Lessons/lesson.html?lesson=271.
Cousland, J. R. C. "Tobit: A Comedy in Error?" *CBQ* 65 (2003) 535–53.
Coxe, A. Cleveland. *The Apostolic Fathers with Justin Martyr and Irenaeus: Chronologically Arranged with Brief Notes and Prefaces*. In *The Ante-Nicene Fathers* 1. Edited by Alexander Roberts and James Donaldson. American reprint. Grand Rapids, MI: Eerdmans, 1993.
Culpepper, R. Alan. *The Anatomy of the Fourth Gospel: A Study in Literary Design*. Philadelphia: Fortress, 1983.
———. "Cognition in John: The Johannine Signs as Recognition Scenes." *PRSt* 35 (2008) 251–60.
———. "The Gospel of John as a Document of Faith in a Pluralistic Culture." In *"What is John?" Readers and Readings of the Fourth Gospel*, 107–27. JBL Symposium Series 3. Edited by Fernando F. Segovia. Atlanta: Scholars, 1996.
Dana, H. E., and Julius R. Mantey. *A Manual Grammar of the Greek New Testament*. Toronto: Macmillan, 1955.
Danby, Herbert. *The Mishnah: Translated from the Hebrew with Introduction and Brief Explanatory Notes*. Reprint ed. Oxford: Oxford University Press, 1985.
Danove, Paul L. *The Rhetoric of the Characterization of God, Jesus, and Jesus' Disciples in the Gospel of Mark*. JSNTSup 290. New York: T. & T. Clark, 2005.
Darr, John A. *Herod the Fox: Audience Criticism and Lukan Characterization*. JSNTSup 163. Sheffield, UK: Sheffield Academic Press, 1998.
———. *On Character Building: The Reader and the Rhetoric of Characterization in Luke-Acts*. Louisville, KY: Westminster John Knox, 1992.
Davies, W. D. "Reflections on Aspects of the Jewish Background of the Gospel of John." In *Exploring the Gospel of John: In Honor of D. Moody Smith*, 43–64. Louisville, KY: Westminster John Knox, 1996.
de Jonge, Marinus. *Jesus: Stranger from Heaven and Son of God: Jesus Christ and the Christians in Johannine Perspective*. Translated and edited by John E. Steely. SBLSBS 11. Missoula, MT: Scholars, 1977.
de la Potterie, Ignace. "Le Bon Pasteur." In *Populus Dei: Studi in onore del Cardinale Alfredo Ottaviani per il cinquantesimo di sacerdozio: 18 marzo 1966*, 2:927–68. Rome: LAS, 1969.
———. "*oîda et ginōskō*: Les Deux de la Connaissance dans le Quatrième Évangile." *Bib* 40 (1959) 709–25.
Di Lella, Alexander A. "The Deuteronomic Background of the Farewell Discourse in Tob 14:3–11." *CBQ* 41 (1979) 380–89.
———"A Study of Tobit 14:10 and Its Intertextual Parallels." *CBQ* 71 (2009) 497–506.
Dodd, C. H. *The Interpretation of the Fourth Gospel*. Reprint ed. Cambridge: Cambridge University Press, 1998.
Draper, J. A. "The Tip of an Ice-Berg: The Temple of the Holy Spirit." *JTSA* 59 (1987) 57–65.
Duke, Paul D. *Irony in the Fourth Gospel*. Atlanta: John Knox, 1985.

Du Rand, Jan A. "A Syntactical and Narratological Reading of John 10 in Coherence with Chapter 9." In *The Shepherd Discourse of John 10 and Its Context*, 94–115. SNTSMS 67. Cambridge: Cambridge University Press, 1991.

Edwards, Ruth B. "Χαριν Αντι Χαριτoς (John 1.16) Grace and the Law in the Johannine Prologue." *JSNT* 32 (1988) 3–15.

Fanning, Buist M. *Verbal Aspect in New Testament Greek*. Oxford Theological Monographs. Oxford: Clarendon, 1990.

Ferreira, Johan. *Johannine Ecclesiology*. JSNTSup 160. Sheffield, UK: Sheffield Academic Press, 1998.

Finkelstein, Louis. "The Origin of the Hallel." *HUCA* 23 (1951) 319–37.

Fish, Stanley. *Is There a Text in This Class? The Authority of Interpretive Communities*. Cambridge, MA: Harvard University Press, 1980.

Fitzmyer, Joseph A. "The Aramaic and Hebrew Fragments of Tobit from Qumran Cave 4." *CBQ* 57 (1995) 655–75.

Foerster, Werner. "*diabolos*. Linguistic." In *TDNT*, 2:72–73. Edited by Gerhard Kittel. Grand Rapids, MI: Eerdmans, 1999.

——— "*diabolos*. The NT View of Satan." In *TDNT*, 2:79–81. Edited by Gerhard Kittel. Grand Rapids, MI: Eerdmans, 1999.

Forster, E. M. *Aspects of the Novel*. New York: Penguin Books, 1962.

Gaffney, James. "Believing and Knowing in the Fourth Gospel." *Theological Studies* 26 (1965) 215–41.

Gignac, Francis T. "The Use of Verbal Variety in the Fourth Gospel." In *Transcending Boundaries: Contemporary Readings of the New Testament*, 191–200. Edited by Rekha M. Chennattu and Mary L. Coloe. Biblioteca di Scienze Religiose 187. Rome: Libreria Ateneo Salesiano, 2005.

Grassi, Joseph A. "The Role of Jesus' Mother in John's Gospel: A Reappraisal." *CBQ* 48 (1986) 67–80.

Grayston, Kenneth. "The Meaning of *Paraklētos*." *JSNT* 13 (1981) 67–82.

Grigsby, Bruce. "Washing in the Pool of Siloam—A Thematic Anticipation of the Johannine Cross." *NovT* 27 (1985) 227–35.

Grisanti, Michael A. "Inspiration, Inerrancy, and the OT Canon: The Place of Textual Updating in an Inerrant View of Scripture." *JETS* 44 (2001) 577–98.

Gutmann, Joseph. *The Synagogue: Studies in Origins, Archaeology and Architecture*. New York: KTAV, 1975.

Hare, Douglas R. A. *The Theme of Jewish Persecution of Christians in the Gospel according to St. Matthew*. Cambridge: Cambridge University Press, 1967.

Harris, R. Laird. "The Book of Job and Its Doctrine of God." *Presbyterian* 7 (1981) 5–33.

Hawkin, David J. "The Johannine Concept of Truth and its Implications for a Technological Society." *EvQ* 59 (1987) 3–13.

Hawthorne, Gerald F. "The Concept of Faith in the Fourth Gospel." *BSac* 116 (1959) 117–26.

Hendricksen, William. *A Commentary on the Gospel of John*. London: Banner of Truth Trust, 954.

Horbury, William. "The Benediction of the *Minim* and Early Jewish-Christian Controversy." *JTS* 33 (1982) 19–61.

Hornung, Erik. *Conceptions of God in Ancient Egypt: The One and the Many*. Translated by John Baines. Ithaca, NY: Cornell University Press, 1982.

Horsley, Richard A. "Synagogues in Galilee and the Gospels." In *Evolution of the Synagogue: Problems and Progress*, 46–69. Edited by Howard C. Kee and Lynn H. Cohick. Harrisburg, PA: Trinity Press International, 1999.

Hoskins, Paul M. *Jesus as the Fulfilment of the Temple in the Gospel of John*. Paternoster Biblical Monographs. Eugene, OR: Wipf & Stock, 2006.

House, Paul R. *Old Testament Theology*. Downers Grove, IL: InterVarsity, 1998.

Howard, John M. "The Significance of Minor Characters in the Gospel of John." *BSac* 163 (2006) 63–78.

Howard, Kevin, and Marvin Rosenthal. *The Feasts of the Lord*. Nashville: Thomas Nelson, 1997.

Hunt, Harry. "An Examination of the Current Emphasis on the Canon in the Old Testament Studies." *Southwestern Journal of Theology* 23 (1980) 55–70.

"Iranian Poetry." No pages. Online: http://www.iranyellowpages.net/En/about_iran/Culture/poets/iranian_poetry01.shtm.

Isaac, E. "The Book of Enoch." In *The Old Testament Pseudepigrapha: Apocalyptic Literature and Testaments*, 1:13–89. Edited by James H. Charlesworth. Garden City, NY: Doubleday, 1983.

Kaiser, Walter C. *The Messiah in the Old Testament*. Grand Rapids, MI: Zondervan, 1995.

Kanagaraj, Jey J. *'Mysticism' in the Gospel of John: An Inquiry into its Background*. JSNTSup 158. Sheffield, UK: Sheffield Academic Press, 1998.

Kee, Howard C. "Defining the First-Century C.E. Synagogue: Problems and Progress." In *Evolution of the Synagogue: Problems and Progress*, 7–26. Edited by Howard C. Kee and Lynn H. Cohick. Harrisburg, PA: Trinity Press International, 1999.

Kennedy, George A. *New Testament Interpretation through Rhetorical Criticism*. Chapel Hill: University of North Carolina, 1984.

Kim, Hyun Chul Paul. "Interpretative Modes of Yin–Yang Dynamics as an Asian Hermeneutics." *Biblical Interpretation* 9 (2001) 287–308.

Kim, Stephen S. "The Literary and Theological Significance of the Johannine Prologue." *BSac* 166 (2009) 421–35.

Kimball, Dan. *They Like Jesus But Not the Church: Insights from Emerging Generations*. Grand Rapids, MI: Zondervan, 2007.

Kinnaman, David, and Gabe Lyons. *Unchristian: What a New Generation Really Thinks about Christianity . . . and Why It Matters*. Grand Rapids, MI: Baker Books, 2007.

Klein, William W., Craig L. Blomberg, and Robert L. Hubbard. *Introduction to Biblical Interpretation*. Reprint ed. Nashville: Thomas Nelson, 2004.

Klink, Edward W., III. "Expulsion from the Synagogue? Rethinking a Johannine Anachronism." *Tyndale Bulletin* 59 (2008): 99–118.

Koester, Craig R. *The Dwelling of God: The Tabernacle in the Old Testament, Intertestamental Jewish Literature, and the New Testament*. CBQMS 22. Washington, DC: Catholic Biblical Association of America, 1989.

———. "The Spectrum of Johannine Readers." In *"What is John?": Readers and Readings of the Fourth Gospel*, 5–19. SBL Symposium Series 3. Edited by Fernando F. Segovia. Atlanta: Scholars, 1996.

———. *Symbolism in the Fourth Gospel: Meaning, Mystery, Community*. Minneapolis: Fortress, 1995.

Köstenberger, Andreas J. *John*. Zondervan Illustrated Bible Backgrounds Commentary. Grand Rapids, MI: Zondervan, 2002.

———. *A Theology of John's Gospel and Letters*. Grand Rapids, MI: Zondervan, 2009.

Kushner, Harold S. *When Bad Things Happen to Good People.* New York: Schocken, 1981.
Kuyper, Lester J. "Grace and Truth: An Old Testament Description of God, and Its Use in the Johannine Gospel." *Int* 18 (1964) 3–19.
Kysar, Robert. *John: The Maverick Gospel.* Revised ed. Louisville, KY: Westminster John Knox, 1993.
Larsen, Kasper Bro. *Recognizing the Stranger: Recognition Scenes in the Gospel of John.* Biblical Interpretation Series 93. Leiden, Neth.: Brill, 2008.
Lee, David. *Luke's Stories of Jesus: Theological Reading of Gospel Narrative and the Legacy of Hans Frei.* JSNTSup 185. Sheffield, UK: Sheffield Academic, 1999.
Lee, Dorothy. "In the Spirit of Truth: Worship and Prayer in the Gospel of John and the Early Fathers." *VC* 58 (2004) 277–97.
Lehtipuu, Outi. "Characterization and Persuasion: The Rich Man and the Poor Man in Luke 16.19–31." In *Characterization in the Gospels: Reconceiving Narrative Criticism,* 73–105. Edited by David Rhoads and Kari Syreeni. London: T. & T. Clark International, 1999.
Liddell, H. G., and Robert Scott. *A Greek-English Lexicon: Revised and Augmented Throughout by Sir Henry S. Jones with the Assistance of Roderick McKenzie.* Reprint ed. Oxford: Clarendon, 1968.
Lieu, Judith M. "The Mother of the Son in the Fourth Gospel." *JBL* 117 (1998) 61–77.
Lightfoot, J. B. No pages. Online: http://web.archive.org/web/20041214085105/www.earlychristianwritings.com/lightfoot/pt1vol2/translation1.html.
Lincoln, Andrew T. *The Gospel according to Saint John.* Black's New Testament Commentaries. New York: Hendrickson, 2005.
———. *Truth on Trial: The Lawsuit Motif in the Fourth Gospel.* Peabody, MA: Hendrickson, 2000.
Lindars, Barnabas. *The Gospel of John.* London: Oliphants, 1972.
Lindsay, Dennis R. "What Is Truth? *Alētheia* in the Gospel of John." *ResQ* 35 (1993) 129–45.
Mansfield, Stephen. *ReChurch: Healing Your Way Back to the People of God.* Carol Stream, IL: Tyndale House, 2010.
Marshall, I. Howard. *The Epistles of John.* NICNT; Grand Rapids, MI: Eerdmans, 1978.
Martyn, J. L. *History and Theology in the Fourth Gospel.* Third ed. Nashville: Abingdon, 2003.
Masterpiece Theatre. "Jane Eyre." No pages. Online:http://www.pbs.org/wgbh/masterpiece/janeeyre/index.html.
Matera, Frank J. *New Testament Christology.* Louisville, KY: Westminster John Knox, 1999.
McCracken, David. "Character in the Boundary: Bakhtin's Interdividuality in Biblical Narratives." *Semeia* 63 (1993) 29–42.
———. "Narration and Comedy in the Book of Tobit." *JBL* 114 (1995) 401–18.
McHugh, John. *The Mother of Jesus in the New Testament.* London: Darton, Longman & Todd, 1975.
McKay, Kenneth L. "On the Perfect and Other Aspects in New Testament Greek." *NovT* 23 (1981) 289–329.
Meeks, Wayne A. "The Man from Heaven in Johannine Sectarianism." *JBL* 91 (1972) 44–72.
Metzger, Bruce M. *A Textual Commentary on the Greek New Testament.* Second ed. Stuttgart: UBS, 1994.

"The Miracle Times: It's Your Window to the Real World, A Course In Miracles and Marianne Williamson." No pages. Online: http://www.themiracletimes.com/A-Course-In-Miracles/Marianne-Williamson-Oprah-Winfrey-Radio-Show.htm.

Moloney, Francis J. *Belief in the Word: Reading John 1–4*. Minneapolis: Fortress, 1993.

———. "Excursus: Theories of Johannine Community History." In *An Introduction to the Gospel of John* by Raymond E. Brown, 69–86. Edited, updated, introduced, and concluded by Francis J. Moloney. New York: Doubleday, 2003.

———. *The Johannine Son of Man*. Rome: LAS, 1978.

———. *Signs and Shadows: Reading John 5–12*. Minneapolis: Fortress, 1996.

Morris, Leon. *The Gospel according to John*. Revised ed. NICNT. Grand Rapids, MI: Eerdmans, 1995.

Mou, Bo. "Becoming-Being Complementarity: An Account of the *Yin-Yang* Metaphysical Vision of the *Yi-Jing*." In *Comparative Approaches to Chinese Philosophy*, 86–96. Edited by Bo Mou. Aldershot, UK: Ashgate, 2003.

Mullins, Michael. *The Gospel of John*. Dublin: Columba, 2003.

Neyrey, Jerome H. "The 'Noble Shepherd' in John 10: Cultural and Rhetorical Background." *JBL* 120 (2001) 267–91.

Nielsen, Kirsten. "Old Testament Imagery in John." In *New Readings in John: Literary and Theological Perspectives. Essays from the Scandinavian Conference on the Fourth Gospel*, 66–82. JSNTSup 182. Sheffield, UK: Sheffield Academic, 1999.

Noble, Alan. "Rethinking the Stumbling Block: Christian Culture as a Barrier." No pages. Online: http://www.christandpopculture.com/featured/rethinking-the-stumbling-block-christian-culture-as-a-barrier-part-2/.

Novenson, Matthew V. "The Jewish Messiahs, the Pauline Christ, and the Gentile Question." *JBL* 128 (2009) 357–73.

Novick, Tzvi. "Biblicized Narrative: On Tobit and Genesis 22." *JBL* 126 (2007) 755–64.

O'Brien, Mark A. "The Contribution of Judah's Speech, Genesis 44:18–34, to the Characterization of Joseph." *CBQ* 59 (1997) 429–47.

O'Day, Gail R. "'I Have Overcome the World' (John 16:33): Narrative Time in John 13–17." *Semeia* 53 (1991) 153–66.

———. "Narrative Mode and Theological Claim: A Study in the Fourth Gospel." *JBL* 105 (1986) 657–68.

Oegema, Gerbern S. *The Anointed and his People: Messianic Expectation from the Maccabees to Bar Kochba*. JSPSup 27. Sheffield, UK: Sheffield Academic, 1998.

Operation World. "Operation World: Asian Countries." No pages. Online: http://www.operationworld.org/region/asia/owtext.html.

"Oprah Winfrey: Jesus Did Not Come To Die On The Cross." Video clip: http://sg.video.search.yahoo.com/search/video?ei=UTF-8&p=oprah+Jesus&fr2=tab-web&fr=yfp-t-712.

"The Oprah Winfrey Show: United States Viewership." No pages. Online: http://www.answers.com/topic/the-oprah-winfrey-show.

O'Rourke, John J. "Asides in the Gospel of John." *NovT* 21 (1979) 210–19.

Painter, John. "Johannine Symbols: A Case Study in Epistemology." *JTSA* 27 (1979) 26–41.

———. "John 9 and the Interpretation of the Fourth Gospel." *JSNT* 28 (1986) 31–61.

Pancaro, Severino. *The Law in the Fourth Gospel: The Torah and the Gospel, Moses and Jesus, Judaism and Christianity According to John*. NovTSup 42; Leiden, Neth.: Brill, 1975.

Patte, Daniel. "Jesus' Pronouncement about Entering the Kingdom Like a Child: A Structural Exegesis." *Semeia* 29 (1983) 3–42.

Petersen, Norman R. "'Point of View' in Mark's Narrative." *Semeia* 12 (1978) 97–121.

Phillips, Rob. "LifeWay Research finds American 'Millennials' are Spiritually Diverse." No pages. Online: http://www.lifeway.com/article/170233/.

Pomykala, Kenneth E. *The Davidic Dynasty Tradition in Early Judaism: Its History and Significance for Messianism*. SBLEJL 07. Atlanta: Scholars, 1995.

Porter, Stanley E. *Idioms of the Greek New Testament*. Reprinted second ed. London: Continuum, 2007.

———. *Verbal Aspect in the Greek of the New Testament, with Reference to Tense and Mood*. Studies in Biblical Greek 1. New York: Peter Lang, 1989.

Portier-Young, Anathea. "Alleviation of Suffering in the Book of Tobit: Comedy, Community, and Happy Endings." *CBQ* 63 (2001) 35–54.

Preisker, Herbert. "*kleptō, kleptēs*." In TDNT, 3:754–56. Edited by Gerhard Kittel. Reprint ed. Grand Rapids, MI: Eerdmans, 1999.

Quasten, Johannes. "The Parable of the Good Shepherd: Jn. 10:1–21." *CBQ* 10 (1948) 1–12.

Reinhartz, Adele. "Judaism in the Gospel of John." *Int* 63 (2009) 382–93.

Rengstorf, K. H. "*lēstēs*," TDNT, 4:257–62. Edited by Gerhard Kittel. Grand Rapids, MI: Eerdmans, 1999.

———. "*pēlós*." In TDNT 6:118–19. Edited by Gerhard Friedrich. Reprint ed. Grand Rapids, MI: Eerdmans, 1999.

Resseguie, James L. "Reader-Response Criticism and the Synoptic Gospels." *JAAR* 52 (1984) 307–24.

Ridderbos, Herman N. *The Gospel according to John: A Theological Commentary*. Translated by John Vriend. Grand Rapids, MI: Eerdmans, 1997.

Rivkin, Ellis. "The Meaning of Messiah in Jewish Thought." *USQR* 26 (1971) 383–406.

Robertson, A. T. *A Grammar of the Greek New Testament in the Light of Historical Research*. Nashville: Broadman, 1934.

Roth, S. John. *The Blind, the Lame, and the Poor: Character Types in Luke-Acts*. JSNTSup 144. Sheffield, UK: Sheffield Academic, 1997.

Rubenstein, Jeffrey L. "Sukkot, Eschatology and Zechariah 14." *RB* 103 (1996) 161–95.

Sanders, E. P. *Judaism: Practice and Belief 63 BCE–66 CE*. Philadelphia: Trinity Press International, 1992.

Schneiders, Sandra M. "Death in the Community of Eternal Life: History, Theology, and Spirituality in John 11." *Int* 41 (1987) 44–56.

———. "History and Symbolism in the Fourth Gospel." In *L'evangile de Jean: Sources, Redaction, Theologie*, 371–76. Edited by M. de Jonge. Louvain: Louvain University Press, 1977.

Schnelle, Udo. *History and Theology of the New Testament Writings*. Translated by M. Eugene Boring. Minneapolis: Fortress, 1998.

Scholnick, Sylvia H. "The Meaning of *mišpāt* [Justice] in the Book of Job." *JBL* 101 (1982) 521–29.

Schwartz, Benjamin I. *The World of Thought in Ancient China*. Cambridge, MA: Harvard University Press, 1985.

Scott, J. Julius, Jr. *Jewish Backgrounds of the New Testament*. Grand Rapids, MI: Baker, 1995.

Segovia, Fernando F. *The Farewell of the Word: The Johannine Call to Abide.* Minneapolis: Fortress, 1991.

———. "John 15:18—16:4a: A First Addition to the Original Farewell Discourse?" *CBQ* 45 (1983) 210-30.

———. "The Structure, *Tendenz*, and *Sitz im Leben* of John 13:31—14:31." *JBL* 104 (1985) 471-93.

Shepherd, Michael B. "Targums, the New Testament, and Biblical Theology of the Messiah." *JETS* 51 (2008) 45-58.

Sigal, Phillip. *Judaism: The Evolution of a Faith.* Revised and edited by Lillian Sigal. Grand Rapids, MI: Eerdmans, 1988.

Smick, Elmer B. "Another Look at the Mythological Elements in the Book of Job." *WTJ* 40 (1978) 213-28.

———. "Mythology and the Book of Job." *JETS* 13 (1970) 101-8.

Smith, D. Moody. *John.* Nashville: Abingdon, 1999.

Smith, Warren. "'Oprah and Friends' to Teach Course on New Age Christ." No pages. Online: http://www.crossroad.to/articles2/007/smith-oprah.htm#sin#sin.

Soo Hoo, Gilbert. *The Pedagogy of the Johannine Jesus: A Comparative Study of Jesus' Pedagogy to the World and to His Own.* Saarbrücken, Ger.: VDM Verlag Dr. Müller Aktiengesellschaft, 2009.

Staley, Jeffrey L. *The Print's First Kiss: A Rhetorical Investigation of the Implied Reader in the Fourth Gospel.* SBLDS 82. Atlanta: Scholars, 1988.

———. "Stumbling in the Dark, Reaching for the Light: Reading Character in John 5 and 9." *Semeia* 53 (1991) 55-80.

Stroumsa, Sarah, and Gedaliahu G. Stroumsa. "Aspects of Anti-Manichaean Polemics in Late Antiquity and Under Early Islam." *HTR* 81 (1988) 37-58.

Stuckenbruck, Loren T. "Messianic Ideas in the Apocalyptic and Related Literature of Early Judaism." In *The Messiah in the Old and New Testaments*, 90-113. Edited by Stanley E. Porter. Grand Rapids, MI: Eerdmans, 2007.

Talbert, Charles H. *Reading John: A Literary and Theological Commentary on the Fourth Gospel and the Johannine Epistles.* New York: Crossroad, 1994.

Tannehill, Robert C. "The Gospel of Mark as Narrative Christology." *Semeia* 16 (1979) 57-95.

———. "Introduction: The Pronouncement Story and Its Types." *Semeia* 20 (1981) 1-13.

———. "Varieties of Synoptic Pronouncement Stories." *Semeia* 20 (1981) 101-19.

Taylor, Theophilus M. "Kingdom, Family, Temple, and Body: Implications from the Biblical Doctrine of the Church for the Christian Attitude Amid Cultural and Racial Tensions." *Int* 12 (1958) 174-93.

Tenney, Merrill C. "The Footnotes of John's Gospel." *BSac* 117 (1960) 350-64.

Thatcher, Tom. "A New Look at Asides in the Fourth Gospel." *BSac* 151 (1994) 428-39.

———. *The Riddles of Jesus in John: A Study in Tradition and Folklore.* SBLMS 53. Atlanta: SBL, 2000.

Thompson, Marianne M. "'God's Voice You Have Never Heard, God's Form You Have Never Seen': The Characterization of God in the Gospel of John." *Semeia* 63 (1993) 177-204.

———. *The Incarnate Word: Perspectives on Jesus in the Fourth Gospel.* Peabody, MA: Hendrickson, 1988.

Tomasino, Anthony J. *Judaism Before Jesus: The Events & Ideas that Shaped the New Testament World.* Downers Grove, IL: InterVarsity, 2003.

Tsevat, Matitiahu. "The Meaning of the Book of Job." *HUCA* 37 (1966) 73–106.
Vanderkam, James C. *From Revelation to Canon: Studies in the Hebrew Bible and Second Temple Literature.* Leiden, Neth.: Brill Academic, 2002.
van der Merwe, Dirk G. "Towards a Theological Understanding of Johannine Discipleship." *Neot* 31 (1997) 339–59.
von Rad, Gerhard. "*diabolos*. The OT View of Satan." In *TDNT*, 2:73–75. Edited by Gerhard Kittel. Grand Rapids, MI: Eerdmans, 1999.
Weitzman, Steven. "Allusion, Artifice, and Exile in the Hymn of Tobit." *JBL* 115 (1996) 49–61.
Whitters, Mark F. "Discipleship in John: Four Profiles." *WW* 18 (1998) 422–27.
Wise, Michael O. *The First Messiah: Investigating the Savior Before Jesus.* San Francisco: Harper Collins, 1999.
Witherington, Ben, III. *John's Wisdom: A Commentary on the Fourth Gospel.* Louisville, KY: Westminster John Knox, 1995.
Wolters, Al. "The Messiah in the Qumran Documents." In *The Messiah in the Old and New Testaments*, 75–89. Edited by Stanley E. Porter. Grand Rapids, MI: Eerdmans, 2007.
Yeoh, Brenda S. A. "Singapore: Hungry for Foreign Workers at All Skill Levels." No pages. Online: http://www.migrationinformation.org/Profiles/display.cfm?ID=570.
Zerwick, Maximilian. *Biblical Greek: Illustrated by Examples.* Rome: Editrice PontificioIstituto Biblico, 1994.
Zimmerman, Frank. *The Book of Tobit: An English Translation with Introduction and Commentary.* New York: Harper & Brothers, 1958.

www.ingramcontent.com/pod-product-compliance
Lightning Source LLC
Chambersburg PA
CBHW052102230426
43662CB00036B/1766